NY PUBLIC LIBRARY THE BRANCH LIBRARIES
3 3333 02663 7138

REFERENCE

REFERENCE

S0-DTC-482

CAMBRIDGE TEXTS AND STUDIES IN THE HISTORY OF EDUCATION

*General Editors*

A. C. F. BEALES, A. V. JUDGES, J. P. C. ROACH

# ROBERT LOWE AND EDUCATION

## IN THIS SERIES

*Texts*

*Fénelon on Education*, edited by H. C. Barnard

*Friedrich Froebel*, a selection edited by Irene Lilley

*Matthew Arnold and the Education of the New Order*, edited by Peter Smith and Geoffrey Summerfield

*Robert Owen on Education*, edited by Harold Silver

*James Mill on Education*, edited by W. H. Burston

*Samuel Hartlib and the Advancement of Learning*, edited by Charles Webster

*Thomas Arnold on Education*, edited by T. W. Bamford

*English for the English*, by George Sampson edited by Denys Thompson

*T. H. Huxley on Education*, edited by Cyril Bibby

*H. E. Armstrong and the Teaching of Science*, edited by W. H. Brock

*Studies*

*Education and the French Revolution*, by H. C. Barnard

*Public Examinations in England, 1850–1900*, by John Roach

*The Rise of a Central Authority for English Education*, by A. S. Bishop

*Education and Society in Nineteenth-Century Nottingham* by David Wardle

# ROBERT LOWE AND EDUCATION

D. W. SYLVESTER

*Lecturer in Education*
*University of Leeds*

CAMBRIDGE UNIVERSITY PRESS

Published by the Syndics of the Cambridge University Press
Bentley House, 200 Euston Road, London NW1 2DB
American Branch: 32 East 57th Street, New York, N.Y. 10022



Library of Congress Catalogue Card Number: 73-82446

ISBN 0 521 20310 4

First published 1974

Printed in Great Britain
by William Clowes & Sons, Limited
London, Beccles and Colchester

# CONTENTS

# TABLES

# PREFACE

I wish to thank the many people who have helped me in the preparation of this book. First, the Editors of this series, Professor A. C. F. Beales, Professor A. V. Judges and Professor J. P. C. Roach, who have given most helpful advice. Secondly, the librarians and staffs of many libraries, especially Mr J. R. V. Johnston and the staff of the library of the Institute of Education, University of Leeds, the staff of the University and Brotherton Library, Leeds, the staff of the Public Record Office, the staff of the British Museum Manuscripts Room and the staff of the Victoria and Albert Museum Library. I would also like to thank Mrs R. T. Sneyd of The Malt House, Hinton Charterhouse, near Bath, for permission to use the Lowe Papers in her possession, and also the Editor of *The Times* for permission to use *The Times* archives.

Finally I would like to thank my wife, for without her forbearance and encouragement the book would not have been written.

1973 D.W.S.

# ABBREVIATIONS

| | |
|---|---|
| B.M. | British Museum |
| *Parliamentary Debates* | *Hansard's Parliamentary Debates*, Third Series |
| *P.P.* | *Parliamentary Papers* |
| P.R.O. | Public Record Office |
| S.I.C. | Schools Inquiry Commission. *Report of the Royal Commission on Schools*, 1867–8 (Taunton Report) |

TO MY PARENTS

# INTRODUCTION

The 'whig interpretation of history' is a common temptation for historians of education. Educational ideas and practices of the past are often considered in the light of the values and aspirations of the present, and there is a tendency to write the history of education as a struggle for progress. The social, economic and political context of educational institutions and policies is either ignored or given only cursory treatment, and consequently a limited account of the past results.

Robert Lowe, in particular, has been a victim of this kind of historical writing and almost invariably he has been condemned by educationists. There have been some sympathetic accounts of Lowe[1] but as yet no published study has treated his educational ideas and policies in the context of his times.

Lowe was in many ways a typical mid-Victorian figure. He was a second-generation utilitarian attempting to apply the ideas of philosophical radicalism to the problems of an increasingly complex industrial society. The task was not an easy one; partly because the administrative framework, which succeeding generations have found essential to the task, was lacking, and partly because there was a contradiction in the tenets of philosophical radicalism which had to be resolved. Ideas of *laissez-faire*, self-help and free competition were seen to hinder the utilitarian desire to achieve effective reform. Lowe belonged to a generation which had to compromise its *laissez-faire* ideology and accept some collective state action to achieve the reforms it wanted.

Lowe's response to educational problems was influenced and, to some extent, conditioned by his environment, but it would be a mistake to see him as a mere puppet of his times. His intellectualism, his considerable administrative talents and his adherence to the idea of a meritocracy combined with a basic empiricism to produce policies and attitudes towards education which were distinctly

[1] For example, J. E. G. de Montmorency's article on Lowe in *Encyclopedia of Education*, ed. Foster Watson, London, 1921, II, pp. 1014–16; C. Duke, 'Robert Lowe. A Reappraisal', *British Journal of Educational Studies*, XIV (Nov. 1965), 19–35; Asa Briggs, 'Robert Lowe and the Fear of Democracy', *Victorian People*, Penguin 1965, pp. 24–271; J. Hurt, *Education in Evolution. Church, State, Society and Popular Education 1800–1870*, London 1971.

personal. Thus while the Revised Code was in some ways the natural and only possible policy for elementary education at the time, the logic and vigour with which it was framed and applied owed much to Lowe. However it must also be added here that Ralph Lingen, Secretary to the Education Department was even more important in deciding in actual detail how the Revised Code was to be applied.[2] Similarly, the 1870 Act was a legislative measure for a national system of education which would necessarily have come, sooner or later, but Lowe played a significant part in campaigning for it to come when it did and in structuring the form which it eventually took. His views about secondary education reflected free-trade and utilitarian attitudes, but Lowe made an individual contribution in his demand for curriculum reform, and in his willingness to impose state interference upon all secondary schools through a system of inspection and examination. Finally, his ideas for university reform were part of a general mid-nineteenth-century reassessment of the universities, but they were also unique in the emphasis they gave to the universities as community-service centres producing a meritocratic elite for society.

Considered in the light of his times the picture so often painted of Lowe as an educational reactionary takes on a less malevolent hue. The logic and realism of his thought may be appreciated, his administrative skills recognised and his position established as a pioneer in the application of economics to education.

[2] A. S. Bishop, *The Rise of a Central Authority for English Education*, Cambridge 1971, pp. 70–3.

# 1
# BIOGRAPHICAL SKETCH

Robert Lowe was born at Bingham, Nottinghamshire, on 4 December 1811. He was the second son of Robert Lowe, Rector of the parish of Bingham, and his wife Ellen. The living was a good one and Lowe's father also had some property of his own[1] so his boyhood was in no sense poor. However, Lowe began life with one great disadvantage: he had the misfortune to be born an albino.

His eyesight was so poor that no attempt was made to teach him his letters until he was six years old and he was eight before he began what he called 'the great business of life',[2] namely the study of Latin grammar. Though unable to shine at games, he persevered with his reading, and what had been initially a great difficulty became a great pleasure to him. In 1822 he went to a private school at Southwell for two years and then to a school at Risley in Derbyshire for a year, before proceeding in September 1825 to Winchester College. This was, as Lowe later reflected, a crucial test for a boy with his particular disabilities. Lowe has left a graphic account of the Winchester of his day, and there is no doubt that life was hard there. The boys were ill-fed, over-crowded and lacking freedom and space so 'the high spirits of youth', as Lowe called them, 'missing their natural vent, found employment in mutual torment'. Lowe suffered perhaps more than most, but he survived, and to his own mind it was the signal that he could be successful in public life. 'I had', he afterwards wrote, 'effectually solved the problem as to whether I was able to hold my own in life, and proved by a most crucial experiment that I was not too sensitive nor too soft for the business.'[3]

From Winchester Lowe went on to University College, Oxford, matriculating on 16 June 1829. He enjoyed his university years. He became a prominent member and notable speaker in the Union Debating Society and he took to rowing and was chosen to represent the university in a race against Cambridge – though the event

[1] A. Patchett Martin, *Life and Letters of the Rt. Hon. Robert Lowe, Viscount of Sherbrooke*, 2 vols. London 1893, I, p. 4.
[2] *Ibid.* p. 5. [3] *Ibid.* p. 10.

never came off. He also worked hard to take a double first-class degree. In this he failed. In 1833 he gained his Bachelor of Arts degree with a first class in classics and a second class in mathematics. It was a great disappointment to him but not insurmountable.

Of the three main professions open to him, the Church, academic life and the law, Lowe's determined objection to taking Holy Orders precluded him from the first two, and so he decided to go to the Bar. This was on the face of it unwise. Lowe later maintained that if he had had a friend who had asked such questions as these – 'Can you see the face of a witness?' 'Can you watch the countenance of a jury so as to judge whether what you say finds acceptance with them or no?' 'Can you find your place readily in a long brief or report?'[4] – then he would have decided against the Bar. However, he lacked such a friend and so to support himself while he studied law he became a private tutor at Oxford. In an effort to raise money quickly, Lowe took on more pupils than was usual for a private tutor and often he had ten pupils at a time, each of whom had an hour's tutorial each day. Lowe was extremely successful as a tutor – that is, if it is allowed that success can be judged by the examination results of his pupils – and for seven years he took as many pupils as he felt he could do justice to in the time at his disposal. In 1835 he held for a while a lay Fellowship at Magdalen College, which was confined to candidates from Nottinghamshire, but he relinquished this within a year in favour of his younger brother, when he married Georgina Orred on 26 March 1836. Lowe took his MA in 1836 and continued to teach and to study but about this time his eyes began to warn him that he must give up all idea of reading by candlelight and, momentarily, he questioned his plan of going to the Bar. Indeed in 1838 he applied for the Professorship of Greek at the University of Glasgow. He later wrote that his 'testimonials were, as I believe testimonials always are, a splendid instance of what Bentham calls the fallacy of indiscriminate laudation',[5] and he spent a month making himself known in Glasgow prior to the election. However, despite his efforts, he failed to secure the chair, when his principal supporter, the Professor of Ecclesiastical History, deserted him in favour of his rival, Mr Lushington. The change was part of some interior university politics by which in return for his desertion of

[4] *Ibid.* p. 24. [5] *Ibid.* p. 31.

Lowe, the Professor of Ecclesiastical History would himself secure his desired translation to the Chair of Moral Philosophy. Lowe was bitterly disappointed, though he soon took a calmer view of the affair and could later admit that Lushington was 'a better scholar' than himself.[6]

For the next two years, Lowe continued to teach, taking his pupils off on reading holidays to Ambleside in 1839 and to Dinan in 1840, and learning Sanskrit in his spare time. Then in the latter year, having failed to secure an academic post at Oxford, the Praelectorship of Logic, he moved to London in order to intensify his studies for the Bar, though he still made time to concern himself with Oxford affairs and in particular came out in opposition to Newman and the Tractarians, publishing an anonymous pamphlet *The Articles Construed by Themselves* in answer to Newman's *Tract 90* and also *Observations Suggested by 'A Few More Words in Support of No. 90'* in answer to two pamphlets by W. G. Ward. On 28 January 1842 Lowe's studies were rewarded when he was called to the Bar as a member of Lincoln's Inn. However, almost at the same time, oculists whom he consulted prognosticated that he would be completely blind within seven years, and suggested that he should go to Australia or New Zealand.

Apart from being a wrong diagnosis this was poor advice, since as Lowe later wrote, his 'eyes being unprotected by a *pigmentum nigrum* and having nothing but white lashes to screen them, were particularly subject to injury from the blazing sky of Australia, which is one of the brightest and most trying in the world'.[7] However, to Australia Lowe and his wife went, setting sail on 8 June 1842.

Lowe was in Australia[8] from 1842 to 1850 and he soon acquired a busy and lucrative practice in the law courts of Sydney. On medical advice he was obliged to give up his practice and refrain from reading for some eight months in 1843, but after this enforced holiday, returned to his profession. He also entered politics, and in November 1843, on the nomination of Sir George Gipps, the Governor, he acquired a seat in the Legislative Council of New South Wales. Lowe was active in various issues but most notably

[6] *Ibid.* p. 32. [7] *Ibid.* p. 37.

[8] The authoritative account of Lowe's life in Australia is: Ruth Knight, *Illiberal Liberal. Robert Lowe in New South Wales 1842–50*, Melbourne 1966.

in securing the abolition of imprisonment for debt, in pressing for a national and unsectarian system of education, in protesting against the monopoly which a comparatively few squatters held over thousands of acres of land and in opposing the British Government's attempt to renew the system of convict transportation. However, Lowe had no intention of remaining in Australia for the rest of his life and when his wife's health became increasingly disturbed he decided to return to England. On 27 January 1850 Lowe and his wife set sail for England together with the two orphan Jamieson children, whom Lowe had adopted in 1844 after unsuccessfully trying to defend their mother's murderer, John Knatchbull, on a plea of insanity. In May they were safely back in London.

It is likely that Lowe had previously decided to embark upon a political career in England, and on 4 June 1850, as a necessary preliminary, he was nominated a member of the Reform Club. In April 1851 Lowe joined the staff of *The Times*, and began his work as a regular *Times* leader writer on 4 April 1851 with an article on Chancery reform. Meanwhile he hoped for a parliamentary seat. In 1852 a chance meeting with an old Oxford friend, the Reverend David Melville, led to Lowe's introduction to Lord Ward, afterwards Earl of Dudley, and his successful election on 10 July 1852 to the seat at Kidderminster, a borough constituency in which Lord Ward held great political influence.

Lowe quickly made his mark in the House of Commons and in his party. He made his maiden speech on 29 November 1852 on the Courts of Common Law (Ireland) Bill,[9] he spoke in favour of legalising the principle of limited liability on 7 December,[10] and on 13 December 1852 contributed to the debate on Disraeli's second budget.[11] Disraeli had completely thrown over Protection in the hope of detaching Peelites from the opposition to the Derby–Disraeli side of the House, but it was in vain. On 17 December the Government was defeated, Lord Derby resigned and Lord Aberdeen became Prime Minister. In the new administration Lowe received the office of Joint Secretary of the Board of Control for India, under Sir Charles Wood as President.

Immediately Lowe was involved in legislation and he helped

[9] *Parliamentary Debates*, CXXIII, col. 755.
[10] *Parliamentary Debates*, CXXIII, col. 1079.
[11] *Parliamentary Debates*, CXXIII, col. 1350.

to prepare the Government of India Bill which was successfully passed in July 1853. The most notable feature of the Bill was the opening of writerships in the Indian Civil Service to competition instead of the system of nomination which had previously operated. As Lowe said in his speech of 23 June 1853, open competition to civil appointments was 'new in this country' but he hoped that it would succeed and gradually acquire acceptance as the normal method of filling all official posts.[12] Subsequently he played an important part in the extension of open competition throughout the Civil Service.

When in January 1855 Lord Aberdeen fell and Lord Palmerston came into office, Lowe decided not to keep his former post and for six months he was out of office. He was not, however, inactive in the House and he spoke on various issues, opposing the introduction of decimal coinage,[13] supporting the Public Libraries Bill[14] and objecting to the way in which it was proposed to remodel the governments of New South Wales and Victoria.[15] Meanwhile the Government was occupied with the Crimean War, and Palmerston had trouble with his ministry when on 23 February 1855 three notable Peelites, Sir James Graham, Sidney Herbert and Gladstone, withdrew in opposition to the appointment of a Select Committee to inquire into the condition of the army before Sebastopol. Lowe also objected to this Select Committee as inappropriate in the middle of a war when all the accused generals and officers were absent.[16] However, putting this on one side, he continued to support Palmerston in the war against Russia.[17] Eventually in August 1855 Palmerston was obliged to reconstruct his Cabinet and Lowe gained some reward for his loyalty when he was given office as Vice-President of the Board of Trade.

Lowe held this position until February 1858 and successfully carried through Parliament the Joint Stock Companies Act of 1856 and 1857 and the Joint Stock Banking Companies Act of 1857. He was unsuccessful at the time in his attempt to abolish local

[12] *Parliamentary Debates*, CXXVIII, cols. 639–40.
[13] *Parliamentary Debates*, CXXXVIII, col. 1885.
[14] *Parliamentary Debates*, CXXXVII, col. 211.
[15] *Parliamentary Debates*, CXXXVIII, cols. 719, 1959.
[16] *Parliamentary Debates*, CXXXVI, col. 1779.
[17] *Parliamentary Debates*, CXXXVIII, col. 1213.

shipping dues[18] but he certainly aired the whole question of property rights in his attack on 'musty parchments' of title deeds which allowed certain classes, corporate bodies and individuals, to hold rights which could not be held to be in the public interest.[19] In the general election of 1857, Lowe retained his seat, though he was badly injured by flying stones in a riot which occurred on election day at Kidderminster.[20] On 25 February 1858 Palmerston resigned, and Lowe left the Board of Trade, but when in June 1859 Palmerston returned to office Lowe came with him, this time as Vice-President of the Committee of Council on Education. Lowe had meanwhile changed his constituency. It was now as the Member of Parliament for Calne, a 'pocket borough' under the influence of Lord Lansdowne, that Lowe took his seat and not for Kidderminster. His relations with the Kidderminster constituency, recently disturbed by his unhappy experience at the 1857 election, were now finally severed.

In his new post Lowe was responsible for the Board of Health in addition to education; and he ensured the passage of a Bill which made certain that the Public Health Act of 1858 had a permanent effect by making the office of Medical Officer under the Privy Council a permanent rather than an annual tenure. However, his most notable work was at the Education Department where in 1862 he introduced the Revised Code of Regulations under which parliamentary grants were administered to schools. It immediately aroused opposition but Lowe rode the storm and the Code went into operation.

It was a separate though related issue which eventually brought Lowe's resignation from the Vice-Presidency of the Education Committee. Dispute arose as to whether or not Her Majesty's Inspectors' reports on schools should be printed as submitted, or subjected to censorship by Education Department officials. The matter was raised on 27 March 1863 in a question by Sir John Pakington on the fate of Mr Watkins' report for Yorkshire. In his reply Lowe pleaded that the Department had operated the policy which had been enunciated in a Minute of the Committee of Council of 31 January 1861. By this Inspectors' reports were to be confined to 'the state of the schools inspected by them and to

[18] *Parliamentary Debates*, CXL, col. 153.
[19] Patchett Martin, II, pp. 122–5, also *Parliamentary Debates*, CXL, cols. 165–73.
[20] Patchett Martin, II, pp. 153–5.

practical suggestions for their management and improvement'[21] and if reports did not conform to this, they were to be returned to the Inspector for revision. Originally the Minute of 31 January 1861 had resulted from Lowe's attention being drawn to a report of Mr J. R. Morell, a Roman Catholic Inspector, in which the Inspector had discussed the comparative morality of Roman Catholic and Protestant countries, concluding that Protestant countries had more illegitimate births and more capital crimes.[22] Lowe could not see why Inspectors should have their views on such matters 'printed at the public expense'.[23] Now in 1863, he went further and suggested to the House that Inspectors should not 'enter into speculative and controversial matters on such a delicate subject as education'.[24] On 11 June 1863 W. E. Forster raised the matter again and Lowe once more justified his position,[25] suggesting that it was a question of the 'discipline'[26] of the Department. Lowe said:

Men do not necessarily agree in opinion because they act together. They reserve those opinions on which they do not agree; and no public Department but particularly one which has a most difficult and even invidious duty to perform, can be expected to carry on its operations with success, if it is obliged to print controversies maintained against itself by the very persons whom it employs to carry out the objects intrusted to its charge.[27]

Nevertheless the matter was not allowed to drop, and on 12 April 1864 Lord Robert Cecil moved a resolution that

in the opinion of this House the mutilation of the reports of Her Majesty's Inspectors of Schools, and the exclusion from them of statements and opinions adverse to the educational views entertained by the Committee of Council, while matter favourable to them is admitted, are violations of the understanding under which the appointment of the Inspectors was originally sanctioned by Parliament and tend to destroy the value of their reports.[28]

[21] *Parliamentary Debates*, CLXX, col. 23.
[22] *Report of Select Committee appointed to inquire into the practice of the Committee of Council on Education with respect to the reports of H.M. Inspectors of Schools*, 1864, p. iv. [23] *Ibid.* Minute of 31 January 1861.
[24] *Parliamentary Debates*, CLXX, col. 25.
[25] *Parliamentary Debates*, CLXXI, cols. 720–2.
[26] *Parliamentary Debates*, CLXXI, col. 720.
[27] *Parliamentary Debates*, CLXXI, col. 722.
[28] *Parliamentary Debates*, CLXXIV, col. 897.

Lowe denied the charge of mutilation, pointing out that reports were returned 'to make the Inspectors their own censors';[29] but he was poorly supported by the Government and the motion was carried by 101 votes to 93.

Lowe took the matter as a reflection upon him personally and resigned,[30] demanding a Select Committee of Inquiry, on 18 April 1864. The same day the House exonerated Lowe from blame and the subsequent Report of the Select Committee, issued on 11 July 1864, concluded that the Committee of Council had acted fairly in its treatment of Inspectors' reports and quite within its powers.

If passages occur in the reports, as printed, consisting of inference or arguments which may tend to support the educational view of the Department, other passages may be found which have a contrary bearing. No objection is made to statements of facts observed by the Inspectors within the circle of their official experience, whatever may be their bearing on the policy of the Committee of Council.[31]

On 26 July 1864 the House rescinded its former vote on Lord Robert Cecil's resolution without a division.

Lowe now entered upon a period of four years in which he was not only out of office but also unpopular with the majority in the House of Commons. His support of compensation from public funds for farmers hit by cattle plague[32] in 1866 brought opposition from members led by J. S. Mill and Bright, and his campaign against the 1867 Reform Bill,[33] while welcomed by some and acknowledged to be brilliantly conducted by more, was certainly against the opinions of most members.

After the passage of the Bill, Lowe embarked upon a series of public speeches on the question of education. On 1 November 1867, before the Philosophical Institution of Edinburgh, he delivered his address on *Primary and Classical Education*, and followed it on 22 and 23 January 1868 with two speeches on *Middle Class and Primary Education* to the annual dinner of the Liverpool Philomathic Society and to a conference on education at the Town Hall, Liverpool. He also published in 1868 his pamphlet, *Middle Class Education. Endowment or Free Trade.*

[29] *Parliamentary Debates*, CLXXIV, col. 905.
[30] *Parliamentary Debates*, CLXXIV, cols. 1203–11.
[31] *Report from the Select Committee on Education* (Inspectors' Reports), p. v.
[32] *Parliamentary Debates*, CLXXI, cols. 483–8; see also Patchett Martin, II, p. 250.
[33] R. Lowe, *Speeches and Letters on Reform*, London 1867.

The Reform Act of 1867 had swept away the constituency of Calne, but in 1868 Lowe was returned to the House as Member of Parliament for the University of London. He severed his connection with *The Times* in April 1868 and on 9 December returned to office as Chancellor of the Exchequer in Gladstone's first ministry, having, it seems, impressed Gladstone by a review he had written of Gladstone's views on finance.[34] As a Chancellor, Lowe was very much in the Gladstonian tradition, making it his constant concern in his budgets to reduce public expenditure.[35] In 1869 income tax was reduced by 1*d*., the shilling duty on a quarter of corn abolished, and the duty on fire insurance removed. In 1870 another 1*d*. was taken off the income tax, stamp duties were consolidated, and the duty on sugar was reduced by a half. By 1871, the revenue had recovered and Lowe's standing in the House of Commons was high. However, the Franco–Prussian war led to a demand, supported by Gladstone,[36] for increased expenditure upon the army, and so Lowe proposed to raise a million by a tax on matches. It proved his undoing. His proposal was defeated, not so much by economic arguments as the march of a body of women match-makers from the East End to Westminster. This so affected the House that Lowe was obliged to withdraw his proposal and raise income tax instead. Though Lowe reduced income tax again in 1873 his reputation never really recovered from the proposed tax on matches, which seemed to many to be yet another of Lowe's attacks upon the working class – in line with those he had pursued when opposing the extension of the franchise.[37] Lowe lost more popularity by refusing to use public funds either for the purchase of Epping Forest or the provision of gardens on the Thames Embankment. He also alienated his colleagues and disturbed his superior, Gladstone, by his boastful speech at Sheffield in September 1873 in which he claimed that no previous Chancellor in British history had ever reduced taxation by so much.[38] Lowe was a firm supporter of Gladstone's abortive Irish University Bill of 1873,[39] but the discovery of financial irregularities at the Post Office led to difficulties between the Postmaster-General, Monsell, the Commissioner of Public Works, Ayrton, and Lowe as Chancellor of the Exchequer, and Gladstone took the

[34] John Morley, *Life of William Ewart Gladstone*, 2 vols. London 1908, I, p. 664.
[35] Morley, I, p. 756. [36] *Ibid.* I, p. 756. [37] *Ibid.* I, p. 757.
[38] *Ibid.* I, pp. 758–9. [39] *Parliamentary Debates*, CCXIV, cols. 1481–95.

opportunity to remove Lowe from the office in which he had become so unpopular and transfer him to the Home Office in August 1873. Gladstone wrote to Lowe that 'no man can do his duty in that office (i.e. Chancellor of the Exchequer) and be popular *while* he holds it', and added 'Blessed are ye, when men shall revile you. You have fought for the public, tooth and nail.'[40] Lowe for his part composed in 1876 the following verse on his services:

*Four Years' Work of a Chancellor of Exchequer*

Twelve millions of Taxes, I struck off
Left behind me six millions of gains;
Of Debt forty millions I shook off
And got well abused for my pains.[41]

In February 1874 Gladstone's ministry fell and Lowe was out of office for the last time. He continued in Parliament and achieved notoriety yet again, in April 1876, when in a speech at East Retford he claimed that the Queen had been responsible for the Royal Titles Bill which proposed to add 'Empress of India' to her titles. On 2 May 1876 Disraeli denied it and on 4 May Lowe had to retract.[42] Four years later when Gladstone returned to office, Lowe was omitted from the Cabinet and raised to the Lords though Gladstone did insist that he should be given a viscountcy and not the barony which the Queen, it seemed, thought was enough.[43] On 25 May 1880 Lowe became Viscount Sherbrooke of Sherbrooke in Warlingham, Surrey.

In effect, Lowe had retired from public life. He led a quiet life at home finding his greatest pleasures, as he told Lady Salisbury in 1877, in riding a newly-acquired tricycle and in going once again through Icelandic literature.[44] He continued to travel abroad and to attend various functions at home but he was no longer a public figure. He realised this with some regret. He wrote to A. C. Tupp: 'When I was in the House of Commons and could make myself disagreeable I could do something. Now I do nothing, and no attention would be paid to me. Now I am like Giant Despair in

[40] Morley, II, pp. 50–54. [41] Patchett Martin, II, p. 371.
[42] *Parliamentary Debates*, CCXXIX, col. 52. [43] Morley, II, p. 178.
[44] Lady Burchlere, *A Great Lady's Friendships: Letters to Mary, Marchioness of Salisbury, Countess of Derby, 1862–1890*, London 1933, p. 470.

*Pilgrim's Progress* who could only grin at people whom he once could have eaten.'[45]

On 3 November 1884 his wife died and in the following year he married his second wife, Caroline Sneyd. He was made a Knight Grand Cross of the Order of the Bath on 30 June 1885 at Gladstone's nomination, and this crowned the various public honours he had received in his lifetime. In 1867 he had been made a Fellow of the Royal Society and given the honorary degree of LL.D at Edinburgh University. In 1870 Oxford University had conferred upon him the honorary degree of D.C.L. and in 1872 the freedom of Glasgow had been bestowed upon him. Robert Lowe died on 27 July 1892.

[45] Patchett Martin, II, p. 455, 28 September 1881.

# 2

# POLITICAL AND SOCIAL PHILOSOPHY

Lowe published no substantial volume of educational theory. His educational views arose in the heat of the day: in debate, in pamphlets or in newspaper articles upon some current issue. They were grounded in the political and social realities of his time. They were closely related to Lowe's general views on the nature of society, politics and economics. To understand them they must be seen in this wider context.

Lowe's political, economic and social philosophy owed much to the influence of philosophical radicalism, that brand of Liberalism which flourished in England in the latter part of the eighteenth and the earlier part of the nineteenth century. Lowe had a high regard for philosophical radicals, such as Bentham, and he admired the logic with which they pursued their principles. 'Our Radicals in former times', he wrote, 'used at least to be true to one set of principles. Trained in the school of Bentham they were at least loyal to the doctrines of Economical Truth. They worshipped their goddess according to the straitest sect of her religion.'[1] For his own part he regretted that since the dying out of the free trade controversy the attention of men had been much less turned to the 'principles of economical science'.[2] Lowe's attachment to philosophical radicalism emerged most obviously in his respect for Adam Smith and his adoption of many of Smith's viewpoints. From 1853 Lowe was a member of the Political Economy Club which had been founded in 1821 as a meeting point for radical thinkers. On 31 May 1876, to commemorate the hundredth anniversary of Adam Smith's *The Wealth of Nations* the club met, with W. E. Gladstone in the chair, and Lowe addressed them with a eulogy of Adam Smith.[3] Prior to that Lowe's discipleship of Adam Smith had been made clear in some of his speeches and attitudes. For example, on 3 May 1865, in a speech upon the

[1] R. Lowe, *Middle Class Education. Endowment or Free Trade*, London 1868, p. 5. [2] *Ibid.* p. 5. [3] Patchett Martin, II, p. 446.

second reading of the Borough Franchise Extension Bill, he opposed manhood suffrage and democracy on the grounds that 'its political economy is not that of Adam Smith',[4] and three years later in a speech on middle-class education he based much of what he had to say on Adam Smith, quoting extensively from the fifth book of *The Wealth of Nations*.[5] Lowe remained firmly attached to the ideas of political economy throughout his life. In 1878 in an article in *Nineteenth Century* entitled 'Recent attacks on Political Economy',[6] he defended his creed with great vigour. It was a notable *apologia*, as well it might be, for it came from one who had gained in early life a core of ideas from philosophical radicalism[7] which had never been relinquished.

At the centre of these ideas was the utilitarianism of Bentham. The social theory of the philosophical radicals was based on the principle of the happiness of the greatest number, which Bentham had outlined in the *Fragment on Government* published in 1776.[8] This greatest-happiness principle, despite any appearance to the contrary, was in fact a deeply individualistic doctrine. For Bentham, assuming that pleasure and pain were the ultimate motivating forces in human life, and pleasure the ultimate value, concluded that since these could only be experienced by individual men and women it was by reference to them that the value of laws and governments should be assessed. If governments and their laws failed to satisfy individual human needs then they should be reformed. It was consequently a battle cry for reform and a prescription for action. It was also a criterion of value which appealed to Lowe.

The economic theory of philosophical radicalism provided Lowe with a belief in the value of individual competition and a distrust of whatever might hinder it. Variously called classical economics or the theory of *laissez-faire*, it derived from Adam Smith's *Wealth of Nations*, through David Ricardo's *Principles of Political Economy* (1817). It was not, however, a homogeneous theory. On the one hand, following Adam Smith, it conceived a society of individual producers who, exchanging their goods freely, would

[4] Lowe, *Speeches and Letters on Reform*, p. 60.
[5] Lowe, *Middle Class Education*, p. 7.
[6] *Nineteenth Century*, IV (November 1878), 858–68.
[7] For a detailed account see E. Halévy, *The Growth of Philosophic Radicalism*, London 1928.
[8] J. Bentham, *A Fragment on Government*, 2nd edn, London 1823, pp. 45–8.

produce a natural harmony of interests and the maximum economic advantage to each individual that circumstances would allow. On the other hand, following Malthus and Ricardo, it conceived a society of classes which, competing with each other for the distribution of the produce of industry as it materialised in the form of rents, profits or wages, produced a society which necessarily precluded any such harmony of interests. The common ground of both these viewpoints was a demand for free trade and in general an opposition to government legislation in either economic or social affairs. There was, however, a conflict here between the individualism of philosophical radicalism and its concern for the good of the greatest number. According to Malthus, for example,[9] it was impossible to improve the lot of the wage-earner by legislation, for since population would always increase faster than the production of food, neither the standard of living nor the wages of the mass of mankind could expect to rise above subsistence level. On the other hand, not all philosophical radicals could support this conclusion. Bentham himself, far from arguing that a harmony of social interests was natural, held that legislation produced social harmony, and the principle of utility and the greater happiness of all justified any amount of legislative interference, whether in trade or in social and industrial relations.[10] This conflict in the economic and social theories of philosophical radicalism remained unresolved. Each man, including Lowe, had to make his own compromise between its individualism and its utilitarian concern for the good of the greatest number.

On the question of education, however, there was almost universal agreement among the classical economists that here there was a proper subject for government intervention. *Laissez-faire* would fail to bring about either the right amount or kind of education which society needed. Moreover, since the returns from investment in education were more social than private, it was always likely to be under-invested and consequently the government was justified in using public revenue to finance it. There was never any doubt among the classical theorists that education had a

[9] T. R. Malthus, *An Essay on the Principles of Population*, 2 vols. London 1806, II, pp. 149–93. Here Malthus discusses the inadequacies of Poor Laws and the relation between wages and prices.

[10] Bentham, pp. 126–8, where he concludes a discussion on the 'right of the supreme power to make laws' by asserting that cases must be judged by the principle of utility.

high socio-economic value. Adam Smith had considered education as a profitable investment for society: an educated man was like a machine, which, though expensive at the outset, eventually repaid that expense with profit by the reduction it achieved in labour and the increase it brought to production. It was also a profitable investment for individuals, bringing them returns in higher wages and also in the form of status and increased opportunities of social mobility.[11] Apart from being an economic productive investment, education was also a social and political good. It prevented crime and disorder: 'an instructed and intelligent people . . . are always more decent and orderly than an ignorant and stupid one' wrote Smith. It was also an essential prerequisite for the proper working of democratic governments, since the people must be educated if they were to make their political choices intelligently.[12] Consequently the State should ensure that the mass of the people were given 'the most essential part of education' – namely, reading, writing and arithmetic.[13] This analysis of education was on the whole followed by other economists of the classical school such as Malthus, Ricardo, J. R. McCulloch and J. S. Mill.[14] It was also the foundation upon which Lowe built his educational ideas.

The political theory of philosophical radicalism was less easily adopted by Lowe. It inherited a tradition of individualism which had been transmitted by Locke from the seventeenth century and which had become common coin in the American Declaration of Independence and the French Revolution's Rights of Man. It held that, ultimately, political sovereignty lay with the people and that government should consist of representative legislatures based on a universal suffrage, once the electorate had been enlightened by education. There was no doubt amongst the early philosophical radicals that all men were educable and that they could be brought to a rational appreciation of their interests. Moreover, such was their faith in reason, they believed that if all men sought their individual interests in a reasonable fashion, then the greatest good of the greatest number would result. James Mill was representative of philosophical radicalism in this respect and his son, John Stuart Mill, left this account of his father's views:

[11] Adam Smith, *An Inquiry into the Nature and Causes of the Wealth of Nations*, London 1875, p. 93. [12] *Ibid.* p. 621. [13] *Ibid.* p. 618.

[14] For a useful summary of the main texts see Pierre N. V. Tu, 'The Classical Economists and Education', *Kyklos. International Review for Social Sciences*, XXII (1969), 691–718.

So complete was my father's reliance on the influence of reason over the minds of mankind, whenever it is allowed to reach them, that he felt as if all would be gained if the whole population were taught to read, if all sorts of opinions were allowed to be addressed to them by word and in writing, and if by means of the suffrage they could nominate a legislature to give effect to the opinions they adopted. He thought that when the legislative no longer represented a class interest it would aim at the general interest, honestly and with adequate wisdom; since the people would be sufficiently under the guidance of educated intelligence, to make in general a good choice of persons to represent them, and having done so, to leave to those whom they had chosen a liberal discretion.[15]

Lowe never acquired such easy optimism, but he did accept the principle implied by Mill that education and the suffrage were necessarily linked, and that an uneducated electorate would not bring about the rule of reason which Mill hoped for.

These doctrines of philosophical radicalism – the principle of the happiness of the greatest number, *laissez-faire* and the education of all men for the suffrage – together with the analysis provided by the classical economists of the role of education in the economy and society, provided the background of Lowe's social and political philosophy. Lowe could never, however, accept philosophical radicalism in its entirety. Partly because of his own character, and partly because of the situation in which he found himself, he was obliged to trim the sails of philosophical radicalism. For, in the first place, Lowe was by nature too much of an empiricist in his approach to politics to adhere strictly to any set of principles. Secondly, he was one of those second-generation radicals whose main concern was to apply utilitarian ideas to the problems of a complex industrial society. It proved no easy task. Lacking the administrative framework of central and local councils which society has since evolved to implement large-scale reform, radicals of Lowe's generation were obliged to make piecemeal efforts at change. They were also forced to reconsider the implications of the individualist *laissez-faire* ideas which stood at the centre of the radical philosophy and review the respective roles of the State and the individual in society. Thirdly, Lowe's belief in the value of a meritocratic form of society gave his political and social philosophy a distinct personal character.

Lowe's educational thought and policies were particularly

[15] J. S. Mill, *Autobiography*, London 1873, p. 106.

influenced by these individual deviations from the more general philosophical radical position. His empiricism, his view of the role of the individual in society and his meritocratic viewpoint dictated the approach to educational problems which he adopted and characterised the solutions he proposed. They warrant further examination.

## EMPIRICISM

Lowe had a complete distrust of abstract *a priori* arguments and his approach to politics was one of empiricism and realism. His speeches on the Reform Question of 1865–7 make this abundantly clear. In his preface to the published collection of his speeches he wrote:

> When I find a book or a speech appealing to abstract *a priori* principles I put it aside in despair, being well aware that I can learn nothing useful from it. Such works only present to us the limited and qualified propositions which experience has established, without their limitations and qualifications, and elevate them into principles by a rash generalisation which strips them of whatever truth they originally possessed. Thus the words *right* and *equality* have a perfectly clear and defined meaning to the administration of justice under a settled law, but are really without meaning, except as vague and inappropriate metaphors, when applied to the distribution of political power.[16]

In his speech upon the second reading of the Borough Franchise Extension Bill, 3 May 1865, Lowe gave a more explicit account of the thinking processes which he would have men use in determining political and social questions. Theories should be constantly tested by facts, and corrected or abandoned in so far as they prove unsound. Decisions on human affairs must be based on experience and historical thinking.[17] Neither inductive nor deductive methods would suffice. In an article he wrote in 1878, in defence of political economy against the then newly-born study of sociology, Lowe applauded the triumph of scientific method in the natural and physical sciences but questioned its value as an approach to human affairs.[18]

[16] Lowe, *Speeches and Letters on Reform*, pp. 4–5. [17] *Ibid.* pp. 41–2.

[18] Lowe, 'Recent Attacks on Political Economy', *Nineteenth Century*, IV (Nov. 1878), 861–2.

Government, it seemed to Lowe, was an art and not a science. It had to grapple with particular problems as they arose and solve them in what seemed to be the best possible way at the time, rather than attempt to apply general laws of universal application for their solution. In his speeches during the debates on the extension of the franchise 1866–7, Lowe repeatedly asserted that politicians should judge in their decisions what was practical and possible, having in mind that the ultimate object of government was peace, security and good government rather than the implementation of idealistic theories.

Honourable gentlemen will, I think, concur with me in thinking that the true view of the science of government is, that it is not an exact science, that it is not capable of *a priori* demonstration; that it rests upon experiment, and that its conclusions ought to be carefully scanned, modified, and altered so as to be adapted to different states of society, or to the same state of society at different times . . . When Mr. Mill . . . speaks of every citizen of a State having a perfect right to a share in its government, he appeals to some *a priori* considerations, in accordance with which every man would be entitled not only to be well governed, but to take part in governing himself. But where are those *a priori* rights to be found? The answer to that question would lead me into a metaphysical inquiry which I shall not now pursue, contenting myself with saying that I see no proof of their existence, and that the use of the term arises from a bungling metaphor, by which a term appropriate to the rights arising under civil society is transferred to moral considerations antecedent to it. Can those alleged rights form a ground on which a practical, deliberative assembly like the House of Commons can arrive at a practical conclusion?[19]

In Lowe's view those who regarded the giving of the franchise as a matter of morality were possibly 'inspired apostles of a new Religion of Humanity', but they were not politicians. They had mistaken the means for the end, and inferred that because the elective franchise was a good thing for the purpose of obtaining the end of good government, it was necessarily a good thing in itself. They had the great advantage, in common with all enthusiasts, of emancipating themselves from the necessity of looking at consequences, and as a result were free from 'those complicated, embarrassing, and troublesome considerations of the collateral and future effects of measures, which perplex ordinary mortals'. Lowe

[19] Lowe, *Speeches and Letters on Reform*, pp. 34–6.

preferred to look to consequences and concluded that the franchise, like every other political expedient, was not a right but a means to an end, the end being 'the preservation of order in the country, the keeping of a just balance of classes, and the preventing of any dominance or tyranny of one class over another'.[20]

Lowe's empiricist approach to human affairs was a constant factor in his political life. His opposition to democracy was based not on principle but on a consideration of circumstances. In his speech of 3 May 1865 on the Borough Franchise Extension Bill he said,

> I am no proscriber of Democracy. In America it answers its purpose very well: in States like those of Greece it may have been desirable; but for England, in its present state of development and civilisation, to make a step in the direction of Democracy appears to me the strangest and wildest proposition that was ever broached by man.[21]

The same empiricism led him later to accept the Reform Act once it was passed. Though he regretted the triumph of the theory of rights over his theories of expediency and of what he called 'quantity over quality, numbers over property and intelligence' he thought it better 'to help to make the thing work' and accordingly was prepared to vote for the disfranchisement of boroughs with populations under 5,000.[22] Empiricism, too, governed his approach to educational problems. His educational policies were developed in response to the educational needs of his time and with due consideration of the financial resources which society was then willing to contribute towards education. They were not blueprints for an ideal world, but they were practical and they were possible.

## THE STATE AND THE INDIVIDUAL

The second feature of Lowe's social and political philosophy which contributed to his educational ideas was his view of the respective roles of the State and the individual in society. Here Lowe held views which were typical of those held by many of his mid-Victorian contemporaries. He was suspicious of the State as either a regulator or a benefactor of society. He wanted to keep its role

[20] *Ibid.* p. 104. [21] Lowe, *Speeches and Letters on Reform*, pp. 57–8.
[22] Lady Burchlere, pp. 128–9.

limited so that individual liberty and independence could have free reign. Society for him was no more than the sum of those individuals who composed it,[23] and its health and prosperity, or alternatively its sickness and poverty, depended solely upon the exertions of those individuals. The State should not be the agent of social change: rather the individuals who composed society were their own agents and the changes effected were in direct proportion to the efforts of self-help which these individuals made. The following passage shows Lowe's viewpoint quite clearly.

The theory of uneducated or half educated persons in general is, that Government is almost omnipotent, and that when an evil is not remedied the fault lies in the indolence, the selfishness, or the shortsightedness of Parliament. It is much pleasanter to an audience of non-electors to be told that the franchise would enable them to remedy the evils of their condition than to be told the real Truth that the evils they endure are remediable by themselves in their individual rather than in their collective capacity – by their own thrift and self-denial, not by pressing on Government to do that for them which they are able, if they will, to do without it.[24]

Lowe, like most of his contemporaries, believed in the value for society of individual competition and of the stimulus to effort which life, its fortunes and misfortunes, could provide. This he took to be the basic teaching of political economy. When others differed in their views from Lowe, he could only conclude that they were ignorant of this subject. In a leading article which he wrote for *The Times* on 24 November 1860, he chided John Bright for his unwillingness to consider political economy and in so doing gave his view of the limited role which the State should pursue in society. He wrote:

Here, again, political economy would have pointed out, if Mr. Bright would only deign to consult it, that to raise the people from poverty to wealth is not the duty, because it is not in the power of a Government. When Government has removed all obstacles to the accumulation of property, has given security to the person and a good administration of justice, it has done its part; and if people do not get on in the world they must lay the blame elsewhere. A man must be the architect of his own

[23] Cf. J. S. Mill, 'the worth of a State in the long run, is the worth of the individuals composing it', *Essay on Liberty*, London 1859, p. 207.

[24] Lowe, *Speeches and Letters on Reform*, p. 7.

fortune and rise by his own energy. All Government can do is to remove obstacles from his path.[25]

Lowe accepted what seemed an obvious truth in mid-Victorian England – that the free operation of the law of supply and demand in trade and business brought success and achievement – and he could see no reason why the same law should not be allowed to operate in social life.

Political economy was a subject whose field of study was wider than that of mere economics, and in Lowe's view, it could be successfully applied to various areas of social and economic life, including education. In 1868 in a letter to Sir John Simon, Lowe wrote about an article he had written, that it contained 'a great Economical Truth – that Education is no exception to the general Rules of Political Economy'.[26] This sentence provides the key for the understanding of most of Lowe's educational ideas and policies. In the light of this it is possible to see them not merely as measures hastily conceived for administrative convenience as some have asserted, nor as instruments forged for use in a class war as others have implied, but as exercises in the application of economics. This is not to deny Lowe's interest in devising administrative procedures. He had considerable administrative talent and it was a factor in all his policies, but his concern for economics dominated.

Lowe was much indebted to political economy in general and to Adam Smith in particular for his educational views. When in 1878 Lowe wrote an account of the achievements of political economy, it is notable that he included amongst them 'payment by results';[27] and ten years previously in developing his views on the education of the middle classes, Lowe founded his views on those of Adam Smith, attacking endowments and pressing for free trade in secondary education.[28]

However, it was not only political economy which led Lowe to emphasise the value of competition and free enterprise in economic and social life, including education. A moral and psychological viewpoint also supported his thinking about the respective

[25] *The Times*, 24 November 1860, second leader.

[26] Lowe (Viscount Sherbrooke) Mss. A.14, 31 October 1868, letter to Sir John Simon. [27] Lowe, 'Recent Attacks on Political Economy', p. 868.

[28] Lowe, *Middle Class Education*, p. 7, quoting Adam Smith, *The Wealth of Nations*, 1875 edn, p. 601.

roles of the State and the individual. Like most of his contemporaries, Lowe had a fear of demoralising people by giving them too much. He saw the connection between material and moral progress as a close one, and he would have contended that material wealth and comforts gained without effort not only went unappreciated by the gainer but degraded rather than helped the recipient's character. Payment by results was thus a natural policy for mid-Victorians like Lowe. Political economy recommended it and moral and psychological considerations upheld it.

Lowe's own personal life reinforced these views. Born an albino, he had found his deficient eyesight a great hindrance in his own struggle to win first, scholastic success, and later, a successful legal and political career. His triumph convinced him of the virtue which came from the individual's struggle in life, though it also left him a little self-righteous in addition. For example, in 1838 when he was only 27 years old, his eyes became so poor that he had to give up all idea of reading by candlelight. He afterwards wrote in his memoir: 'From that time till now, some forty years, I have never been able to read by candlelight, and when I think of all the things I might have known if I had not had this misfortune, I am astonished how persons who have all their winter evenings to themselves contrive to know so little.'[29]

It is likely that Lowe was also influenced by his father in his approach to life. For the Reverend Robert Lowe had begun in 1818 in his parish of Bingham, Nottinghamshire, 'the system of forcing independence upon paupers by means of a workhouse'.[30] This was later taken as the principle on which the Poor Law of 1834 was based and indeed Lowe always considered that his father was the author of that measure. Certainly Lowe was at one with his father in his adoption of the principle of discipline and self-help.

Lowe's opposition to the free granting of universal suffrage and his belief in the need for individual self-denial in order to achieve the franchise indicates his strong views in this matter and makes clearer his thinking about the State's provision of education. His views on the franchise and his views on education have much in common, for while they differ in details, basically Lowe's attitude is the same: people must help themselves to reach certain standards. In the following quotation Lowe is speaking about the achievement of the right to vote but it also makes clear the

[29] Patchett Martin, I, p. 33. [30] *Ibid.* I, pp. 48–51.

underlying philosophy which he brought to other issues, such as educational provision.

Not to take an extreme case, the Chancellor of the Exchequer says that 600 quarts of beer is a fair average consumption for every adult male in the course of the year, and, taking beer at 4*d.* a pot, the consumption of 240 quarts represents an annual outlay of 4*l.* If, therefore, persons who live in 8*l.* houses would only forgo 120 quarts annually, they might at once occupy a 10*l.* house, and acquire the franchise. That is the exact measure of the sacrifice which is required on their part to obtain this much-coveted right, to raise themselves from the position of slaves, to wipe off from their characters the mark of degradation and all other horrors that have been so feelingly depicted.[31]

Lowe is obviously naive here in assuming that there is enough work to go round, enough £10 houses to rent, enough room for all individuals to 'get on', so that in the end there is no need for poverty, but that is what he and many of his contemporaries believed. There was an essential optimism among the mid-Victorians that all could be well if individuals exerted themselves sufficiently to that end.

It is important to stress that Lowe's views about the individual and the State were not unusual but rather typical of most of the mid-Victorian contemporaries who belonged to his social class.[32] For a summary of the spirit and thinking of that age there is no better book than Samuel Smiles' *Self Help*, published in 1859, and that Lowe's views coincided with those of Smiles is readily apparent. Smiles wrote:

'Heaven helps those who help themselves' is a well tried maxim, embodying in a small compass the results of vast human experience. The spirit of self help is the root of all genuine growth in the individual; and exhibited in the lives of many, it constitutes the true source of national vigour and strength. Help from without is often enfeebling in its effects, but help from within invariably invigorates. Whatever is done for men or classes, to a certain extent takes away the stimulus and necessity of doing for themselves; and where men are subjected to over-guidance and over-government, the inevitable tendency is to render them comparatively helpless.[33]

[31] Lowe, *Speeches and Letters on Reform*, p. 48.

[32] For further discussion of this see W. L. Burn, *The Age of Equipoise*, London 1964, chap. 3, pp. 92–131.

[33] S. Smiles, *Self Help*, John Murray, London Centenary edn 1958, pp. 35–6.

Smiles and Lowe said what most men believed. It would be considered subversive in some quarters today to proclaim that society is no more than the sum of its individual persons, or that the State should seek to minimise its activities, that institutions and services should be efficient and pay for themselves or perish, and that the individual is responsible for his own actions. It is therefore all the more important, in considering Lowe's beliefs and policies, to recognise their context and not judge them by twentieth-century notions. Moreover it is important to realise that the social philosophy which Lowe maintained was not conceived negatively in a spirit of abdication and escape from social responsibility. Rather the balance of limited state action, individual self-help and individual voluntary philanthropy was seen as the most beneficial way, both morally and materially, of improving society. It must also be remembered that this balance was far from fixed. In the mid-Victorian period Liberalism changed from a philosophy of individualism which seemed to assert, as Marxist critics have held, middle-class interests, into a philosophy of a national community in which the interests of all classes and sections should be protected. To achieve this men were coming to see the need for an increased amount of state intervention in social and economic life. Just where and to what extent this should take place was a matter for continued debate, but in principle it was admitted. For example, contrary to Marxist expectation, Liberalism, having achieved complete freedom for industry and the enfranchisement of the middle class, went on to the enfranchisement of the working class and their protection against the worst features of industrialisation. Robert Lowe stood in the middle of this, and his own ideas and attitudes show this general transition. In particular he came to see the need for the expenditure of more public help in the interests of children. He wrote in 1878:

There is a point where the doctrine of *laissez-faire* ceases to be applicable, as in the case of children. As to when that point is reached, honest and able men may reasonably differ, but no-one ever claimed for political economy, though it may suit the interests of baffled sociologists to say, that it has any right to encroach on the domain of charity or mercy.[34]

Political economy formed many of Lowe's ideas on education, but together with his ever-present empiricism it also prevented him

[34] Lowe, 'Recent Attacks on Political Economy', p. 868.

from holding hard-and-fast doctrines which time and circumstances could not change. Thus, as mid-Victorian Liberalism changed, Lowe relented in his adherence to the principle of self-help, and in education, for example, he became a campaigner for a national system of secular education. In so doing Lowe was answering no visionary, progressive or socialist call. His views arose from the contemporary situation, and if they showed transition a little more quickly than those of many of his contemporaries, this was only a temporary difference. In the end his contemporaries caught up, and Robert Lowe's views may be seen to be no better, but also no worse, than those of many of his fellow mid-Victorians.

## MERITOCRACY

The third feature of Lowe's social and political philosophy, his belief in the value of meritocracy, was an individual viewpoint which was not necessarily shared by his contemporaries. Nevertheless, it developed logically from the position that individual character and development were of prime importance, by postulating that the best individuals should rule in society. To decide who were the best individuals Lowe accepted the traditional standards used in England, those of property and intellect, and of these the greatest for Lowe was intellect.

It was this which made Lowe so antagonistic to the granting of the franchise to the working class. 'It appears to me', he said, 'that nothing can be more manifest, looking to the peculiar nature of the working classes, than in passing a Bill such as is now proposed, you take away the principal power from property and intellect, and give it to the multitude who live on weekly wages.'[35] For Lowe, power in the State should belong to those who were intelligent and able to think. Moreover – and this is where property came into the argument – it was more likely that those who had property or capital would have more leisure to think constructively about the affairs of government, than those who had to spend all their time in manual work, earning enough to keep themselves and their families. Here Lowe was once again following a train of thought which Adam Smith had begun. Smith had suggested that the man who lived by manual labour, particularly in an industrialised

[35] Lowe, *Speeches and Letters on Reform*, pp. 53–4.

society, necessarily developed a 'torpor of his mind' which made him incapable of judging 'the great and extensive interests of his country'.[36] Lowe accepted this and took it to the logical conclusion that only the educated should have a share in government. Another conclusion, equally logical, which he might have drawn – that all men should be educated – he preferred to ignore at least until after 1867. Instead Lowe opposed the extension of the franchise under the Reform Act of 1867, on the grounds that this would give to the uneducated, to those incapable of judging the nation's interests, the ultimate power of deciding them. He asserted that:

> So far from believing that Democracy would aid the progress of the State, I am satisfied it would impede it. Its political economy is not that of Adam Smith and its theories widely differ from those which the intelligent and clear-headed working man would adopt, did his daily avocation give him leisure to instruct himself . . . because I am a Liberal, and know that by pure and clear intelligence alone can the cause of true progress be promoted, I regard as one of the greatest dangers with which the country can be threatened a proposal to subvert the existing order of things and to transfer power from the hands of property and intelligence, and to place it in the hands of men whose whole life is necessarily occupied in daily struggles for existence.[37]

In addition Lowe's adherence to the utilitarian philosophy of self-interest, according to which all men were seeking their best interests with all the means in their power, made him fearful of what the newly-enfranchised electors might do. He assumed that they would be intelligent enough to know their own interests and to act upon them and consequently he feared for the future. As it happened, those newly enfranchised after 1867 did not realise their potential and enter upon a course of violence and change. Lowe, however, was not to know that they would still be content to remain passive spectators of the game of politics and continue to allow others to play it for them. In his philosophy, moved by self-interest, the new electors should have become the new rulers. Consequently Lowe's first tactic was to oppose the proposed Reform Bill. Later, when he saw that despite opposition some measure of reform would be passed, he turned to support those

[36] Adam Smith, p. 616.
[37] Lowe, *Speeches and Letters on Reform*, pp. 60–61.

who, like John Stuart Mill, would wish to 'diminish and counteract the tyranny of majorities'[38] by establishing some system of proportional representation. This, in Lowe's view, was the last arrow left in the quiver of those who wanted an intellectual elite to rule, 'so that if this does not hit, there will be nothing left but one simple uniform franchise to be entrusted to, and left in, the hands of the lowest class of society'.[39] However, when the Reform Bill did pass, Lowe realised that in fact there was one other weapon remaining. If the educated were not to rule, then the rulers must be educated, and Lowe embarked upon a campaign for a better system of national education.

Lowe's concern for the rule of intelligence derived from his own intellectual abilities and experience. Highly intelligent himself, he had gone through Winchester College and Oxford University with distinction. He had been a successful private tutor at Oxford and it was only by chance that he was led away from the academic career for which he was so ably suited when he failed to obtain the Chair of Greek in the University of Glasgow.[40] With this background it is not surprising that Lowe should value intelligence and intellect in others and wish it to have first place in the government of society. Benjamin Jowett, the Master of Balliol College, Oxford, testified to this in the memoir he wrote of Lowe in 1893.

Of all Mr. Lowe's qualities, some of his friends have thought his natural love of intelligence to have been the most charming and characteristic. He was perhaps a little severe on the dull, the prejudiced or the commonplace; he was not one of those who 'suffer fools gladly'. But he lighted up at once when he met with a congenial spirit, and he was always ready to welcome anyone who would give him valuable information. A glow of satisfaction came over him whenever any new idea occurred to his mind; he rejoiced at any fresh discovery in Science, as if he himself had had a part in it . . . From youth upward, this striving after intelligence had been his chief pleasure and solace. His early years were a time of struggle to him, for he had been unlike other boys and young men. But he had always been sustained by absorbing intellectual interests; this was the golden thread which ran through his life.[41]

Another contemporary, while admitting the force of Lowe's own

[38] *Parliamentary Debates*, CLXXXVIII, col. 1103.

[39] *Parliamentary Debates*, CLXXXVIII, col. 1037.

[40] See above, p. 4.

[41] Patchett Martin, II, pp. 499–500. Jowett was a great admirer of Lowe and had dedicated his edition of Thucydides to him.

intellect, interpreted his attitude differently. James Bryce wrote of Lowe:

> He had a most unchristian scorn for the slow and the dull and the unenlightened . . . He did not conceal his contempt for the multitude . . . The very force and keenness of his intellect kept him aloof from other people and prevented him from understanding their sentiment.[42]

There is some truth in this. Lowe disliked intensely what he knew of the workings of the masses in the past and what he could see of their actions in the present. Lowe was born into the generation which grew up in the knowledge of the French Revolution and in fear of what a similar revolution might achieve in England. Even as a schoolboy, he had conceived a dislike of 'mobocracy' and he continued to hold to this throughout his life. At Winchester College in 1828, when he was then seventeen years of age, Lowe had written a poem entitled 'The Fidelity of the Swiss Guards to Louis XVI'. It shows clearly the genesis of his views.

> Not theirs to wish to break the regal chain
> To bid the many-headed Monster reign
> To plunge the land in anarchy and blood
> For vain chimeras of ideal good.[43]

It was the view of Lowe's niece, Mrs Chaworth Musters, that Lowe's horror of 'mobocracy' was strengthened in 1831 when he saw the sacking of Colwick Hall, Nottinghamshire, in some Reform riots.[44] This may be so. It is likely too that he was similarly affected by the attack he suffered at the Kidderminster election of 1857 when, though winning the poll, his face and head were cut and his skull fractured by the stones thrown at him by a mob of non-electors. Since 1832 Kidderminster as a constituency had been accustomed to wholesale bribery at elections, but in 1852 when Lowe secured the seat, he had refused to run up such extensive election expenses. It is true that the influence of Lord Ward, afterwards the Earl of Dudley, had helped to secure his success in the constituency, but Lowe refused to follow the example of previous candidates and buy beer freely. As one observer put it, 'Lowe appealed to rectitude and reason; the mob desired the bribe and the beer-barrel.'[45]

[42] James Bryce, *Studies in Contemporary Biography*, London 1903, p. 303.
[43] Patchett Martin, I, p. 74. [44] Patchett Martin, II, p. 159.
[45] *Ibid.* II, p. 154.

What Lowe saw and heard of democracy in America during his visit there from August to October 1856, what he knew of its working in Australia where he had lived for eight years from 1842 to 1850,[46] and what he saw at home in England of the trade union movement in the sixties, confirmed him in his distrust of the rule of the multitude in politics. The efforts of trade unions to secure the employment of union members only, their opposition to over-time, piece-work, and 'chasing' (where one worker strives to work faster than his fellows) appalled him. He concluded that the aim of the unions was: 'to enclose as many men as can be got into these societies, and then to apply to them the strictest democratic principle, and that is to make war against all superiority, to keep down skill, industry, and capacity, and make them the slaves of clumsiness, idleness and ignorance'.[47]

This fear and distrust of the masses crystallised into fervent opposition to the extension of the franchise. His opposition to the Reform Bill of 1867 is well known, but he also opposed later attempts to widen the franchise. On 4 September 1876 Lowe wrote to his brother: 'I am glad Dizzy is out of the House. It may be the means of staving off a little longer electoral districts and universal suffrage',[48] and in the following year, in opposition to Gladstone, he wrote an article against the extension of the franchise to agri-cultural labourers, reiterating his plea for the rule of 'the educated and experienced'.[49]

Lowe's views have sometimes been interpreted to suggest that he had a complete contempt for the working classes,[50] but this is to misunderstand Lowe's position. In this, as in most of his views, Lowe had a rational basis for his attitude. His opposition to trade union activities, for example, was not so much hostility to the

[46] In his speech on the Representation of the People Bill, 13 March 1866, Lowe said: 'I did not want to say anything disagreeable, but if you want to see the result of democratic constituencies, you will find them in all the assemblies of Australia, and in all the assemblies of North America.' Lowe, *Speeches and Letters on Reform*, p. 88.

[47] Lowe, *Speeches and Letters on Reform*, pp. 143–4.

[48] Patchett Martin, II, p. 439.

[49] R. Lowe, 'A New Reform Bill', *Fortnightly Review*, XX, N.S. No. CXXX, (1 October 1877), 449.

[50] Bryce, p. 303; B. W. Johnson, 'The Development of English Education 1856–1882 with special reference to the work of Robert Lowe, Viscount of Sherbrooke', unpublished M.Ed. thesis, University of Durham, 1956, pp. 324–6.

lower classes as 'hostility to any violation of economic laws to the inevitable detriment of society, by whatsoever means'.[51] His opposition to the extension of the franchise was a response to his basic premiss that the most intelligent and the best educated should rule.[52]

Lowe lived in a period when classes were more consciously stratified than in the present. Mark Pattison said 'class-education would seem to be as rooted an idea in the English mind as denominational religion'.[53] Consequently most of Lowe's utterances on the subject refer to classes in a positive, direct way which is neither possible nor acceptable in the more egalitarian society of today. However, as a result, to the charge that Lowe despised the lower classes as a whole, has been added the further charge that he wished to keep the existing class stratification and that he moulded and used his educational policies to this end. It is doubtful if Lowe was prejudiced against the lower classes as a whole. Whatever the strata of class men had been born to, those who worked hard and tried to improve themselves earned his praise and respect.[54] There is also some evidence that Lowe tried to avoid class discrimination in his political actions. In 1875, for example, when discussing the Conspiracy and Protection of Property Bill, he was much concerned that 'breach of contract' should apply to contractors and employers as well as to employees. Legislation should not show bias towards one class or another. 'Everybody must feel that it was extremely desirable that there should be one law for both the rich and the poor, and that there should be no ground given for the accusation or the suspicion that they were passing laws for their poorer fellow countrymen to which they themselves were not willing to submit.'[55] Nevertheless, evidence has been quoted against Lowe to suggest that he was prejudiced against the lower classes, and this needs to be considered.

Two passages in particular from Lowe's speeches have been used in this connection. The first comes from his speech on the Representation of the People Bill of 13 March 1866. On that occasion Lowe said:

[51] Duke, 'Robert Lowe. A reappraisal', p. 19.
[52] Johnson, p. 327, also admits this point.
[53] Mark Pattison, *Suggestions on Academical Organisation*, Edinburgh 1868, p. 326. [54] Lowe, *Speeches and Letters on Reform*, pp. 47–8.
[55] *Parliamentary Debates*, CCXXV, col. 1342.

Let any gentleman consider – I have had such unhappy experiences and many of us have – let any gentleman consider the constituencies he has had the honour to be concerned with. If you want venality, if you want ignorance, if you want drunkenness, and facility for being intimidated; or if, on the other hand, you want impulsive, unreflecting, and violent people, where do you look for them in the constituencies? Do you go to the top or to the bottom?[56]

This passage was construed at the time by some of Lowe's constituents[57] as an indication of his contempt for the masses, and later commentators[58] have used the passage in the same way. However, if it is seen in its context, this interpretation becomes less tenable. Lowe was asserting that many of the non-electors in the constituencies did exhibit the features he named, and no doubt he was partly remembering his own experiences at Kidderminster in 1857. He was also suggesting that if the Bill to lower the franchise qualification passed, then there would be an increase 'of corruption, intimidation and disorder, of all the evils that happen usually in elections',[59] but he was not castigating the working classes as a whole. Lowe's own written reply to the charge which Mr John D. Bishop and sixty other electors of the borough of Calne made in a letter to Lowe of 4 April 1866,[60] is still valid. Lowe wrote:

You observe 'with pain and regret the unjust and ungenerous satire which I have flung on the masses of my fellow-countrymen', and you assert that, speaking of them, I say 'If you want venality, ignorance, drunkenness, and the means of intimidation; if you want impulsive unreflecting, violent people, where would you look?' These words are in the middle of a sentence, the beginning and end of which have been omitted; had the passage been submitted to you in full, I think you would have seen that it did not refer to the masses of my working fellow-countrymen at all, but only to practices which notoriously exist in some boroughs among the poorer classes of electors. I was arguing that the proposed Franchise Bill would increase corruption and other malpractices at elections . . . The whole passage as reported in *The Times*, stands thus: '*I have had opportunities of knowing some of the constituencies in this country*, and I ask, if you want venality, ignorance, drunkenness, and the means of intimidation; if you want unreflecting violent people, where will you go to look for them – *to the top or to the bottom*?' – of what? of the constituencies of course. You will see by

56 Lowe, *Speeches and Letters on Reform*, p. 74.
57 *Ibid.* p. 22.
58 Johnson, p. 326
59 Lowe, *Speeches and Letters on Reform*, p. 76.
60 These letters are printed in *ibid.* pp. 21–7.

comparing this passage with the portion quoted in the protest you have signed, that its import is entirely changed by the omissions of the beginning and end, and instead of being pointed, as it was intended to be, at abuses notoriously existing in many constituencies, and daily exposed before the Election Committees now sitting, it is made to appear as an indiscriminate censure of a whole class, of which I was not speaking . . . I entirely agree with you, gentlemen, as to the possession by large numbers of the masses of my fellow working countrymen of great prudence, self-reliance, and perseverance, and, indeed, of many other qualities to which we owe the present position of England among the nations of the world. But you will now see that, as I was not, as you suppose, speaking of those masses, I cannot be correctly said to 'ignore' these good qualities because I did not mention them.

The second passage, which has been interpreted as showing Lowe's concern to preserve the existing class stratification, occurs in an address on *Primary and Classical Education* which he delivered to the Philosophical Institution of Edinburgh on 1 November 1867. It reads in full as follows, though often it is quoted only in part and this may in some measure explain the limited interpretations which have been placed upon it.

I have said that I am most anxious to educate the lower classes of this country, in order to qualify them for the power that has passed, and perhaps will pass in a still greater degree, into their hands. I am also anxious to educate, in a manner very different from the present, the higher classes of this country, and also for a political reason. The time has gone past evidently when the higher classes can hope by any direct influence, either of property or coercion of any kind, to direct the course of public affairs. Power has passed out of their hands, and what they do must be done by the influence of superior education and superior cultivation: by the influence of mind over mind – 'the sign and Signet of the Almighty to command', which never fails being recognised wherever it is truly tested. Well, then gentlemen, how is this to be done? Is it by confining the attention of the sons of the wealthier classes of the country to the history of these old languages and these Pagan republics, of which working men never heard, with which they are never brought into contact in any of their affairs, and of which, from the necessity of the case, they know nothing. Is it not better that gentlemen should know the things which the working men know, only know them infinitely better in their principles and in their details, so that they may be able, in their intercourse and their commerce with them, to assert the superiority over them which greater intelligence and leisure is sure to give, and to conquer back by means of a wider and more enlightened cultivation some of the influence? I confess, for myself, that, whenever I talk with an intelligent workman, so far from being able to assert any such superiority, I am always tormented with the conception, 'What a fool the man must think me when he finds me, upon whose education thousands of pounds have been spent, utterly ignorant of the matters which experience teaches him, and which he naturally thinks every educated man ought to know.' I think this ought easily to be managed. The lower classes ought to be educated to discharge the duties cast upon them. They should also be educated that they may appreciate and defer to a higher cultivation when they meet it; and the higher classes ought to be educated in a very different manner, in order that they may exhibit to the lower classes that higher education to which, if it were shown to them, they would bow down and defer.[61]

This passage has been quoted and commented upon in various ways. S. J. Curtis quoted an extract from it to show that Lowe's views on education 'were simply the product of his political and economic outlook, which in some ways belonged to the end of the 18th century'.[62] J. P. Sullivan in his thesis took the view that 'the masses were as canaille to Lowe'[63] and after commenting on the above passage, concluded that Lowe was dominated by 'his fear of the lower classes'[64] and consequently wished to hinder rather than develop a system of primary education. Professor B. Simon quotes the passage with the following comment: 'Lowe is quite clear that political reasons must dictate educational change, and equally clear about the political end educational reform is to serve.' He goes on to imply that Lowe wanted one education for the rich and another for the poor so that the two classes would be effectively separated,[65] and suggests that Robert Lowe wanted to use elementary education as a means 'to stabilise class society'.[66]

It has been pointed out that if Lowe's words, 'the higher classes ought to be educated in a very different manner' are read in the context of the argument of the whole passage, it will be seen that 'different' means different from the existing higher-class education[67] rather than different from lower-class education. Thus it

[61] R. Lowe, *Primary and Classical Education*, Edinburgh 1867, pp. 31–2.

[62] S. J. Curtis, *History of Education in Great Britain*, University Tutorial Press, 3rd edn London 1953, pp. 255–6.

[63] J. P. Sullivan, 'The Educational Work and Thought of Robert Lowe', unpublished MA (Education) thesis, University of London 1952, p. 67.

[64] *Ibid.* p. 238.

[65] B. Simon, *Studies in the History of Education 1780–1870*, London 1960, p. 356.

[66] *Ibid.* p. 365.

[67] This point is made by Duke, 'Robert Lowe. A Reappraisal', p. 30.

may be suggested that the overall argument of the passage is for curriculum reform to secure a meritocracy rather than the establishment of different forms of education for the different classes in an effort to stabilise class society.

Nevertheless, there can be no question that Lowe heartily disliked the idea of social revolution. Even if his main aim was not to preserve the existing class divisions but to secure meritocratic government, he hoped that the effect would be the same. In wanting a meritocratic elite he assumed that the traditional upper classes of society would be able to supply it. Ultimately this assumption was misguided. Lowe's concern for rule by a meritocracy and his reforms of the Civil Service during the years from 1869 to 1873 which initiated its establishment, progressively caused a social revolution which undermined the existing class structure. Lowe, though he did not intend it, sounded the death knell of the old class system. Once a government career was admitted to be open to talent it was ultimately possible that any man could rise to a foremost position in the State no matter what his station at birth had been.

As for the existing class stratification, Lowe did not rigidly uphold it. He even favoured the mixing of some of the classes in schools. On 13 June 1865, while giving evidence before the Schools Inquiry Commission, Lowe said that he thought it was 'extremely desirable' to educate middle-class children with those of the labouring class.[68] He envisaged government schools with sliding scales of fees appropriate to the incomes of the various parents and added that the middle classes might well choose government schools for their children since he thought it unlikely that either the endowed schools or private schools could compete with those assisted by the government.[69] Lowe also wanted to establish scholarships to enable poorer boys to go to schools which would give them a secondary education.[70] Lowe was quite prepared for social mixing and in addition his belief in self-help led him to expect social mobility, since individuals by their own efforts might well improve their respective stations in life. It is true that he did not consider that educational policies should be deliberately framed to achieve particular social ends, but if social mixing oc-

[68] S.I.C. IV, *Minutes of Evidence 1868*, p. 633, Q. 6572. [69] *Ibid.*
[70] *Ibid.* p. 638, Q. 6612.

curred as an incidental part of the process, then he was not opposed to it. Lowe conceived the purposes of education too much in terms of individual mental development to use it deliberately either to stratify the classes on the one hand or to promote social mobility on the other.

Lowe's position was well summarised, as his Victorian biographer pointed out, in an article in the *Standard* of 28 July 1892, written just after Lowe's death: 'He was an aristocrat to the core, in no class signification, but in the solid and substantial sense that he believed in Government by the best, and utterly disbelieved in the sagacity or superior wisdom of the crowd.'[71] Lowe was trying to uphold what he thought to be the values of culture, intellect and humanity, and to prevent them from being submerged by what he considered to be alien developments such as manhood suffrage. He made this quite clear in an article he wrote in answer to Gladstone[72] in 1877.

> Here then are the arguments in favour of manhood suffrage, as revised and corrected by the Minister [Gladstone][73] who proposed a £7 franchise in 1866. 1. Every man must directly, or indirectly, contribute to the revenue. The same thing may be said of every dog. A man satisfies the qualification by paying for a glass of beer. 2. Every man by his labour contributes to the public wealth. The same thing may be said of every carthorse. 3. Nine out of ten are fathers of families. This qualification is the condition of the continuance of the species which we share with the lower animals. 4. Every man is possessed of the power of doing a great deal of mischief. So is almost every animal. We have known houses where everything that was broken was attributed to the agency of the cat. It will hardly be believed that these four arguments, expounded, of course, and amplified, are the four Corinthian pillars which are destined to support the enormous fabric of universal suffrage . . . We sigh for some reason for submitting ourselves to the will of the many which is drawn at least from qualities peculiar to the human race, to which after all, the poorest and most ignorant among us do belong.[74]

Beneath the facetious tone of this passage Lowe was asserting his Platonic view that wisdom and virtue should rule. He believed in this strongly and was not afraid to take his stand by it.

[71] Patchett Martin, II, p. 160.

[72] W. E. Gladstone, 'The County Franchise and Mr. Lowe Thereon', *Nineteenth Century*, II (November 1877). [73] *Ibid.* p. 544.

[74] R. Lowe, 'Mr. Gladstone on Manhood Suffrage', *Fortnightly Review*, XXII. N.S. No. CXXXII (1 December 1877), 738.

Other Victorians such as Carlyle, John Stuart Mill and Matthew Arnold held a similar view but few upheld it as consistently as Lowe. It was a factor in the formulation of all his educational ideas, whether for the education of the poor, the reform of the public and endowed schools or the reform of university education. It also motivated his advocacy of open competition in appointments to the public services and the importance he gave to examinations at all levels of educational provision. Indeed Lowe's views on the virtue of a meritocracy crystallised most notably in the important role he ascribed to examinations.[75] He pressed for their adoption in various fields. In 1853, as Secretary of the India Board, he helped to establish them as a means of securing the best entrants to the Indian Civil Service,[76] and in 1870, largely due to the efforts of Lowe,[77] this precedent was followed when all branches of the Civil Service – except the Foreign Office and ironically some posts in the Education Department – were thrown open to competition by examination. Lowe's Revised Code of 1862 was based on the use of examinations as a means of ensuring efficiency in schools under the payment by results scheme. Lowe also advocated the use of government sponsored examinations in the private secondary schools of his day, as a means of giving parents a standard by which they could judge the value of the schooling for which they were paying.[78] At the university level too, Lowe pressed for state administered examinations as a means of raising standards.[79] The importance Lowe assigned to examinations reflected his acceptance of competition as a natural feature of the human condition. Most of his contemporaries would have agreed with this[80] and Lowe could dismiss opponents of examinations in a few terse words: 'there is no objection so frequently urged against competitions as the rather superficial one, that it is, in its nature competitive'.[81] The value of competition was, to Lowe, self-evident, and by using it in an ever-widening system of examinations Lowe considered

[75] For a discussion of the origin of examinations and their role in 19th-century life see J. Roach, *Public Examinations in England 1850–1900*, C.U.P. 1971, pp. 8–12. [76] Patchett Martin, II, pp. 62–3.

[77] M. Wright, *Treasury Control of the Civil Service 1854–74*, Oxford 1969, pp. 74–109. [78] *The Times*, 8 January 1864, third leader.

[79] R. Lowe, 'Shall we create a New University?', *Fortnightly Review*, XXI, N.S. No. CCXXII (1 February 1877), 170.

[80] See for example, J. S. Mill's view of the need for examinations: Mill, *On Liberty*, pp. 191–2. [81] *The Times*, 4 April 1860, first leader.

that merit would come to hold the supreme positions of influence in State and society.

In conclusion then, Lowe's views and policies on education arose largely from his own background and the climate of opinion in which he lived. They cannot be fully understood or interpreted fairly without reference to his political realism, his ideas about the relative roles of the individual and the State in society, and his concern to secure government by the most intelligent and the best educated.

# 3

# THE GENESIS OF PAYMENT BY RESULTS

Robert Lowe's name will always be associated with the system of 'Payment by Results' which he inaugurated in the Revised Code of 1862. Probably no man has been so universally condemned by educationists as Lowe.[1]

This combined statement and verdict is substantially true. Payment by results has brought Lowe into almost complete disrepute among writers on education. It faced criticism from the moment of its birth and it has continued to attract it ever since. To educationists the attitudes embodied in the administrative system which Lowe established have seemed stultifying in the extreme, reducing the content of primary education in schools to a minimum of reading, writing and arithmetic, and encouraging teaching methods of so mechanical a nature that the classrooms were emptied of any creative learning and enjoyment. Similarly, to later generations with more egalitarian and collectivist views of the role the State should play in providing education, the cheese-paring attempts of Lowe to cut expenditure on education have seemed heartlessly illiberal.

If, however, payment by results is considered historically, in the context of its times, a different view of it emerges. It may be seen then not as an alien substance suddenly injected by Lowe into a healthy system in such a way as to injure it, but rather as a change which grew naturally from the prevailing environment. For most mid-Victorians of the dominant middle and upper classes, payment by results was an acceptable, practical and very necessary answer to a pressing problem. Public money was being spent to provide education for those too poor to provide it for themselves, and most of the available evidence suggested that the public were not getting value for money. To remedy this a system which demanded results, as measured by examinations, before state grants were paid, commended itself to the *laissez-faire* capitalist society

[1] Curtis, p. 253.

of the day. It was natural, too, that such a system would attract Lowe for it accorded well with his views about popular education and also his general political and social philosophy. It is important, however, to stress that Lowe did not invent the idea of payment by results. It arose from the existing ideals and practical problems of mid-Victorian society, and there were precedents for its use long before Lowe decided to implement it as a policy. Payment by results was in fact Lowe's response to two particular circumstances which confronted him on taking office as Vice-President of the Committee of Council on Education in 1859: first, the conclusions which had emerged from the parliamentary debates of the fifties about education, and secondly the evidence gained from the various experiments which had already been made in applying the principle of payment by results.

## PARLIAMENTARY OPINION

During the fifties the House of Commons became increasingly concerned with the question of popular education and the existing pattern for its provision was the subject of long debates. The basic principle of the existing provision was that education was primarily the duty of parents, though where parents could not afford to do this they could be assisted by the voluntary contributions of others who were financially better placed. By 1850 most voluntary contributions were channelled through school societies: the inter-denominational British and Foreign Schools Society, the National School Society of the Church of England and the school agencies of the Roman Catholic Church had established between them 1,943 schools providing elementary education for the poor throughout the country. Of these 1,562 were National (Church of England) schools, 282 were British and Wesleyan schools and 99 were Roman Catholic, though there was, of course, no systematic foundation of schools which ensured any equality of provision for the population as a whole.[2] Since 1833 the State had assisted this work with financial grants, beginning in that year with a grant of £20,000 to be distributed between the British and Foreign School Society and the National Society for the purpose of building schools. In 1847 financial help was extended to Roman Catholic schools and over

[2] *Minutes of Report of Committee of Council on Education 1850*, p. iii.

the years the size of the grant had increased so that when Lowe took office in 1859 it stood at £668,000.[3]

From the various parliamentary debates on this pattern of provision, certain conclusions emerged which commanded so large a measure of support from Members of Parliament that Lowe could not ignore them. Firstly, there was concern about the deficiencies of educational provision in England, particularly as it compared with other countries. On 16 March 1855, Sir John Pakington, MP for Droitwich, in proposing a 'Bill for the better encouragement and promotion of Education in England' pointed out that of the nation's children about 41 per cent were at school, some 12 per cent were at work and over 46 per cent were neither at school nor at work.[4] He went on to claim that in making comparisons with other countries as to the quantity and quality of elementary education – the latter being measured in terms of the range of the curriculum in primary schools – 'with the exception of Russia, Spain, Italy and the Slave States of America, England is at the bottom of the scale'.[5] Pakington continued with arguments to convince the House of the need for more educational provision, and it is notable that these were framed in social rather than economic terms. It was not that England should fear to fall behind other nations industrially, but rather that its crime would increase and the quality of its social and personal life diminish if better schooling was not implemented. Pakington quoted the example of Austria where 'in one of the best educated countries in Europe, crime is greatly less than in England'.[6] He contrasted with this the position in England where

> we find in one year, in one gaol an aggregate of 800 persons who never heard the name of the Saviour. We find in one year, in one gaol, 300 persons who did not know the months of the year. This . . . is ignorance not only of religion, but of everything, both secular and religious which can tend to elevate human beings and make them worthy of the name.[7]

It may be that after the Paris Exhibition of 1867 and the Franco–Prussian War, England did begin to feel, as it is so often asserted, that industrial and military power might depend upon the extent

[3] *Parliamentary Debates*, CLV, col. 313.
[4] *Parliamentary Debates*, CXXXVII, col. 649.
[5] *Parliamentary Debates*, CXXXVII, col. 650.
[6] *Parliamentary Debates*, CXXXVII, col. 654.
[7] *Parliamentary Debates*, CXXXVII, col. 657.

of its educational provision, but in the fifties there is little evidence of such considerations. There was a great concern to reduce illiteracy and give the population as a whole the benefits of an elementary education, but these benefits were seen in moral and religious terms and in the context of social life. Sir John Pakington's views on this were typical of many.

A second conclusion of the educational debates of the fifties was, paradoxically enough, a concern to cut the increasing costs of education. Consequently the question arose that if more schools were to be provided to remedy the deficiencies, how were they to be financed? One repeated answer was to allow the raising of local rates for education, with local school boards to share it out among the various denominational bodies which sponsored schools. The Manchester and Salford Bill, for example, proposed to levy a 6*d.* rate for this purpose, but it was rejected on 21 February 1854 because of the religious difficulties involved in the granting of rate aid to denominations which not all the rate-payers could in conscience support.[8] Similarly, Sir John Pakington's Bill of 16 March 1855, for the establishment of local administrative boards – popularly elected, to administer grants and build new schools in which the religious teaching should be in accord with the religion of the majority in the district[9] – was eventually withdrawn in July 1855 because of the religious difficulties involved.[10] Lord Russell's Resolutions introduced on 6 March 1856 for local rates, more Inspectors, more schools and a conscience clause[11] also failed to gain sufficient support in the House of Commons. In short, the idea of local rates for education was repeatedly shown to be a non-starter at this time. Not only did it arouse the opposition of those with allegiances to particular religious denominations but it also antagonised those who supported the voluntary principle, and favoured this and self-help rather than state or local rate subsidies. There were not a few who held with G. Hadfield, a Member for Sheffield, that 'voluntary efforts, properly regulated, were sufficient to provide for the educational wants of the country'.[12]

[8] *Parliamentary Debates*, CXXX, cols. 1045–111; also *Report from the Select Committee on Manchester and Salford Education, 1852, Minutes of Evidence*, p. 264. [9] *Parliamentary Debates*, CXXXVII, col. 667.

[10] *Parliamentary Debates*, CXXXIX, col. 388.

[11] *Parliamentary Debates*, CXL, cols. 1955–80.

[12] *Parliamentary Debates*, CXXXVII, col. 673. As for example, Edward Baines, MP for Leeds. See *Parliamentary Debates*, CLV, col. 323.

If there was no general desire to turn to local rates for education similarly there was no wish to increase the costs to the central government. When Lowe took office the pressure for financial retrenchment, which had followed the end of the costly Crimean War, was still strong and already education had been marked out as a field where cuts should be made. In June 1858, under the Derby administration, the Newcastle Commission had been set up 'to inquire into the present State of Popular Education in England, and to consider and report what measures, if any, are required for the Extension of sound and cheap elementary instruction to all classes of the People'. The implication in these terms of reference was that the costs of popular education should be kept to a minimum. Apart from this, there was direct pressure from his Cabinet colleagues on Lowe to restrict educational expenditure. In particular the Chancellor of the Exchequer, W. E. Gladstone, was continually battling for economy in all directions. Early in 1860 he was pressing the Cabinet for economy, particularly in the field of military estimates and the construction of fortifications,[13] but his concern spread to government expenditure as a whole. Gladstone argued for economy on moral as much as financial grounds and nowhere was his viewpoint better expressed than in his budget speech of 15 April 1861. 'For my own part', he said, 'I am deeply convinced that all excess in the public expenditure beyond the legitimate wants of the country is not only a pecuniary waste – for that, although important, is yet a comparatively trifling matter – but a great political, and above all, a great moral evil.'[14] Already Gladstone had shown his reluctance to grant public money for education in 1853, when he had been Chancellor of the Exchequer in a previous administration. He had opposed Lord Granville's desire to increase government aid to education then, and more particularly had refused aid to Kneller Hall, a non-denominational training college near Richmond for Poor Law school teachers.[15] He had also expressed his desire to control educational expenditure in a Commons debate on 22 July 1859, when he regretted that since the appointment of a Vice-President of the Committee of Council on Education in 1856, the Treasury did not see the Minutes authorising expenditure, as they had done

[13] Morley, I, pp. 506–9. [14] *Parliamentary Debates*, CLXII, col. 595.

[15] Lord Edmond Fitzmaurice, *The Life of Lord Granville 1815–1891*, 3rd edn, 2 vols. London 1905, I, pp. 415–16.

previously.[16] His speech of 17 July 1860 on the abortive Education Bill to secure universal schooling at least part-time for children under twelve made explicit his desire to keep down the costs of education. In Gladstone's view:

The passing of the Bill at the present moment was as much out of the question as a Bill to abolish the House of Commons . . . Such were the threatening circumstances arising from the heavy expenditure for education that had been going on for some years, that he was not willing to interfere with, or prejudge, the right consideration by premature discussions like the present. The public mind was absolutely unprepared to deal with the question.[17]

Such was the attitude of perhaps the most formidable of Lowe's Cabinet colleagues. It could not help but encourage Lowe to seek a means of reducing the education estimates. It is likely, however, that Gladstone's influence was even more specific in deciding educational policy. When he heard that a full implementation of the recommendations of the Newcastle Commission would entail great public expenditure he seems to have favoured the Revised Code as a measure of economy which would also go some way towards meeting those recommendations. According to Lord Edmond Fitzmaurice's *Life of Earl Granville*, the Chairman of the Newcastle Commission wrote

warning Lord Granville that their recommendations would mean great expense, and that in order to avoid public odium it would be necessary before proposing them to Parliament to make large corresponding reductions if possible in other branches of public expenditure. This warning naturally found a responsive listener in the mind of Mr Gladstone, who was again at the Exchequer; but he acknowledged that other reasons, besides economy weighed with him.[18]

In the Cabinet papers and memoranda on Lowe's Revised Code[19] there is no record of Gladstone's views. However from other evidence it seems that he supported Lowe, particularly because the Code was likely to reduce public expenditure. Certainly in 1864, in a letter to Palmerston, Gladstone expressed his wholehearted approval of Lowe's measure. Pointing out that expenditure had been greatly reduced since 1859 when there had

[16] *Parliamentary Debates*, CLV, col. 342.
[17] *Parliamentary Debates*, CLIX, cols. 2024–5. [18] Fitzmaurice, I, pp. 421–2.
[19] See Russell Papers, Public Record Office, P.R.O. 30/22/27.

been great need for 'the operation of the pruning knife' he went on to state that

> in one very important point, the economy effected has been accompanied with a great and salutary reform, I mean the Administration of the Vote for Education in Great Britain. I am far from thinking that all, which is desirable and practicable has been effected; but it is something to say that we have checked what was almost an inveterate tendency to rapid expansion of change, without the smallest decline (but the contrary) in the efficiency of the expenditure.[20]

In the House of Commons there was little doubt that Gladstone was behind Lowe in the Revised Code. He was seen, perhaps not unfairly, as the villain behind all restrictions on educational expenditure.[21]

Apart from Gladstone, Lowe also had the support of most of his Cabinet colleagues. Sir George Grey, Chancellor of the Duchy of Lancaster, Lord Stanley of Alderley, the Postmaster-General, Sir Charles Wood at the India Office and the Duke of Argyll, the Lord Privy Seal, all welcomed Lowe's policy.[22] Lord Granville, the Lord President of the Council, was totally in agreement with Lowe's views[23] and continued to hold that the Revised Code was an 'excellent' measure which produced an economy in the public grant to education and increased the efficiency of teaching in the schools.[24] There were, however, two notable exceptions to this fulsome support. Earl Russell, the Foreign Secretary, objected strongly to the way in which it was now proposed to distribute grants, and considered that Granville and Lowe were attempting 'to limit the extent and degrade the quality of popular education'.[25] However he did want some retrenchment in the expenditure on education and suggested that in future the total amount for education should be limited to £800,000 by refusing any new applica-

[20] Palmerston Papers, *Gladstone and Palmerston. The Correspondence of Lord Palmerston with Mr Gladstone, 1851–1865*, ed. P. Guedella, London 1928, p. 293.

[21] See the comment of Sir J. Pakington 11 July 1861 that cuts 'arose out of the systematic determination of the Chancellor of the Exchequer to reduce the amount even for education purposes. Of this they had several proofs.' *Parliamentary Debates*, CLXIV, col. 706.

[22] Russell Papers, P.R.O. 30/22/27, fols. 141–50.

[23] Russell Papers, P.R.O. 30/22/27, fols. 136–7.

[24] *Parliamentary Debates*, CLXXIV, col. 1189, 18 April 1864.

[25] Russell Papers, P.R.O. 30/22/27, fols. 130–32, memorandum 4 January 1862.

tions from schools to receive grants.[26] Russell had held for some time that the original intention of the parliamentary grant was not to set up grant-aided schools all over the country 'but to show what a good school should be'.[27] He had no doubt 'that the progress of the grant system must be slackened and in some instances stopt'[28] but he could not accept the principle of payment by results. Russell's views were, in short, backward looking. The grant was to be reduced, the number of state-aided schools left at its existing level and any expansion in schooling was to be the result of voluntary effort. It was ironic that, holding the views he did, he should criticise Lowe for preventing 'the work, of raising the standard and extending the sphere of popular education'.[29]

The other notable exception to Cabinet support for Lowe was Palmerston himself. It has been alleged that Palmerston was the great stumbling block to increased public expenditure on education. However from a memorandum he wrote on the Revised Code it is clear that on the contrary he accepted such an increase as both inevitable and beneficial. Though aware that the grant for education was increasing every year, he considered that the money was well spent and that the country had full value for its expenditure in the 'improved intelligence and good conduct' of the lower classes to whom it had been given.[30] It was, in his view, quite natural that the amount of grant should be increasing since the birth rate, particularly among the lower classes, was itself steadily increasing. He had no doubt that the annual expenditure would soon exceed £2 million, and he suggested that if in any one year Parliament considered that the expense was too great, then it would just have to limit the yearly vote. Since grants were made to depend upon voluntary contributions this would produce difficulties for some schools, but in Palmerston's view the basis of the existing system with its insistence upon voluntary contributions was intended 'to prevent the whole expense from gradually falling on the public'. He realised that in poor districts where no voluntary subscription was possible and consequently no public grant made, no adequate schooling was likely to exist, but he was resigned to the fact since

[26] *Ibid.*

[27] Granville Papers, P.R.O. 30/29/24, pt. 1, letter from Russell to Granville, 4 January 1860. [28] *Ibid.*

[29] Russell Papers, P.R.O. 30/22/27, fols. 130–32, memorandum 4 January 1862.

[30] Russell Papers, P.R.O. 30/22/27, fols. 128–9, memorandum of 5 January 1862.

'as no human arrangements can be perfect . . . there is no help for this'.[31] Palmerston thought that some improvements possibly could be made in the existing system, though he did not indicate them. However the Revised Code he thought impracticable, and he considered that the most prudent course would be to withdraw it altogether. It might be defended logically and theoretically, but Palmerston considered it open to objection in one of its fundamental principles. He wrote:

It is easy to say that Payment is to be regulated by the number of children who on Examination shall be found able to read, write and cypher well. But the attainment of a child in writing, reading and arithmetic cannot be measured by a fixed and certain standard like his height and weight, and besides the objection with respect to the time which such examinations will take, will not each examiner find it difficult to draw the line which is to separate sufficient from insufficient attainment, and is [it] not likely or indeed certain that different examiners will apply different standards, and that thus inequalities will arise which will cause complaint.[32]

Palmerston also objected to the Revised Code on another level. He did not think that politically it was possible to enforce the measure. There were too many people against it and in his view the wise course was 'to yield to the storm' and withdraw it. In fact Palmerston was proved wrong on all but his first point. The grant over the years did continue to increase but it did not prove impossible either to devise a system of standards or to apply it. Contemporaries did not agree about the suitability of the standards fixed, as the varied evidence given before the Cross Commission of 1888 shows.[33] Nor did Inspectors find it easy to work the system and, as a result, the demand arose for the training of Inspectors for this work, particularly in view of the fact that most of them had no previous experience of school work.[34] Nevertheless, the standards system did prove practicable and if in the view of educationists, such as Matthew Arnold, the system was bad, other equally notable Inspectors, such as Joshua Fitch, were in favour of it.

[31] *Ibid.*

[32] Russell Papers, P.R.O. 30/22/27, fols. 128–9, memorandum of 5 January 1862.

[33] Final Report of *Royal Commission on Education Acts, 1888*, Index to Evidence, pp. 191–7.

[34] *Parliamentary Debates*, CCXLIII, cols. 1607–10, 21 February 1879.

There were other members of Parliament who wanted increased government expenditure on education as money well spent on a worthy cause,[35] but they were in a minority. Most members wanted some retrenchment and saw the Revised Code as a practical way of ensuring it. They also wanted the Government to play a limited role in the provision of education and act as no more than a supplement to parental and voluntary effort. The classic statement of this position was made by C. B. Adderley, who had been Vice-President of the Committee of Council during Derby's ministry (1858–9) and Lowe's predecessor in the office. 'The business of the Government', he told the House of Commons on 22 July 1859,

> was to do as little as it could with reference to what was really the duty of the people themselves. The education of children was naturally a parental function and was not the proper duty of the Government, which only interfered where its interposition was absolutely necessary, and after voluntary action was stimulated and in constant proportion as it become self-acting, the Government's aid should be at the earliest possible period withdrawn. The duty of the right hon. Gentleman (Mr Lowe) was therefore to watch carefully the public expenditure for education and to reduce every unnecessary grant of public money the instant it was found that the object could be attained in some other way.[36]

That such public advice accorded well with Lowe's private opinion was comforting for him. More importantly however, it meant that he could now approach the task of framing new regulations for the administration of the educational grant secure in the knowledge that parliamentary opinion was opposed, not only to any increase in the size of the central grant, but also to local rates as an alternative proposition.

## PRECEDENTS

The other major influence on Lowe in the formulation of his policy was the gradual evolution of the principle of payment by results and the experiments in its application which had taken place in the fifties. The starting point of this was the view, natural enough in a capitalist-dominated entrepreneurial society, that if public money was spent, then some means should be found of

[35] *Parliamentary Debates*, CLV, cols. 323, 340.
[36] *Parliamentary Debates*, CLV, col. 329.

ensuring value for money. Payment by results was the translation of such a viewpoint into educational terms. The Committee of Council on Education first implemented this principle in 1846 when a scheme of payment by results was used as a basis for the financing of the pupil-teacher system. The salaries both of pupil-teachers and of the teachers who instructed them, were made to depend upon their success in annual examinations, and the grants to Normal Schools which gave pupil-teachers further training were also distributed in the same way.[37] Some seven years later the principle was extended as a basis for the payment of school grants. In a Minute of 2 April 1853 the Committee of Council decided to give capitation grants to schools ranging from 3*s*. to 6*s*. the amount depending upon the number and sex of the scholars in a school. One condition of these grants was 'that three-fourths of the scholars above seven and under nine years of age; three-fourths of those above nine and under eleven; and three-fourths of those above eleven and under thirteen respectively pass such an examination before Her Majesty's Inspector or Assistant Inspector, as shall be set forth in a separate minute of details'.[38]

On 20 August 1853 an explanatory circular, signed by Ralph Lingen, the Secretary to the Education Department, was issued to Her Majesty's Inspectors giving the promised details. It is an interesting document in three particular ways. First, it indicates the official view – a view, it may be added, which the majority of all classes would have subscribed to – that the demands of the labour market and the economy should be allowed free operation and that children should be free to work if their parents wished it at the ages of ten or eleven. Secondly, it indicated the growing concern of the Committee to secure value for money by ensuring efficient teaching in state-aided schools. The circular emphasised these two points in the following way: 'it is therefore of great social importance to bring increased attention to bear upon those children in each school who are approaching the age at which their labour becomes valuable, and to make the measure of public assistance depend in some degree upon the connexion between such age and proficiency'.[39] Thirdly, the actual details of the

[37] Minutes of the Committee of Council on Education, 25 August 1846 and 21 December 1846, printed in Sir James Kay-Shuttleworth, *Four Periods of Public Education*, London 1862, pp. 537–8.

[38] *Minutes of Committee of Council 1852–3*, p. 15.

[39] *Minutes of Committee of Council 1853–4*, p. 15.

proposed examination to test the proficiency of pupils are interesting because they indicate the kind of tests which were eventually incorporated in the Revised Code which came into operation in 1863.

It was proposed to examine all children above the age of nine in two divisions; those under eleven years of age and those of eleven and over.[40] The details of the examination were given as follows:

1. In the first division how many were able:
   (a) To read simple narratives with intelligence.
   (b) To work from dictation a sum in simple subtraction, multiplication, or division correctly.
   (c) To write on a slate from dictation, with correct spelling, a simple sentence twice read to them, first consecutively, and then by one word at a time.
2. In the second division how many were able to:
   (a) Read books of general information fluently.
   (b) Work from dictation a sum in one of the four first compound rules of arithmetic correctly.
   (c) Write a paper from dictation in a neat hand and with correct spelling, two or three simple sentences twice read to them, first consecutively, and then by a few words at a time.
   (d) Point out the parts of speech in the same sentence (orally).
   (e) Answer questions in the tables of weights and measures (orally).
   (f) Answer a few elementary questions in geography (orally) and on other subjects of useful information. You should be careful to adapt this part of the examination to the particular course of study pursued in the school.[41]

The circular also added advice about the administration of the examination and emphasised that it 'is not intended to supersede any part of that included in the general examination of the school',[42] which Inspectors already made. This latter point was later reiterated by Lowe and his successors in the Education Department, when the Revised Code authorised the use of an examination as a supplement to general inspection, though the point was ignored by many contemporary critics, and subsequent commentators, too, have often failed to register it. Inspectors were not required to keep or forward examination papers to the Department,

[40] *Minutes of Committee of Council 1853–4*, p. 15. Here is one of the origins of the notorious 11+ examination.
[41] *Minutes of Committee of Council 1853–4*, p. 16.
[42] *Minutes of Committee of Council 1853–4*, p. 16.

but they were asked to record their results on a specially produced form.

This attempt to assess more specifically the education given in state-aided schools did not operate for very long. The results of the first year's operation were tabulated in the Minutes of 1853–4[43] but this was never repeated because it was found that there had been so little uniformity in filling up the form by Inspectors that tabulation of the results was meaningless.[44] In future it was decided merely to ask Inspectors to record which of the listed subjects were taught in schools, together with an indication of how they were taught.[45] A copy of the form on which such records were to be made is given in Table 1. The instructions for its completion were as follows:[46]

The table in the enclosed specimen gives the total number of the children whom the Inspector finds in school, and his opinion *generally*, of the quality of the instruction throughout the school in each of the subjects taught.

This is all that is indispensable, and this much can be given in each school inspected, whatever may be its organisation.

The divisions of the table *into classes* may be regarded as made entirely for the Inspector's own convenience, in affording him stages for the record of his inspections as he proceeds; he may leave them blank, or he may fill them up *with the number of children* whom he examines, as in the line 'Holy Scriptures', or *with qualifying marks* as in the line 'Catechism', or *with both* as in the line 'Liturgy'. These entries under particular classes will *not* be made the basis of any statistical summary, but will merely be regarded as the Inspector's own memoranda of what he did in the school; the only part taken from this table for record will be the total number of children present, and the Inspector's *general* judgment of each subject as expressed in the last column.

The qualifying words are:

| | |
|---|---|
| Excellent .. .. | e. |
| Good .. .. .. | g. |
| Fair .. .. .. | f. |
| Moderate .. .. | m. |
| Imperfect .. .. | i. |
| Bad .. .. .. | b. |
| Not taught .. .. | –. |

43 *Minutes of Committee of Council 1853–4*, p. 77.
44 *Minutes of Committee of Council 1855–6*, p. 26.
45 *Minutes of Committee of Council 1855–6*, p. 26.
46 *Minutes of Committee of Council 1855–6*, pp. 26–7.

TABLE 1 *Specimen report of examination by Inspector, 1854*

| | 1st Class | 2nd Class | 3rd Class | 4th Class | 5th Class | 6th Class | 7th Class | 8th Class | Total present in School |
|---|---|---|---|---|---|---|---|---|---|
| Number present at Examination: Girls | | | | | | | | | 53 |
| Number present at Examination: Boys | | | | | | | | | 61 |
| Number present at Examination: Total in each Class | | | | | | | | | 114 |
| Holy Scriptures | 15 | 11 | 17 | | | | | | g |
| Catechism | g | f | m | | | | | | g |
| Liturgy | 15/m | 11/i | 17/b | | | | | | i |
| Reading: Letters and Mono-syllables | | | | | | | | | f |
| Reading: Easy Narratives | | | | | | | | | f |
| Reading: Books of General Information | | | | | | | | | g |
| Writing: From Copy: On Slates | | | | | | | | | f |
| Writing: From Copy: On Paper | | | | | | | | | |
| Writing: From Dictation: On Slates | | | | | | | | | f |
| Writing: From Dictation: On Paper | | | | | | | | | |
| Arithmetic: Simple Rules | | | | | | | | | g |
| Arithmetic: Compound Rules | | | | | | | | | |
| Arithmetic: Proportion and Practice | | | | | | | | | g |
| Arithmetic: Fractions | | | | | | | | | i |
| Arithmetic: Decimals | | | | | | | | | – |
| Arithmetic: Higher Rules | | | | | | | | | – |
| Geography | | | | | | | | | f |
| Grammar | | | | | | | | | f |
| History | | | | | | | | | e |
| Music from Notes | | | | | | | | | – |
| Drawing | | | | | | | | | – |

As these signs afford ample scope for recording differences of merit, and an indefinite number of such signs defies tabulation, it is particularly requested that none other may be used in expressing quality in the Form No. X.

Her Majesty's Inspectors should test *some* part of the school in *every* subject which purports to be taught in it.

Though the first attempt to establish a more precise system of assessing the efficiency of schools was suspended, a precedent had been set and the idea increasingly commended itself to various individuals and groups. For example on 4 April 1853, W. Johnson Fox, the Member for Oldham, speaking on Russell's resolutions to allow town councils to raise rates for education, suggested that to ensure value for the spending of public money on education a system of payment by results should be established. His statement on this occasion is significant enough to be quoted in full.

To make the application of national grants most conducive to the improvement of education, remuneration should be given, not in reference to the number of children or the mere amount of attendance, but in reference to the attainment; that it should be the result of something like an enquiry by the inspectors into what was actually taught. Let all the schools retain their present denominational character if they would, but if they were always rewarded in this way, if the amount was proportioned to the amount of education actually realised in the school, that would be a stimulus which could operate very strongly indeed towards raising the character of education.[47]

The principle was once again taken up by the Committee of Council when by a Minute of 26 January 1854 they authorised extra payments to teachers whose pupils successfully passed the annual exercises set them in drawing[48] and this was continued by a later amending Minute of 24 February 1857.[49] Precedent became practice when certain Inspectors saw the value of written examinations and began to use them in their inspection of schools. The Reverend M. Mitchell, who inspected Church of England schools in Norfolk, Suffolk and Essex, reported in 1857 that he had used a written examination in all his schools. For all classes able to write – normally about two-thirds of the scholars – the following exercises had been set: written dictation lasting a quarter of an hour, some dictated sums, a map to draw, the parsing of a short

[47] *Parliamentary Debates*, cxxv, col. 557.
[48] *Minutes of Committee of Council 1853–4*, p. 39.
[49] *Minutes of Committee of Council 1856–7*, pp. 26–7.

sentence and the writing out of a question and answer from the Catechism. In addition the Inspector had heard all the classes read and listened to an oral examination of the upper classes in geography, grammar, history and scripture conducted by the master, the pupil-teachers and the local clergyman. Mitchell commented that the result was most satisfactory and that both managers and teachers considered it a great improvement on previous methods of inspection.[50]

It is likely that officials in the Education Department drew Lowe's attention to these earlier essays in payment by results and it should be remembered in this connection that Lowe, with his poor eyesight, was almost wholly dependent upon the various officials and clerks under him to read him any relevant documents.[51] Certainly Lowe would have had read to him the report which the Reverend J. P. Norris submitted in 1860, for it came to the Education Department when Lowe was in office and it was his custom to have his private secretary read Inspectors' reports to him.[52] Norris inspected Church of England schools in Cheshire, Salop and Stafford that year and, commenting on the fact that in his district only a quarter stayed on at school long enough to reach the first class, he pressed for a better use of the time spent in the lower classes, individual examination of children and the payment of the grant according to the results. He accepted that the labouring man would not be able to keep his child at school until he reached the first class and this made him all the more anxious to ensure that if a child passed with regular attendance through the fifth, fourth and third classes of a school, then as a matter of course, he or she should emerge as 'a good reader and writer, or seamstress, and know something of arithmetic'.[53] He considered that the best way to achieve this was to make the capitation grants 'depend on the *results* of the schoolwork', and suggested that assistant examiners, chosen from among the certificated masters and mistresses, should be appointed to help the Inspectors examine the children individually in the elementary subjects of reading, writing, arithmetic and needlework.[54]

Norris reiterated his views in his report for 1860–61, stating categorically that

[50] *Minutes of Committee of Council 1857–8*, p. 346.
[51] *Parliamentary Debates*, CLXXIV, col. 1209. [52] *Ibid.*
[53] *Report of Committee of Council 1859–60*, pp. 109–12. [54] *Ibid.*

the time has come for a commutation of some portion of the annual grants to schools into *grants for work done*. One step in this direction would be taken if the original character of the capitation grant were restored, and if it were paid on account of those children only who attained a certain fixed standard of proficiency in reading, writing and arithmetic.[55]

A year later Lowe was to implement a system of payment by results almost in the same terms and with the same arguments that Norris had used. Norris's influence on Lowe seems obvious and he was equally influential in submitting his views as evidence to the Newcastle Commission, for its Report certainly echoed the views of Norris,[56] and indeed recommended a partial application of the payment by results principle.[57]

Prior to the Newcastle Report of 1861, however, payment by results had been adopted as a principle for dispensing financial aid by the Department of Science and Art. In 1856 the Department had been transferred from the Board of Trade and it had come under the aegis of the Committee on Education. On 10 June 1859 the Board gave approval to a Minute dated 2 June 1859 on Aid to Science Instruction, in which annual payments were to be made to science teachers in augmentation of salaries according to the results their pupils obtained in the award of Queen's Prizes,[58] and earlier than this, in 1857, the principle had been applied for drawing.[59] On 14 July 1859, it was decided at a board meeting of the Science and Art Department, with Lowe present, to apply the same payments as had been agreed under the Science Minute, to navigation schools. Teachers' salaries would be augmented by £3 for each first-class Queen's prize awarded to their pupils, £2 for each second-class prize and £1 for each third-class prize.[60] By 1860 there were thus many precedents for payment by results in the Science and Art Department. Moreover it seems that Henry Cole, the Permanent Secretary of the Science and Art Department was instrumental later, in May 1861, in finally persuading Lowe

[55] *Report of Committee of Council 1860–1*, p. 103.

[56] *Report of the Commissioners appointed to inquire into the State of Popular Education in England, 1861*, I, pp. 244–5. [57] *Ibid.* p. 328.

[58] Science and Art Department Minute Books, P.R.O. Ed. 28/10, fol. 40.

[59] *Report of Select Committee on Schools of Art*, P.P. 1864, XII, p. 17, Ans. 208, and p. 19, Ans. 223.

[60] Science and Art Department Minute Books. P.R.O. Ed. 28/10, fol. 66.

to implement payment for results throughout the state-aided elementary schools. Cole's diaries show that he was on friendly terms with Lowe and record that, on 9 May, Lowe asked him to 'prepare a scheme for paying results in writing, reading and arithmetic'. Cole complied and he records that on 30 May, at a board meeting of the Science and Art Department, 'Lowe thought my plan of results possible and even Lingen thought so but preferred Inspection.'[61] As Cole maintained when giving evidence before the Select Committee on Schools of Art in 1864 'payment upon results is only following out a principle that has been in operation for seven years, a little more extensively than it had hitherto been carried out', and he continued: 'I also venture to say that I think the success of the system of payment for results for drawing especially with reference to poor schools, has operated as an example to induce the primary branch of the Education Department to adopt the same principle in the poor schools for reading, writing and arithmetic.'[62]

It is clear that Lowe did not invent the principle of payment by results. The idea was already common coin when Lowe decided to implement it as a policy for financing public elementary schools. Indeed it would have been very surprising if Lowe had not adopted it when it had already been used in the Science and Art Department, partially employed under various Minutes of the Committee of Council and advocated in the recent Report of the Newcastle Commission. In addition, acceptance of the principle of payment by results was from Lowe's personal standpoint the natural outcome of his own concept of popular education; his views on political economy; the pressure from Gladstone, and others to cut expenditure; the lack or impracticality of viable alternatives such as local education rates; and the prevailing climate of opinion, with its *laissez-faire* and entrepreneurial beliefs in the value of competition and examinations and its overwhelming desire to secure value for money. Payment by results was also seen as a way of overcoming the imminent threat of an administrative breakdown in the central office of the Education Department arising from the complications involved in the existing grant system. In the light of all this, payment by results was almost a necessity which Lowe could not avoid.

[61] Duke, 'Robert Lowe. A Reappraisal', p. 28.
[62] *Report of the Select Committee on Schools of Art, P.P.*, 1864, XII, p. 19.

# 4

# THE PURPOSES OF THE REVISED CODE

If Lowe had not applied payment by results to elementary education, then it seems likely that someone else would have done so. In this sense Lowe was merely the agent for his times. On the other hand, Lowe did make a particular and individual contribution, for it is unlikely that any other politician would have applied the principle as vigorously and logically as Lowe did. In this sense the Revised Code was Lowe's work.

Looking back at the Revised Code, some historians have seen it as part of a grand plan which Lowe had in mind. For example, it has been suggested that Lowe was engaged in a struggle on behalf of the State against the Churches for control over education and that 'the promulgation and enforcement of the Revised Code constituted a significant victory for the State' in this struggle.[1] The Revised Code has also been seen as a deliberate attempt to limit the curriculum to the three Rs so that the poor could be kept in a position of subordination. 'The strategy was to build up a literate (but not skilled) upper working class content to do their allotted work without social or political ambition.'[2] These are interesting and attractive theories, but they credit Lowe with general intentions which it is difficult to find expressed in his own statements. The Revised Code served several immediate purposes, many of them demanded as much by society as by the personal ideas of one man, and Lowe was mainly concerned to achieve these. He was a pragmatist with practical problems to solve. Visions of a secular state-educational system or nightmares about an egalitarian society which he must strive to prevent may have troubled his mind but it is unlikely that they were his main motives in producing the Revised Code. If Lowe had a general purpose, then the evidence of his speeches at the time suggested that it was the application of

[1] J. Hurt, p. 202.

[2] W. P. McCann, 'Elementary Education in England and Wales on the Eve of the 1870 Education Act', *Journal of Educational Administration and History*, II, 1 (Dec. 1969) 21.

political economy to education. The Revised Code was above all an essay in the economics of education.

In the first place the Code was devised to implement the recommendations of the Newcastle Report in so far as this was possible within the existing powers of the Committee of Council on Education and without invoking new legislation. The Newcastle Commission had considered the possibility of establishing a national system of compulsory education but had decided that it was not feasible in England. The administration of education would have to contend with the landed gentry and the employers of labour, both of whom, it was felt, would oppose any such system. Only a police state could enforce it and that was alien to the English.[3] The Newcastle Report recommended therefore the continuance of the present system, though with some administrative changes to make it more economical and efficient.

Lowe accepted this as the premiss from which he must start. He was fully aware that he was not administering a national system, and he knew that the existing system, with its reliance upon voluntary finance and organisation, did not and could not provide schools in the areas of greatest need. As he had told the House of Commons in 1859, only a 'fundamental alteration' in the system could remedy this.[4] However, the Newcastle Report had not recommended any such fundamental change, and Lowe's job was to administer the existing system. In his speech moving the Education Estimates of 11 July 1861 he had this to say about the Commissioners' recommendation to continue the present system:

> . . . in making that recommendation, the Commissioners, so far as I can understand the case, express, I will not say the opinion of the whole country, or of philosophers, or of persons of great powers of abstract thought, but they express the opinion of those to whom education in this country owes almost its existence – of those who gave both time and money to promote education before the present system was called into being. If we have spent £4,800,000 in educating the people, private liberality has spent double that sum . . . So long as it is the opinion of those who contribute to the maintenance of the schools that the present system is the right and the best one, so long will the present system continue . . . it is not the intention of Government to infringe on the organic principles of the present system – namely, its denominational

[3] *Report of the Commissioners appointed to inquire into the State of Popular Education in England, 1861*, I, pp. 198–9.

[4] *Parliamentary Debates*, CLX, col. 317, 22 July 1859.

character, its foundation on a broad religious basis, its teaching religion, and the practice of giving grants from the central office in aid of local subscriptions, the propriety of those grants to be ascertained by inspection.[5]

Here was Lowe at his empirical best. He accepted the situation as it was and left it to others to dream dreams. Here was no fanatical opposition to the Churches but rather an acceptance that he must work with them. Lowe had a true appreciation of his position. He was a junior member of a Government called upon to administer a particular system of educational provision, and even if he had the power and will to initiate new educational legislation, he knew that since the main concern of the Government was to restrict educational expenditure any such move would be doomed to failure. The Revised Code was devised for the limited purpose of implementing those recommendations of the Newcastle Report which it was possible to effect administratively and without major legislation. Both Lord Granville and Lowe made this quite clear in their Report for 1861.[6]

The second purpose of the Revised Code was implicit in the first. The Newcastle Commission had been set up originally to consider what measures were required for the 'extension of sound and cheap elementary instruction', and one purpose of the Revised Code was certainly to control expenditure on education. In his speech of 11 July 1861 on moving the Education Estimates, Lowe drew attention to the first main criticism made by the Newcastle Commissioners – namely 'the great expense of the present system'[7] – and he asserted his wish to economise. Since his appointment to the office of Vice-President of the Committee of Council in 1859 Lowe had been conscious that his government colleagues saw his main task as the limitation of educational expenditure. On 22 July 1859 he noted before the House of Commons that the parliamentary grant for public education had risen from £109,948 in 1849 to £668,000 in 1858 and he estimated that the cost would be £2,500,000 'in a few years'.[8] He expressed his hope then that they would be able to develop a system of popular education without the imposition of additional burdens upon the revenue of the

[5] *Parliamentary Debates*, CLXIV, col. 725.

[6] *Report of Committee of Council on Education 1861–62*, pp. viii–x. See also Lowe's speech of 11 July 1861, *Parliamentary Debates*, CLXIV, col. 737.

[7] *Parliamentary Debates*, CLXIV, col. 721.

[8] *Parliamentary Debates*, CLV, col. 321.

country.[9] However, Lowe's concern to restrict expenditure should not be seen in isolation. There were two factors in the economic problem as he saw it, and if one was cost, the other was efficiency. The following extract from Lowe's speech on the Revised Code of 13 February 1862 has often been quoted:

> I cannot promise the House that this system will be an economical one, but I can promise that it shall be either one or the other. If it is not cheap it shall be efficient; if it is not efficient it shall be cheap. The present is neither one or the other. If the schools do not give instruction the public money will not be demanded, but if instruction is given the public money will be demanded – I cannot say to what amount, but the public will get value for its money.[10]

To represent Lowe as a man whose only aim was to diminish the amount spent on the education of the people, is to do him less than justice. Primarily he wanted an efficient system of popular education and he knew that this might mean an increase in public expenditure on education. Lowe declared this specifically in a later speech to the House of Commons on 5 April 1867. It deserves to be better known.

> I would not grudge the sum of £70,000 per annum, or a much larger sum for the education of the people, if I believed that the money would produce a beneficial effect. I have assisted on more than one occasion in reducing the amount of the grant for public education; but on those occasions I saw the reductions were consistent with – nay, I believed would be the cause of – the greater efficiency of the system. Therefore, I beg that the House will understand that, although I am a friend to economy, I only uphold economy when combined with efficiency. I think that no sum that this House would grant would be too large if by its aid the education of the people would be rendered more efficient.[11]

Thirdly, then, the Revised Code was devised to make popular education efficient, and in Lowe's mind this meant the achievement of certain standards of ability in reading, writing and arithmetic. The Revised Code was a programme of basic education for a country that was as yet still underdeveloped educationally. Two questions immediately present themselves. Why should Lowe apparently limit education to the three Rs, and was England educationally underdeveloped at that time?

[9] *Parliamentary Debates*, CLV, col. 322.
[10] *Parliamentary Debates*, CLXV, col. 229.
[11] *Parliamentary Debates*, CLXXXVI, cols. 1176–7.

Lowe's view of the content of popular education was directly related to economics. As Lowe rightly saw it, there was a limited amount of time available for the education of the labouring classes, given the pattern of society which existed in nineteenth-century England. This being so, children should be taught the most useful basic subjects, and these Lowe concluded were reading, writing and arithmetic.[12] In his first Report as Vice-President Lowe made his attitude clear.

> The first result demanded of the elementary day school is that the generations passing through it shall begin the world with the power to read, write and cipher. With that power everything is open to them: without it nothing. If it be not acquired before work begins, the chances are greatly against its ever being effectively acquired afterwards. It may well be acquired before the end of the tenth year.[13]

It needs to be plainly said that Lowe's insistence that reading, writing and arithmetic are necessary elementary studies is incontrovertible. As Lowe put it in a debate in 1867, if teachers 'cannot teach children to read and write during their school life, what chance have they of teaching them grammar or geography'.[14] Lowe did not object to the teaching of other subjects, but the Revised Code established a necessary minimum.[15]

Lowe easily accepted the situation that limited time for schooling for the working classes meant limited curriculum content. For Lowe it was an economic fact. He asked Parliament to consider

> that the age at which the poor man's child leaves school is generally about eleven: if we ask that during his time of schooling he shall be taught to read, write and cipher, is not that enough? . . . It must never be forgotten that those for whom this system is designed are the children of persons who are not able to pay for the teaching. We do not profess to give these children an education that will raise them above their station and business in life, that is not our object, but to give them an education that may fit them for business. We are bound to take a clear and definite view of the position of the class that is to receive instruction; and having obtained that view, we are bound to make up our minds as to how much instruction that class requires, and is capable of

[12] Lowe discussed this later in *Primary and Classical Education*, pp. 13–14.

[13] *Report of Committee of Council on Education 1859–60*, p. xxi.

[14] *Parliamentary Debates*, CLXXXVI, col. 1179.

[15] *Parliamentary Debates*, CLXV, col. 237.

receiving and we are then bound to have evidence that it has received such instruction.[16]

This passage is offensive in later egalitarian times but for Lowe and most of his contemporaries it was sound sense. Few in the middle of the nineteenth century held that the State should provide an education which promoted social mobility, though Robert Owen had sown the seed of this idea and it was beginning to spread among working-class organisations.[17] Lowe was not a socialist egalitarian but then it is unhistorical to expect him to be. Lowe accepted the economic and social structures of his age and the Revised Code was devised to fit in with them. If Lowe cannot be praised for being a visionary nor can he be blamed for being a creature of his times.

As for the second question, it has been argued that in terms of *quantity* of school provision England was not underdeveloped in the nineteenth century.[18] Day schooling, it has been calculated, accounted for about 1 per cent of the net national income in 1833 and this percentage was still about the same between 1920 and 1945, though by 1965 it had risen to 2 per cent.[19] If this is accepted as a satisfactory indicator of educational growth then England was no more underdeveloped in 1833 than a century later. Nevertheless, despite this, it is difficult to maintain that in terms of *quality* England was not underdeveloped in 1860. The Newcastle Report had concluded that only about one quarter of the children who went to school were taught the three Rs efficiently[20] and if other criteria are also considered, such as the lack of continuity in education owing to irregular school attendances, the lack of moral and religious training, the size of classes and the physical condition of the schools, then more doubts may be raised about the state of educational development of England in the nineteenth century.

Similarly, arguments from the evidence for literacy in the nineteenth century that by about 1870 almost 90 per cent of the working classes were literate[21] should not be interpreted to suggest that

[16] *Parliamentary Debates*, CLXV, cols. 237–8.

[17] H. Silver, *The Concept of Popular Education*, London 1965, pp. 157–200.

[18] E. G. West, 'Resource Allocation and Growth in Early Nineteenth Century British Education', *Economic History Review*, second series, XXIII, 1 (April 1970), 68–95. [19] *Ibid.* p. 87.

[20] *Report of the Commissioners appointed to inquire into the State of Popular Education in England*, 1861, I, p. 273.

[21] E. G. West, *Education and the State*, Institute of Economic Affairs 1965, pp. 131–2.

Lowe was fighting a problem which was not there. It may be doubted whether the measures used to arrive at literacy figures, such as marriage register marks, were as searching as those Lowe was to use in his system of standards. Complete illiteracy there may not have been but Lowe was basically right in his assessment of the situation. The country did need a programme for the extension of literacy and numeracy and the Revised Code was devised to provide it.

Lowe accepted the evidence of the Newcastle Commission 'that not one-fourth of our children is properly taught, that the younger and lower boys are neglected for the sake of the upper classes, and that each child ought to be able to read, write and cipher in an intelligent manner when he leaves school'.[22] From it he concluded that the country needed an increase, 'not of the quality, but of the quantum of education. We want not better schools, but to make them work harder, and we seek by an incentive and stimulus, to get the greatest possible number out of every 100 children properly educated.'[23] The contrast which Lowe made here between quality and quantity does not mean that he favoured an inferior type of education for the mass of the people. The point of the passage is that in the context of the sixties, it was the wide extension of a basic education which the country needed rather than the production of a few 'better' schools which educated its most able pupils to higher levels but neglected the mass of the children. Paradoxically enough, and in contrast to his reputation as a man who cared little for the education of the people, Lowe was pressing in the Revised Code for more attention to be paid to the less able and the under-privileged. 'We want to make them educate', said Lowe, 'not children in the first class, for that is done already, but those who now leave schools without proper education.'[24]

This concern to achieve an efficient mass education in basic literacy and numeracy dictated the main features of the Revised Code: payment by results; the use of examination to supplement inspection; the emphasis upon the three Rs; the establishment of standards; the attempt to stimulate greater teacher productivity and the changes in teacher-training.

Payment by results and the assessment of results by examination

[22] *Parliamentary Debates*, CLXIV, col. 722, 11 July 1861.
[23] *Parliamentary Debates*, CLXV, col. 215.
[24] *Parliamentary Debates*, CLXV, col. 215.

rather than by Inspectors' reports, derived directly from the Newcastle Report. It had proposed that 'distinct inducements should be offered to school teachers so that they would bring up their individual scholars, junior as well as senior, to a certain mark'.[25] It had also criticised the existing system with its reliance upon Inspectors, as unable 'to secure a thorough grounding in the simplest but most essential parts of instruction'.[26]

As a remedy the Newcastle Report proposed two grants in aid of schools. The first was to be a charge upon public money as administered by the Treasury and was to be given on condition that the average attendance of children over the year reached a certain level and that the Inspector at his visit could report satisfactorily on the school. The second was to be 'paid out of the county rates, in consideration of the attainment of a certain degree of knowledge by the children in school during the year preceding the payment'.[27] The examiners were to be appointed by County Boards of Education, and the examination was to be in reading, writing and arithmetic with the addition of plain work (needlework) for the girls.[28] The Revised Code implemented these recommendations to a considerable extent. A grant of 4*s.* per scholar was given to a school provided that the individual scholar had attended for two hundred morning or afternoon sessions. In addition, for those who satisfied the attendance conditions, a further grant of 8*s.* was given to the school for each child who passed in reading, writing and arithmetic, though this grant was reducible at the rate of 2*s.* 8*d.* per subject failed. Thus a pupil who failed in one subject earned only 5*s.* 4*d.*[29] Certain other conditions also governed the payment of this grant: particular building regulations had to be fulfilled, the principal teacher had to be certificated, the girls had to be taught plain needlework and the school register had to be kept accurately.[30]

However, Lowe could not agree with the Newcastle Commission about the recommended machinery for the payment of the second 'result' grant. It threw a national burden of expense upon local areas and it failed to give local ratepayers adequate control over

[25] *Report of the Commissioners appointed to inquire into the State of Popular Education in England*, 1861, I, p. 274.

[26] *Ibid.* p. 296. [27] *Ibid.* p. 328. [28] *Ibid.* p. 330.

[29] *Report of Committee of Council on Education 1861–2*, pp. xxi–xxii, arts. 40–45 of the Revised Code. [30] *Ibid.* p. xxiv, art. 51 of the Revised Code.

the expenditure, since they would merely be obliged to pay out whatever the appointed examiners requested.[31] Moreover, it would have meant the establishment of County Councils in some form and since this would have necessitated major legislation, Lowe naturally shied away from it. Apart from this, Lowe's realistic appreciation of the contemporary situation convinced him that any attempt to base educational provision on local rating was impractical since it raised religious difficulties which at that time seemed insurmountable.[32] Even Sir J. Kay-Shuttleworth, who objected to much of the Revised Code, at least agreed with Lowe on this point.[33] Finally, Lowe objected to the Newcastle scheme on the grounds that it did not ensure a proper examination of the education given in schools. The Report envisaged that the examiners would be schoolmasters appointed by County Boards, and Lowe doubted their impartiality as examiners. As a result the County Boards would, if established, become 'mere paying machines' with no real responsibility, and as Lowe told the House of Commons the 'only discretion which it appears to me will be left to any one is that which will rest with the schoolmasters, who may make a favourable report or otherwise, as they please, and thus influence the amount to be paid out of the county rates'.[34] Lowe therefore preferred that the 'result' grant should come from central parliamentary funds and that the examination should be conducted by Inspectors appointed by the Committee of Council, for government Inspectors would conduct examinations more effectively than schoolmasters.[35]

It was basic to the Revised Code that examination should replace inspection as a means of assessing the results of the education given in schools. 'I have come to the conclusion', said Lowe, 'that inspection as opposed to examination is not, and never can be, a test of the efficiency of a system of national education.'[36] He felt that Inspectors' reports dealt too much with the general rather than the particular to be an adequate means of assessing the efficiency

[31] *Parliamentary Debates*, CLXV, col. 215.

[32] *Parliamentary Debates*, CLXIV, cols. 740–2.

[33] Letter to Earl Granville on the Recommendations of the Commissioners appointed . . . to inquire into the Present State of Popular Education, dated April 24, 1861, in Kay-Shuttleworth, *Four Periods of Public Education*, p. 571.

[34] *Parliamentary Debates*, CLXIV, col. 727. See also *Parliamentary Debates*, CLXV, col. 215.

[35] *Parliamentary Debates*, CLXV, col. 737.

[36] *Parliamentary Debates*, CLXV, col. 203.

of a school.[37] He noted that there was in the reports of individual Inspectors as compared with the Newcastle Report a conflict of evidence about the efficiency of the existing system.

The Inspectors reported that in 90 per cent of the schools the reading was taught 'excellently or well'; that in 89 per cent, writing was taught 'excellently or well' and that in 83 per cent arithmetic was taught 'excellently or well'. Lowe reconciled this with the Commissioners' report by suggesting that the Inspectors were referring to the quality of the teaching and not to the extent of the learning,[38] but he remained sceptical of the ability of inspection to raise the standards of educational achievement. 'What is the object of inspection?' Lowe asked.

Is it simply to make things pleasant, to give the schools as much as can be got out of the public purse, independent of their efficiency; or do you mean that our grants should not only be aids, subsidies, and gifts, but fruitful of good? ... The Commissioners said that only one-fourth of the children were properly instructed, while the Inspectors contended that ninety per cent of the schools were either excellently or fairly taught. And the Department of Education had to judge between the two. What were we 'to do'? ... We said, we will appeal to facts, and not go on reasoning *a priori*. We said we will go to the schools, examine the children child by child, and have a complete report, and then we shall know whether the Inspectors or the Commissioners are right.[39]

This decision to test and ensure the efficiency of the system by a process of examination reinforced the dominant place which was given to the three Rs. For not only were they the most useful basic subjects but also, it seemed to Lowe, the subjects which could be assessed with some precision. They therefore formed a natural basis for a payment by results parliamentary grant. Lowe describes this dual function which the three Rs served, in a letter written on 17 March 1882 to Lingen, his former colleague at the Education Department in the sixties.

As I understand the case, you and I viewed the three R's not only or primarily as the exact amount of instruction which ought to be given, but as an amount of knowledge which could be ascertained thoroughly by examination, and upon which we could safely base the Parliamentary

[37] *Parliamentary Debates*, CLXV, col. 204.
[38] *Parliamentary Debates*, CLXV, col. 203.
[39] *Parliamentary Debates*, CLXV, cols. 205–6.

grant. It was more a financial than a literary preference. Had there been any other branch of useful knowledge, the possession of which could have been ascertained with equal precision there was nothing to prevent its admission. But there was not.[40]

The emphasis given to the three Rs led both contemporaries and subsequent historians to label Lowe as a secularist. In one sense he was. He certainly wanted the schools to offer an efficient practical secular education. He was not, however, against religious education in schools. In his speech on the Revised Code of 13 February 1862 Lowe assumed that schools did and should provide a religious education but he pointed out that it 'is not the specific thing for which the grant is given'.[41] Because he did not make religious education a grant-earning subject it was assumed unjustly that he did not value it. On the contrary, Lowe's view was that a school could not qualify for any grant at all unless its general state – and in this he included its religious education – was satisfactory. Clauses 49, 50 and 51 of the Revised Code allowed the withholding of the grant from a school on this ground and a footnote to Clause 51 specifically includes religious education in Church of England schools as one of the factors to be taken into consideration by Inspectors.[42] The omission of religious education from the grant-earning subjects was not so much an indication of Lowe's secularism as a reflection of his political realism. Any attempt to pay a grant for religious education would have aroused all the denominational quarrels that local rate schemes had provoked in the fifties. Lowe was too wise to touch such political dynamite. Lowe, it should be remembered, was trying to make the existing system work more efficiently, and that system was provided mainly by the voluntary subscriptions of religious societies. In those circumstances Lowe's attitude was a perfectly logical one; let the clergy run the religious education, and let the State ensure that the schools also provide a secular education. Lowe was not, however, trying to secularise education completely. His view of the situation was made clear in the evidence he gave to the Schools Inquiry Commission in 1865.

You have the clergy, who have an object in view, and a very excellent object, that of the religious instruction of the people; and you have the

[40] Patchett Martin, II, p. 217. [41] *Parliamentary Debates*, CLXV, col. 216.
[42] *Report of Committee of Council 1861–2*, p. xxiv.

Government, which makes the best bargain it can for secular instruction with the clergy, presuming they will see after the religious part of it, and giving its assistance on the condition that so much secular instruction should be mixed with it . . . The Government is not to be considered irreligious nor the clergy enemies to secular instruction because religion comes rather from the one and secular instruction from the other.[43]

The most notable feature of the Revised Code was its attempt to define and enforce educational standards. It was in effect the origin of standardised tests of scholastic attainment. Viewed in the light of subsequent psychological research, the framing of the standards was open to criticism. The Consultative Committee's *Report on Psychological Tests of Educable Capacity* in 1924 noted that the standards of the Revised Code were based not upon experimental inquiry into what children of a given age actually knew, but upon an *a priori* notion of what they ought to know. They largely ignored the wide range of individual capacity in children and the detailed formulations for the several ages were not always precise or appropriate.[44] However, considered as standards, whether framed *a priori* or not, they were on the whole sensible and appropriate. The same Consultative Committee admitted in its report on *The Primary School* in 1931 that the scheme of standards was skilfully graded and that impossibilities were not demanded of the teachers. It also suggested that once the mass of young illiterate children which formed the body of most schools had been passed through the first two standards 'the remaining requirements of the Code could be fulfilled with reasonably hard work, except in schools with inadequate staffs, bad attendance or a very poor class of children'.[45] Since 1931 it seems that educationists have lost confidence in their ability to define standards. The Plowden Committee on Primary Schools reported in 1967 that it had considered whether they could lay down the standards that should be achieved by the end of the primary school but had concluded that 'it is not possible to describe a standard of attainment that should be reached by all or most children'.[46] Such a

[43] S.I.C. IV, *Minutes of Evidence 1868*, p. 632, Q. 6567.

[44] *Report of the Consultative Committee on Psychological Tests of Educable Capacity*, 1924, p. 44.

[45] *Report of the Consultative Committee on The Primary School*, 1931, p. 8.

[46] *Children and their Primary Schools*, H.M.S.O. 1967, *Report of the Central Advisory Council of Education (England)*, I, p. 221, para. 55.

view provides an illuminating contrast to that of Lowe, but it by no means invalidates his standpoint. For in fact as a programme of basic education Clause 48 of the Revised Code, which laid down the standards, has much to recommend it. It may seem from some viewpoints to be extremely limited, but in the context of the newly emerging industrial society of nineteenth-century England it amounted, as Lowe told the Commons, to a New Deal.[47]

Following the recommendations of the Newcastle Report[48] Lowe at first conceived the system of examination by standards according to age. When he introduced the Revised Code to the House on 13 February 1862 Lowe gave his reason for his decision with the following example:

> supposing capitation to be claimed on a boy of eleven who has passed in the infant class. That boy is about to leave school; he can read words of one syllable, can make letters on a board, and count twenty. Is that result worth paying for? It will not abide with him six months . . . What we mean is that the children should be taught, not a smattering only, but that they should leave school so grounded in elementary knowledge that it may be of use to them during the whole of their life.[49]

Ultimately, however, this proposal to examine children for grants according to their age had to be withdrawn. Lowe accepted this most reluctantly and in the *Report of the Committee of Council 1861–2* he and Lord Granville gave a full account of the reasons for their regret. They had wanted examination according to age to ensure that managers and teachers concentrated their attention on those who were disproportionately backward for their age. They were also of the opinion that the amount of knowledge required by Standard VI was the minimum of 'book instruction which can be put to practical use in life' and so they wanted to ensure that as many children as possible reached that standard before economic necessity forced their parents to send them out to work. A child of ten on leaving school should be able to pass according to Standard IV, and similarly an eleven year old and a twelve year old should be able to pass according to Standards V and VI, respectively. Schools, they concluded, which failed to enable a child to do this had 'done little or nothing to better him in life'.[50]

[47] *Parliamentary Debates*, CLXXXVI, col. 1179, 5 April 1867.
[48] *Report of Committee of Council on Education 1861–2*, p.x.
[49] *Parliamentary Debates*, CLXV, col. 239.
[50] *Report of Committee of Council on Education 1861–2*, pp. x–xi.

TABLE 2 *Revised Code. Clause 48*

| Cl. 48 | Standard I | Standard II | Standard III | Standard IV | Standard V | Standard VI |
|---|---|---|---|---|---|---|
| Reading | Narrative in monosyllables. | One of the Narratives next in order after monosyllables in an elementary reading book used in the school. | A short paragraph from an elementary reading book used in the school. | A short paragraph from a more advanced reading book used in the school. | A few lines of poetry from a more advanced reading book used in the first class of the school. | A short ordinary paragraph in a newspaper, or other modern narrative. |
| Writing | Form on blackboard or slate, from dictation, letters, capital and small manuscript. | Copy in manuscript character a line of print. | A sentence from the same paragraph, slowly read once and then dictated in single words. | A sentence slowly dictated once by a few words at a time, from the same book, but not from the paragraph read. | A sentence slowly dictated once by a few words at a time, from a reading book used in the first class of the school. | Another short ordinary paragraph in a newspaper, or other modern narrative, slowly dictated once by a few words at a time. |
| Arithmetic | Form on blackboard or slate, from dictation, figures up to 20; name at sight figures up to 20; add and subtract figures up to 10: orally from examples on blackboard. | A sum in simple addition or subtraction and the multiplication table. | A sum in any simple rule as far as short division (inclusive). | A sum in compound rules (money). | A sum in compound rules (common weights and measures). | A sum in practice or bills of parcels. |

Source: *Report of Committee of Council on Education 1861–2*, the Revised Code, p. xxiii.

Throughout his life, Lowe refused to relinquish this concern for the maintenance of standards. In 1874 when the Education Department were proposing to substitute the Third Standard of the Education Code for the Fifth Standard, as the standard to be reached by the children of out-door paupers, Lowe attacked it in the House of Commons as a backward step, and a 'deadly blow at education'. It was tantamount to saying that the children of the poor were sufficiently educated to be sent out into the world with an education suitable for a child of nine. Lowe would have none of this and his opposition[51] shows a concern for the education of the poor which suggests that Lowe's reputation as a man who had no real interest in popular education needs some reconsideration. For example, in the light of this it is difficult to sustain the conclusion of one writer that Lowe 'never seriously contemplated that the whole of the child population would be educated in however elementary a fashion'.[52]

To achieve this basic education for all, the Revised Code attempted to stimulate greater productivity among teachers. It is questionable whether the process of teaching is amenable to analysis in economic terms, but Lowe assumed that in certain respects it was. In particular he considered that pecuniary incentives operated for teachers in the same way that they did for men in other trades and professions, and that they would stimulate teachers to greater efforts in their work. It is difficult to deny that there is much truth in this assumption. Lowe objected to the view that all teachers should be paid the same whether they were lazy or not and consequently payment by results seemed to him to be a fair basis on which to remunerate teachers. He failed, or rather was unwilling, to see that often in teaching, extensive efforts might bring little in the way of examinable results. For example, an extremely conscientious teacher in a school where pupils attended irregularly might find it difficult to procure the necessary results in even the First Standard. As one of Lowe's critics put it, to pay teachers by results was like paying 'physicians only for the patients they have cured'.[53] Society would never adopt this policy for its its physicians so why should it for its teachers? Lowe remained

[51] *Parliamentary Debates*, CCXVIII, col. 1733.

[52] Sullivan, 'The Educational Work and Thought of Robert Lowe', p. 244.

[53] Miss Hume, *Brief Comments on the Revised Speech of the Rt. Hon. Robert Lowe on The Revised Code, Feb. 13, 1862*, London 1862, p. 26.

deaf to such pleas. Lowe wanted to maximise effort in what amounted to a war against illiteracy, and he used a weapon which had had a long history of success in motivating men – pecuniary incentive. It has recently been argued that Lowe's system of testing the efficiency of teachers by results is not necessarily a *laissez-faire*, or free-trade attitude, that 'economic deployment of resources and the desire to get value for money expended, are not the hall marks of free traders',[54] and that it merely shows that the State in this period was 'cost-conscious' and willing to use payment by results as 'a productivity reward'. This may be true generally but in Lowe's mind the question was specifically related to free trade and he used the language of protection and free trade in his discussion of the matter. As he told the Commons, 'hitherto we have been living under a system of bounties and protection; now we propose to have a little free trade.'[55]

The purposes of the Revised Code with regard to teacher-training were two-fold. On the one hand, it aimed to reduce, if possible, the cost of teacher-training, and on the other hand it desired to change the content of teacher-training so that teachers would be specifically equipped to achieve an efficient mass education in basic literacy and numeracy.

The system of teacher-training in operation in 1860 was basically that established by the Minutes of the Committee of Council in 1846. Government assistance was given to the training colleges – Normal Schools – by offering them grants for every student who trained there and successfully passed the examination carried out by Her Majesty's Inspectors. A student who stayed one year earned £20 for his college, and if he stayed for a second and third year then a further £25 and £30 respectively was earned. During his course through the college a student received certificates of merit at the end of every year that he completed successfully, and this entitled him to an increase in the salary he eventually earned from the school to which he was appointed, to the extent of £15 to £20 for the first certificate, £20 to £25 for the second and £25 to £30 for the third.[56] Teachers who had not been through Normal

[54] N. Morris, 'State Paternalism and laissez-faire in the 1860's', in History of Education Society, *Studies in the Government and Control of Education since 1860*, London 1970, p. 15. [55] *Parliamentary Debates*, CLXIV, col. 736.

[56] Minutes of Committee of Council, August and December 1846, in Kay-Shuttleworth, *Four Periods of Public Education*, p. 538.

Schools were also allowed to take an examination and gain a certificate which would qualify them for augmentation of salary.[57] To ensure that the Normal Schools had a supply of good candidates, the Minutes further established a scheme of pupil-teachers whereby scholars were apprenticed at the age of thirteen to the master or mistress of school for a period of five years. They were to assist in the schools and also receive instruction from the teachers of at least seven and a half hours a week in various subjects. At the end of each year the pupil-teacher was examined by an Inspector according to a syllabus laid down in the Minute[58] and at the end of his apprenticeship, received a certificate to this effect, if he had been successful in the annual examinations.[59] Pupil-teachers received a salary of £10 for their first year and this increased by £2 10*s*. each year over the five-year period to a total of £20.[60] Teachers of successful pupil-teachers also received £5 per annum for one, £9 for two, £12 for three pupil-teachers and £3 for every additional apprentice.[61] Successful apprentices could then compete for the award of exhibitions of £20 to £25 to enable them to go as 'Queen's Scholars' to a Normal School.

By 1859 the cost of this two-tier system of teacher education was considerable, and rising steadily. In 1851 the total paid both for augmentations of salary and for pupil-teachers had been £96,190 10*s*. 10*d*.[62] In 1853 the cost in payments to pupil-teachers and in gratuities to teachers for their instruction alone had been £139,040 4*s*. 0*d*. and in addition £26,777 10*s*. 10*d*. had been paid in augmentation of salary.[63] By 1859 when Lowe took office as Vice-President these figures respectively stood at £252,550 12*s*. 11*d* and £86,328 1*s*. 10*d*.[64] At the same time the cost in annual grants to training colleges had risen from £19,196 19*s*. 3*d*. in 1853 to £89,587 10*s*. 6*d*. in 1859.[65] Lowe wanted to cut these costs as much as possible.

Lowe's other concern to change the content of teacher-training followed criticisms which had been levelled at the colleges for the irrelevance of their studies to the future tasks of school teaching.

[57] *Ibid*. p. 543. [58] *Ibid*. p. 533. [59] *Ibid*. p. 537.
[60] *Ibid*. p. 535. [61] *Ibid*. p. 537.
[62] *Minutes of Committee of Council 1850–1*, p. c.
[63] *Minutes of Committee of Council 1853–4*, p. 73.
[64] *Report of Committee of Council 1859–60*, p. xxxi.
[65] *Minutes of Committee of Council 1853–4*, p. 73; *Report of Committee of Council 1859–60*, p. xxxi.

The curriculum in the colleges had gradually evolved under the influence of the various principals and Her Majesty's Inspectors. At first the Certificate examinations at Normal Schools were not uniform throughout the country but were tailored by the Inspectors to fit the studies at the particular schools.[66] However, by the end of 1854 an official syllabus was in operation and an examination common to all the colleges had been held. A full and revised syllabus came into operation in 1857. From the outset the curricula in the colleges seemed to many to be pretentious, and as early as 1847 one Inspector pleaded for a less ambitious content more related to the future tasks of the trained master.[67] However, most principals were graduates of Oxford and Cambridge and under their influence the syllabus became inappropriately academic.[68] A Minute of 20 August 1853 offered an augmentation of salary of £100 to lecturers proficient in history, English literature, geography, physical science and applied mathematics, provided that they showed 'skill in adapting them to the purposes of elementary instruction'. However, this seemed to some Inspectors to be a measure which only increased the academic content. In 1856 the Reverend F. Temple, for example, pressed for the addition of 'method' to the list of subjects which carried an increase in salary.[69] The following year the Education Department took positive action and in a circular to principals on its new syllabus stressed that certain subjects such as arithmetic were to be more highly valued than others such as history or Euclid because of their utility for the purposes of elementary education. Thus a student who failed in arithmetic would fail overall, but a failure in history would not be considered fatal.[70]

The dichotomy of purpose in teacher-training institutions between providing on the one hand a personal education for the students and equipping them on the other with a rigorous professional training was the constant problem then as now. Students who were knowledgeable about literature but ignorant of the techniques of teaching pupils to read, often seemed incongruous products of colleges financially assisted by the State primarily to

[66] Minutes of August & December 1846, in Kay-Shuttleworth, *Four Periods of Public Education*, p. 538.

[67] *Minutes of Committee of Council 1847–8*, II, p. 537, report of Reverend Alex Thurtell.

[68] Newcastle Report, I, pp. 118–19.

[69] *Minutes of Committee of Council 1856–7*, p. 703.

[70] *Minutes of Committee of Council 1856–7*, p. 7.

provide an effective body of teachers for elementary schools. Lowe in particular felt that with the pressing need to provide an efficient basic education for children before they left school the teachers should be trained for that specific purpose. He wrote in *The Times* for 9 June 1860.

> We cannot force parents – and we ought not if we could – to keep their children at school beyond the age when they become available for work, at a sacrifice the magnitude of which we can scarcely estimate to themselves and their families. Nor can we by any process impart to a child of 9 or 10 years old even the rudiments of the whole education that we should wish it to possess; but we can, if we please, teach most children at that age to read well and to write and cipher tolerably. These, then should be the principal objects of our schools, and to their attainment everything else should be subordinated. But then it follows that for these humble ends our whole system of public education is vastly too ambitious and expensive, and that the high training which the schoolmaster receives at the public expense does not return to the public a corresponding utility.[71]

It was a view that other influential publications shared.[72]

Lowe's remedy came in 1863 with the new syllabus for Normal Schools. This emphasised that the subjects taught in the Normal Schools should be identical with those taught in the elementary schools and added that they were not to be more 'advanced in degree than marks the interval by which the teacher ought to precede the scholar'.[73] The syllabus of the Normal Schools was accordingly narrowed and this laid Lowe open to the charge that he was denying teachers the value of a liberal education. The colleges, as the Principal of St Mark's College, Chelsea, put it, should educate men not machines and provide a class of free agents not 'a caste of elementary schoolmasters'.[74] Lowe was fully aware of the advantages of a wide liberal education, and in fact he was at this same time busy advocating it for factory inspectors.[75] Why then did he deny it to teachers?

There were two main reasons for this. First Lowe was not

[71] *The Times*, 9 June 1860, p. 8, second leader.
[72] See for example *Government Education*, reprinted from *The Edinburgh Review*, No. 231, London 1861, p. 25.
[73] *Report of the Committee of Council 1862–3*, p. xii.
[74] Rev. Derwent Coleridge, *The Teachers of the People. A Tract for the Time*, London 1862, p. 15.
[75] *The Times*, 7 June 1860, p. 8, first leader.

sympathetic to teaching as a profession. He quoted with approval the opinion of the Newcastle Commission that on the whole teachers were boys who would otherwise go to work at mechanical trades at the age of 12 but who were educated at the public expense up to an age of 20 or 21 and then given a salary of about £100 a year for what amounted to only a 39½ hour week with a vacation of 6 or 7 weeks in the course of a year.[76] Lowe thought that teachers were well paid for what they did[77] and on the whole over-educated for what was in his view an unintellectual trade.[78] This attitude hardened in the course of the drafting of the Revised Code when the Committee of Council was besieged with letters and deputations from teachers objecting to the loss of augmentation grants for their salaries. Lowe combated them vigorously, pointing out that the augmentation grant was not a property, that no vested interest could arise from it, and that it was part of a system which could be changed if 'economical laws' which the Government could not control, demanded it.[79] Secondly, Lowe knew that he must economise on central expenditure, and teacher-training seemed to be an area where he could do it.[80] The financial squeeze had begun in 1859 with a reduction in the number of pupil-teachers, and the withdrawal of building grants for Normal Schools,[81] and the Revised Code continued it. A Minute of 21 March 1863 reduced the grants available to Normal Schools and abolished Queen's Scholarships.[82] Grants paid to Normal Schools were not to exceed 75 per cent of their total expenditure and the colleges were not to expand above their numbers for the year 1862. 'If it be true, as we believe it is, that our teachers are overtrained and over educated', wrote Lowe, 'it is on their training and their education that economy would most naturally fall.'[83]

Finally the Newcastle Commission had criticised the administrative 'complexity' of the existing system of government grants and one of Lowe's purposes in the Revised Code was to simplify it.[84] Lingen had pointed out to the Commission the difficulties of

[76] *Parliamentary Debates*, CLXV, col. 231.
[77] *Ibid.*
[78] Lowe, *Middle Class Education*, p. 8.
[79] *Parliamentary Debates*, CLXV, col. 234.
[80] *The Times*, 28 Sept. 1861, p. 8, first leader.
[81] *Report of Committee of Council 1859–60*, p. xi.
[82] *Report of Committee of Council 1862–3*, pp. xliv–xlvii.
[83] *The Times*, 28 Sept. 1861, p. 8, first leader.
[84] *Parliamentary Debates*, CLXIV, cols. 721, 724.

the existing administrative system and Lowe was obviously concerned to make administrative reforms. It has been pointed out[85] that Lowe was also consciously aiming at some decentralisation so that no future political party could dominate both teachers and taught and so gain an 'unconstitutional power'.[86] Similarly, Lowe was equally reluctant to continue a system which in the future might lead to a Government being under the influence of a large body of teachers.[87]

However, the immediate aim in view was to make the administration tidier. Certainly it was complicated. In 1861 there had been 9,957 schools under inspection, 8,698 certificated teachers, 491 probationary teachers, 381 assistant teachers, 16,277 pupil-teachers, and 2,527 Queen's Scholars, 'making altogether', said Lowe, 'if we count one manager for every school, the very respectable army of 38,331 persons all engaging the attention of the Privy Council and most of them receiving money directly from it'.[88] Simplification was achieved by making all grants payable direct to school and college managers. This, however, meant that some means must be found to ensure that these managers used public money properly and Lowe concluded that the only substitute for '"red tape" – the only check on managers – is not to be had by the payment of teachers but by the examination of the pupils'.[89]

Payment by results seemed to be the only way to achieve all the purposes which lay behind Lowe's Revised Code. It would implement the main recommendations of the Newcastle Commission: it would effect economies in educational expenditure, it would secure an efficient basic education for children in school, and all this without changing the essential framework of the existing state-aided but voluntary system. As Lowe admitted, it was neither a perfect system nor even a national system[90] but it was making the best of what existed. Lowe's own account of his situation and purposes at least deserves careful consideration before judgment is passed upon him.

We have endeavoured to meet the case as well as we could; and we hope ... to succeed in giving greater efficiency to the present system. The

[85] G. A. N. Lowndes, *The Silent Social Revolution*, Oxford Univ. Press 1937, 1st edn, pp. 9–11. [86] *Parliamentary Debates*, CLXV, col. 211.
[87] *Ibid.* [88] *Ibid.* col. 199. [89] *Ibid.* col. 202.
[90] *Parliamentary Debates*, CLXV, cols. 198, 240.

Committee must not expect from us impossibilities. We cannot combine in the same system the advantages of the voluntary principle with those of the system of local rating. We want to carry out the present system under present circumstances as far as we can. So far as we can elevate it, so far as we can make it more comprehensive, more efficient and more economical, we are most anxious to do so.[91]

[91] *Parliamentary Debates*, CLXIV, col. 738.

# 5
# THE EFFECTS OF THE REVISED CODE

It is hard to decide when Lowe's responsibility for the effects of the Revised Code ended and the responsibility of others began. He resigned from his office in April 1864, following parliamentary criticism of the way in which his department handled the reports of Her Majesty's Inspectors of Schools. The Code continued, however, until 1890 and though major changes were made in it in 1867, 1875 and 1882, its effects, both short term and long term, owed much to Lowe as its author.

There is also the pitfall of 'the whig interpretation of history' to be avoided in discussing and apportioning personal responsibility for the consequences of past policies. Lowe and the Revised Code have all too often been interpreted in the context of later twentieth-century educational ideas, rather than with reference to Lowe's historical situation. A balanced account of the effects of the Revised Code will only emerge if it is recognised from the outset that Lowe was a particular man, attempting to solve a particular problem at a particular time.

Surprisingly enough, the most perceptive account of the Revised Code is to be found in Edmond Holmes' *What is and What might be*, published in 1911, a book which was in effect wholly devoted to criticism of the Newcastle Report and the Revised Code for recommending and implementing payment by results. Holmes was a former Chief Inspector who had worked under the Revised Code, and his book argued that on educational grounds it was completely misconceived. Its uniformity of syllabus and its concentration upon examinations, produced, he claimed 'a hive of misdirected energy',[1] and the examinations tended 'to arrest growth, to deaden life, to paralyse the higher faculties, to externalise what is inward, to materialise what is spiritual, to involve education in an atmosphere of unreality and

[1] E. Holmes, *What is and What might be*, London 1911, p. 103.

self-deception'.[2] Nevertheless, Holmes realised that he was judging the past too much in terms of the present. He wrote:

It is easy for us of the Twentieth Century to laugh at the syllabuses which the Department issued, without misgiving, year after year, in the latter half of the Nineteenth. We were all groping in the dark in those days . . . But let us of the enlightened Twentieth Century try our hands at constructing a syllabus on which all the elementary schools of England are to be prepared for a yearly examination, see if we can improve appreciably on the work of our predecessors. Some improvement there would certainly be, but it would not amount to very much. Were the 'Board' to re-institute payment by results, and were they, with this end in view, to entrust the drafting of schemes of work in the various subjects to a committee of the wisest and most experienced educationalists in England, the resultant syllabus would be a dismal failure. For in framing their schemes these wise and experienced educationalists would find themselves compelled to take account of the lowest rather than of the highest level of actual educational achievement. What is exceptional and experimental cannot possibly find a place in a syllabus which is to bind all schools and all teachers alike, and which must therefore be so framed that the least capable teacher, working under the least favourable conditions, may hope, when his pupils are examined on it, to achieve with decent industry a decent modicum of success.[3]

A similar attempt to judge the Revised Code in its historical content was made by the Reverend C. D. Du Port in his general report for 1895 on schools in the East Central Division. He welcomed with approval Article 84b of the Code of 1895 which abolished the annual examination of schools in favour of Inspectors' visits. However, he stressed that he did not consider that this welcome change implied that Robert Lowe's Revised Code and the principle of payment by results were mistakes. 'On the contrary, the fact that by slow yearly changes and developments the original bald Code of 1864 has gradually ripened up by evolutionary stages into the Code of 1895, is unquestionable proof that that original move of some 30 years ago had life and power in it.'[4] Du Port went on to contend that in his experience of the pre-Revised Code days only the brightest children had gained the attention of teachers.[5] Had such a 'partial and eclectic' state of affairs been allowed to continue, the demand of the 1870 Act for

[2] *Ibid.* p. 107. [3] *Ibid.* pp. 104–5.
[4] *Report of Committee of Council on Education 1895–6*, p. 64.
[5] *Ibid.* p. 65.

an efficient school in every locality would never have been more than an unrealised paper decree, and Du Port suggested that it was the Revised Code which really made the 1870 Act the educational landmark that it was.

I assert it to be my belief that probably nothing short of the hard and narrow lines of Mr Robert Lowe's first Code, that assigned individual payments for individual examinations passed, and that formulated the somewhat inelastic system of uniform standards of work and of examination in reading, spelling, and arithmetic for adoption from end to end of our land, could have succeeded in crushing out past faults and defects, and in enabling hundreds and afterwards thousands of mere prentice hands to organise quite new schools and to reorganise existing ones almost everywhere, and that upon the quite new principles of educating not merely the privileged few of the wage earning class but all of them, and of teaching not merely the bright and earnest among the children but every child member of the schools.[6]

Considered then in the context of its times the Revised Code may be seen to have had both good and ill effects. Some of them Lowe intended; others he did not foresee.

## REDUCTION IN PUBLIC EXPENDITURE

The most immediate effect of the implementation of the Revised Code was the reduction in the total amount of the parliamentary grant to education. This was one of the results which Lowe had intended. Table 3 shows clearly the substantial and progressive

TABLE 3 *Reduction in Parliamentary grants, 1860–1866*

| | Average attendance | Parliamentary grants |
|---|---|---|
| | | £ |
| 1860 | 803,708 | 724,403 |
| 1861 | 855,077 | 813,441 |
| 1862 | 888,923 | 774,743 |
| 1863 | 928,310 | 721,386 |
| 1864 | 937,678 | 655,036 |
| 1865 | 1,016,558 | 636,806 |
| 1866 | 1,048,493 | 649,307 |

Source: *Final Report of the Commissioners appointed to inquire into the Elementary Education Acts*, 1888, p. 18.

[6] *Ibid.* p. 66.

reduction in the grant, achieved at the same time as the average attendance of children in schools was steadily increasing.

This reduction in the grant was the visible proof of the logic of Lowe's viewpoint in framing payment by results. He had promised the House of Commons that under his system of administering the grant, education would be either efficient or cheap.[7] That it was now seen to be cheaper implied one of two things. First that there had previously existed in the schools a low level of educational achievement as measured by tests of basic literacy and numeracy, which had been either unknown or unrevealed; or secondly that there was currently in existence a falling off in educational achievement. Lowe concluded that the former explanation was the more correct, but in either case, his viewpoint seemed justified that the schools were not very efficient in terms of producing measurable results of basic literacy and numeracy. If they had been, then the total amount of the grant would be expected to increase rather than diminish.

In fact, far from diminishing public expenditure, Lowe's scheme could potentially lead to a great expansion in the total amount of the government grant and Lowe recognised this when he said 'if the system is expensive it will at least be efficient, if it is not efficient it will at least be cheap'. Lowe fixed no upper limit to educational expenditure and if the schools worked efficiently and produced 'results', then Lowe was prepared to pay out to the limit, though he could not forecast that limit.[8] All that was new in Lowe's administration of the Treasury grant was his insistence that money would only be given for value received as measured by examination results. It has been argued that Lowe did not intend to reduce the education grant in 1862 at all, but rather took care to maintain 'the level at which the grant had been running in recent years whilst simplifying . . . its administration'.[9] This argument is based on a consideration of average payments per child. In 1860 they averaged 10*s*. per child, and to maintain this the Newcastle Commission suggested that the earnable maximum per child should be 15*s*. This would probably have produced an average higher than 10*s*. and so under the Revised Code Lowe fixed the earnable maximum at 12*s*. However, as it happened, this

[7] *Parliamentary Debates*, CLXV, col. 229. [8] *Ibid.*

[9] Morris, 'State Paternalism and laissez-faire in the 1860's', p. 19.

produced an average of only 9*s*. and the point of the argument is that though Lowe miscalculated in what was a difficult economic prognostication, there was no overall intention to reduce the grant. This may be true, but it is more likely that Lowe anticipated that the schools would not measure up adequately to the results test he was to impose and that, consequently, there would probably be some saving on the grant at least in the first years of its application.

After 1866 the amount of grant did in fact begin to rise steadily, though this was only partly the result of Lowe's policy, and can in no way be attributed to him as a person, for by that time Lowe had resigned from the Vice-presidency of the Education Committee. The situation had also been changed by the Minute of 20 February 1867 which introduced an increased grant to schools, raising the earnable maximum to 13*s*. 4*d*. and adding specific payments for pupil-teachers. Moreover the Education Act of 1870 served to increase the total amount of grant by adding Board Schools to the existing number already in receipt of government aid. Nevertheless, in principle, payment by results did not necessitate educational cuts. If operated at a higher level than Lowe's maximum per capita of 12*s*. or the 1867 level of 13*s*. 4*d*. – say at £1 – it could have brought affluence to teachers. That it did not was the result of government parsimony rather than the principle itself.

## EXTENSION OF BASIC LITERACY AND NUMERACY

The operation of the Revised Code was also a factor in the growth of basic literacy and numeracy which occurred among the school population between 1860 and 1890. There were of course other causal factors. The increase in the number of schools after the Act of 1870 was one and the gradual enforcement of compulsory education was another. The Act of 1870 gave power – though it did not insist upon its use – to the school boards to frame by-laws for compulsory attendance of children, aged from five to twelve, within their district. Lord Sandon's Act of 1876 set up school attendance committees with similar powers in areas without school boards and also forbade the employment of children below the age of ten and insisted upon certain standards of attainment for children between the ages of ten and fourteen before they could be employed. Mundella's Act of 1880 made school attendance compulsory for children between the ages of five and ten and in 1893 the upper limit was raised to eleven and in 1899 to twelve.

The Revised Code was, therefore, only one of several factors which ensured increased educational provision and school attendance, though the Code did give a grant for attendance and teachers were so conscious of this that, as school log-books from the period show, they often became unpaid school attendance officers, visiting homes to press their children to attend school. Once the children were in the schools they came under the operation of Lowe's Revised Code, and if basic literacy and numeracy did increase, then it must be attributed in large measure to the working of Lowe's policy.

In the *Report of the Committee of Council* for 1863–4 Lord Granville and Lowe analysed at some length the statistics of results compiled from 'the examination of 1,828 schools, with an average attendance of 280,474 day scholars, of whom 180,005 were presented for examination, or about 64 out of every 100'.[10] Table 4 gives the results of this analysis.[11] They indicate the comparatively small number of pupils who were able to satisfy the examiners in Standards IV to VI. Moreover, of those examined 38.96 per cent were over 10 years of age, and these ought, according to age, to have been able to pass Standard VI. In fact, however, only 14.18 per cent of the total number presented above Standard III were over 10 years of age, and of these only 10.09 per cent passed without failure in reading, writing or arithmetic. In other words, the aggregate number of children who passed Standards IV, V and VI was little more than one-fourth of those who ought to have been able to pass.[12]

TABLE 4 *Day scholars presented for examination, 1863–1864*

| Day scholars presented | | | Nos. and percentages of each Standard who failed in: | | | | | |
|---|---|---|---|---|---|---|---|---|
| | | | reading | | writing | | arithmetic | |
| Standard | No. | % | No. | % | No. | % | No. | % |
| I | 70,407 | 39.11 | 14,225 | 20.2 | 12,445 | 17.68 | 18,845 | 26.77 |
| II | 45,180 | 25.1 | 4,900 | 10.85 | 3,635 | 8.05 | 11,406 | 25.25 |
| III | 35,991 | 20.0 | 2,302 | 6.4 | 5,526 | 15.35 | 6,822 | 18.95 |
| IV | 22,137 | 12.3 | 1,017 | 4.6 | 4,342 | 19.62 | 4,047 | 18.28 |
| V | 4,671 | 2.59 | 250 | 5.35 | 659 | 14.11 | 793 | 16.98 |
| VI | 1,619 | 0.9 | 96 | 5.93 | 208 | 12.85 | 267 | 16.49 |
| Total | 180,005 | 100.0 | – | – | – | – | – | – |

[10] *Report of the Committee of Council on Education 1863–4*, p. xviii.
[11] *Ibid.* p. xx. [12] *Ibid.* p. xxi.

During the next twenty-five years the figures show a steady improvement, and in 1888 the Cross Commission concluded that on the whole there had been a 'continued advance' since the authorisation of the Revised Code. Whereas in 1872 only 17.96 per cent of the total children examined had been presented in Standards IV to VI, by 1886 it was 34.68 per cent, or more than a third of the whole. Similarly, the index of backwardness, supplied by the proportion of older children presented in the lower standards, had fallen from 63.71 per cent in 1872 to 36.33 per cent in 1886.[13] There was also an increase in the overall number of children who were examined in Standards I to VII as Table 5 shows, and an increase in the percentage of scholars examined to that of the total population of the nation. The age statistics for the census of 1881 showed that 23.73 per cent of the total population were between the ages of 3 and 13. Assuming, as the Committee of Council on Education did in 1887, that six-sevenths of that population were of the class whose children ought to attend public elementary school, about 20 per cent of the population ought to have been in school. However, the Committee calculated that, after making allowance for absences for various reasons, school seats should be provided for one-sixth of the population.[14] The increase in the percentage of scholars to the total population given in Table 5 shows that schools were by 1890 providing school places well beyond the level considered adequate only three years previously by the Committee of Council. This increase was the result of the 1870 Act and the gradual extension of compulsory education, but taken in conjunction with the operation of the Revised Code in this period it represents a significant attack upon mass illiteracy. Table 6, which shows the numbers of scholars individually examined in the three Rs, indicates the success of Lowe's policy as a programme of basic education.

Figures for the extension of literacy in the nineteenth century as measured by the Registrar-General's returns provide additional evidence for the success of Lowe's policy. Table 7 shows the increase in marriage-registrar signatures and these are a crude but relevant measure of literacy. The figures may be interpreted in two ways. First, as it has been pointed out,[15] the figures for any one

[13] *Final Report of the Commissioners appointed to inquire into the Elementary Education Acts*, 1888, p. 47.

[14] *Report of Committee of Council on Education 1887–8*, p. xii.

[15] West, *Education and the State*, p. 133.

TABLE 5 *Number of scholars examined in Standards, 1872–1890**

| | 1872 | 1875 | 1880 | 1885 | 1890 |
|---|---|---|---|---|---|
| I | 258,946 | 327,412 | 554,188 | 486,073 | 500,489 |
| II | 172,391 | 265,161 | 482,934 | 580,254 | 573,212 |
| III | 111,453 | 186,501 | 398,522 | 529,756 | 543,299 |
| IV | 66,925 | 115,576 | 276,737 | 430,112 | 483,936 |
| V | 36,843 | 58,170 | 139,227 | 240,405 | 315,605 |
| VI | 15,031 | 20,763 | 52,625 | 91,039 | 138,273 |
| VII | – | – | 8,172 | 21,416 | 41,286 |
| Total | 661,589 | 973,583 | 1,912,405 | 2,379,055 | 2,596,100 |
| No. of scholars examined, as percentage of total estimated population | 2.86 | 4.05 | 7.44 | 8.65 | 8.83 |

* Years ending 31 August.
Source: Compiled from the *Reports of Committee of Council on Education 1872–90*.

TABLE 6 *Number of scholars individually examined in the three Rs, 1870–1890*

| Number of scholars individually examined in Standards | Years ending 31 August | | | |
|---|---|---|---|---|
| | 1870 | 1876 | 1885 | 1890 |
| Who passed in reading | 691,763 | 995,046 | 2,185,391 | 2,454,731 |
| Who passed in writing | 680,859 | 907,452 | 1,994,326 | 2,295,376 |
| Who passed in arithmetic | 599,542 | 801,497 | 1,897,095 | 2,233,096 |

Source: *Report of Committee of Council on Education 1892–3*, p. 678.

point in time reflect the schooling gained some seventeen years previously, since on average in this period the age of marriage was about 28 years, that is some seventeen years after leaving school, where presumably the ability to read and write had been gained. Thus it may be suggested that the figure for 1881 indicates that in 1864 about 84 per cent of school leavers (taking an average of the figures for males and females) were already literate, and similarly that the figure for 1891 indicates that the proportion of literates had risen to 93 per cent by 1874. This increase of some 9 per cent may be largely attributed to the effects of the Revised Code since

TABLE 7 *Literacy figures in England and Wales, 1841–1900*

| | Males | | Females | |
|---|---|---|---|---|
| | % of literates | % gain | % of literates | % gain |
| 1841 | 67.3 | | 51.1 | |
| 1851 | 69.3 | 2.0 | 54.8 | 3.7 |
| 1861 | 75.4 | 6.1 | 65.3 | 10.5 |
| 1871 | 80.6 | 5.2 | 73.2 | 7.9 |
| 1881 | 86.5 | 5.9 | 82.3 | 9.1 |
| 1891 | 93.6 | 7.1 | 92.7 | 10.4 |
| 1900 | 97.2 | 3.6 | 96.8 | 4.1 |

Source: R. D. Altick, *The English Common Reader*, University of Chicago Press 1957, p. 171.

in that period the Education Act of 1870, with its increase of educational provision through Board Schools had not yet begun to take effect. Secondly, if the figures are taken as a general indication of the growth of literacy from 1860 to 1890, then the 18 per cent increase in male literacy and 27 per cent increase in female literacy may be attributed at least partially to the working of the Revised Code, though other factors, such as the increase in schools and in public money expended on education, were also operative. The schools after 1860 did produce a greater proportion of literates than earlier, and the financial pressure which the Revised Code put on teachers to ensure that the less able children left school with some basic literacy was probably the main reason for this. The increase in the school population, which undoubtedly occurred in this period, was unlikely of itself to have contributed so much to the decline of illiteracy as the emphasis which Lowe's Code put upon the teaching of all pupils, and particularly of the less able, to learn their letters. Lowe's policy had obvious educational limitations, but as a weapon against illiteracy it was undoubtedly successful. There is already some local evidence in support of this general conclusion,[16] and as local studies in the history of education increase it seems likely that it will be confirmed further.

[16] J. W. Docking, 'The Development of Church of England Schools in Coventry 1811–1944', unpublished Leeds University M.Ed. thesis 1966, pp. 105–10. Also J. W. Docking, *Victorian Schools and Scholars*, Pamphlet No. 3, published by Coventry Branch of Historical Association 1967, p. 21.

### DOMINANCE OF THREE RS

There was, however, a side effect to this. The three Rs came to a position of dominance in the curriculum. Lowe certainly intended that the schools should concentrate on reading, writing and arithmetic, but he hoped that beyond this the schools would also extend the religious, moral and general education of their pupils, and he told the inspectorate that it was their role to ensure that this wider education took place.[17] The Newcastle Report had been prepared to allow all schools to earn grants paid upon results[18] but Lowe objected to this precisely on the ground that the Government would have no means of ensuring 'that the moral teaching, the discipline, and the tone of the school were what they should be'.[19] He therefore insisted that only those schools which had certificated teachers and were subject to inspection could qualify for grants. It is interesting to note that here Lowe was acting counter to strict *laissez-faire* principles. He opposed aid to what he called 'private adventure schools' on the grounds that they were 'mere commercial speculations'.[20] His attitude is an indication of the ambivalent position in which mid-century liberals found themselves when they attempted to use state finances and central powers to ensure reform.

Lowe's hope that schools would do more than give a basic education proved illusory, and indeed it was naive of him to frame regulations which made reading, writing and arithmetic the only grant-earning subjects and yet expect schools to find time for other more general subjects.

The three Rs soon began to dominate the curriculum[21] and after Lowe's departure from the Education Department, the Committee of Council felt obliged to make changes in the Code which would serve to widen the curriculum. In 1867 'specific' subjects were introduced to earn an extra grant which in 1871 was fixed at 3*s*. per scholar who passed up to two additional subjects such as geography, history, grammar, algebra, geometry, natural sciences, political economy or 'any definite subject of instruction'.[22] Only pupils in

[17] *Report of Committee of Council on Education 1862–63*, p. xviii.

[18] *Report of the Commissioners appointed to inquire into the State of Popular Education in England*, 1861, I, p. 96.

[19] *Parliamentary Debates*, CLXIV, col. 729. [20] *Ibid.*

[21] For a full discussion of this see R. J. W. Selleck, *The New Education 1870–1914*, London 1968, pp. 24–77.

[22] *Report of Committee of Council on Education 1870–71*, pp. cviii, cxxiv.

TABLE 8 *The number of departments in day schools in which have been taught the various class subjects, 1884–1898*

| Year ending 31 August | English | Geography | Elementary Science | History | Needlework (Girls) | Welsh | Domestic Economy (Girls) | Object Lessons | Suitable Occupations | Number of departments in which Grants have been Paid | Grants have been Refused | No class Subject has been taken |
|---|---|---|---|---|---|---|---|---|---|---|---|---|
| 1884 | 19,080 | 12,775 | 51 | 382 | 5,929 | – | – | – | – | 18,483 | 597 | 2,538 |
| 1885 | 19,431 | 12,336 | 45 | 386 | 6,499 | – | – | – | – | 18,591 | 840 | 2,400 |
| 1886 | 19,688 | 12,055 | 43 | 375 | 6,809 | – | – | – | – | 18,784 | 824 | 2,411 |
| 1887 | 19,917 | 12,035 | 39 | 383 | 7,137 | – | – | – | – | 19,028 | 889 | 2,320 |
| 1888 | 20,041 | 12,058 | 36 | 390 | 7,424 | – | – | – | – | 19,254 | 787 | 2,284 |
| 1889 | 20,151 | 12,171 | 36 | 386 | 7,620 | – | – | – | – | 19,460 | 693 | 2,261 |
| 1890 | 20,304 | 12,367 | 32 | 414 | 7,758 | – | – | – | – | 19,691 | 613 | 2,212 |
| 1891 | 19,835 | 12,806 | 173 | 750 | 8,026 | – | – | – | – | 19,877 | 688 | 2,044 |
| 1892 | 18,175 | 13,465 | 788 | 1,627 | 7,655 | – | – | – | – | 20,110 | 830 | 1,673 |
| 1893 | 17,394 | 14,256 | 1,073 | 2,209 | 7,612 | – | – | – | – | 20,659 | 866 | 1,139 |
| 1894 | 17,030 | 15,250 | 1,215 | 2,972 | 7,675 | 1 | – | – | – | 21,915 | 753 | 111 |
| 1895 | 16,272 | 15,702 | 1,396 | 3,597 | 7,396 | 8 | 316 | – | – | 22,205 | 560 | 33 |
| 1896 | 15,327 | 16,171 | 2,237 | 4,143 | 7,219 | 18 | 471 | 1,079 | 360 | 22,533 | 389 | 21 |
| 1897 | 14,286 | 16,646 | 2,617 | 5,133 | 7,397 | 31 | 633 | 8,321 | 392 | 22,836 | 234 | 10 |
| 1898 | 13,456 | 17,049 | 2,143 | 5,780 | 7,252 | 12 | 784 | 21,882 | 176 | 22,914 | 127 | 2 |

Source: *Report of Committee of Council on Education 1898–9*, p. 116.

Standards IV to VI were allowed to take these extra subjects and this necessarily limited the effect of the new regulation, but even apart from this, the 'specific' subjects proved on the whole unattractive to schools and failed to widen the curriculum. They were popular at first and in 1872 60.2 per cent of the eligible pupils presented themselves for examination in these subjects but by 1890 this figure had dropped to 15.9 per cent.[23] This failure was to some extent offset by the comparative success of 'class' subjects which were introduced in 1875 as a further attempt to widen the curriculum. Grammar, history, geography and needlework could now be examined on a class basis and, provided that some 75 per cent of the class gave competent answers, a grant of 4*s*. per scholar could be earned.[24] In 1883 science was added to the list of class subjects. Some of these subjects proved popular such as English and geography, but history and science were largely ignored. Table 8 summarises the position over the period 1884–98. In general, it may be concluded that the class subjects presented a challenge to the dominance of the three Rs but they in no way disinherited them. As Lowe had intended, the teaching of reading, writing and arithmetic remained the prime purpose of the elementary school.

Lowe's success has been his undoing in the eyes of subsequent historiography. He has been criticised for impoverishing the curriculum. Two points may be made on this issue. First, there is little evidence to suggest that prior to 1862 the curriculum of elementary schools was as wide and liberal as this criticism of Lowe implies. Table 9 taken from the evidence of the Newcastle Commission, suggests that even before the Revised Code the three Rs – or if one adds religious instruction the four Rs – dominated.

Where other subjects were taught they were often given only to the cleverest and oldest pupils,[25] and if classes were taught geography or history as a whole, it seems likely that the majority did not follow them and the rote-learning and the existing method of examining a class orally only served to conceal this.[26] Secondly, the evidence of Her Majesty's Inspectors as to the decline of the teaching of subjects other than the three Rs after 1862 is by no means unanimous. Some Inspectors found that though initially

[23] Selleck, pp. 37–8.
[24] *Report of Committee of Council on Education 1875–6*, p. 173.
[25] *Ibid.* p. 245.
[26] See for example the report of Rev. C. D. Du Port HMI, *Report of Committee of Council on Education 1868–9*, p. 67.

TABLE 9 *Centesimal proportions of scholars learning various subjects in public weekday schools, 1,824 in number*

| Subjects | Centesimal proportion of scholars |
|---|---|
| Religious | 93.3 |
| Reading | 95.1 |
| Writing | 78.1 |
| Arithmetic | 69.3 |
| Needlework | 75.8 |
| Other industrial work | 3.8 |
| Geography | 39.4 |
| English grammar | 28.0 |
| English history | 19.5 |
| Mechanics | 0.6 |
| Algebra | 0.8 |
| Euclid | 0.8 |
| Elements of physical science | 3.1 |
| Music from notes | 8.6 |
| Drawing | 10.8 |

Source: *Report on the State of Popular Education in England*, 1861, I, p. 660.

the Revised Code caused a decrease in the teaching of the higher subjects such as geography, grammar and history, by 1866 there was a re-introduction of these subjects into the curriculum.[27] Other Inspectors found evidence of increased neglect of the higher subjects.[28]

On balance it seems that Lowe has been wrongly accused of impoverishing a curriculum which pulsated with liberal humanity and wide culture in the years before the Revised Code. It is largely a myth that there was a golden age in elementary schools before Lowe came along. On the other hand, there seems little doubt that Lowe's Revised Code served to prevent the growth of a wider curriculum in elementary schools after 1862. That the Committee of Council should attempt – in 1867 with 'specific' subjects and in 1875 with 'class' subjects – to change this situation is evidence enough of the effect of Lowe's policy. On other evidence Lowe may be accused of limiting the growth of science education by his refusal to admit science as a basic subject to be encouraged in elementary schools. Drawing, too, never developed as much as the Science and Art Department hoped it would, as a result of

[27] *Report of Committee of Council on Education 1866–7*, pp. 91, 101, 140, 233, 306, 324, 339. [28] *Ibid.* pp. 32, 114, 261, 277.

Lowe's attitude.[29] Lowe's policy made certain the dominance of the three Rs. Whether or not he was right to make these the priorities at the primary stage remains a subject for legitimate debate.

## MECHANICAL LEARNING

It is commonly asserted that as a result of the Revised Code the schools became subject to a régime of 'cram' or, in Matthew Arnold's phrase, of 'mechanical' learning.[30] Lowe accepted from the outset that the examination of individual children according to standards must be to a considerable extent mechanical[31] but he did not intend that the teaching preparatory to the examination should be equally mechanical, or that children should learn without understanding. Despite his intention it was soon apparent that much mechanical teaching was taking place and Lowe's successors at the Education Department admitted this, while repeating Lowe's viewpoint that it arose from 'errors in the mode of preparing candidates individually for examination and not from examination itself if properly conducted'.[32] Lowe's Code in no way originated mechanical teaching in schools. The monitorial system of teaching used by Lancaster and Bell at the beginning of the century had established a tradition of mechanical learning, and Charles Dickens had ridiculed such teaching some ten years earlier than the Revised Code in *Hard Times*, published in 1854. Nevertheless, there is substance in Matthew Arnold's criticism that the Revised Code, by making two-thirds of the government grant depend upon a mechanical examination, inevitably gave a mechanical turn to the inspection and affected the intellectual life of the school.[33] Lowe hoped that Her Majesty's Inspectors would be able to reduce these effects by their inspection of a 'school's whole character and work' and he issued special instructions to them, pointing out the dangers attendant upon the Revised Code and the power they had in obviating them.[34] His successors

[29] H. Butterworth, 'South Kensington and Whitehall: A Conflict of Educational Purpose', *Journal of Educational Administration and History*, IV, I (December 1971), 10–11.

[30] *Report of Committee of Council on Education 1867–8*, p. 296.

[31] *Report of Committee of Council on Education 1862–3*, p. xviii.

[32] *Report of Committee of Council on Education 1867–8*, p. xxi.

[33] *Report of Committee of Council on Education 1867–8*, p. 296.

[34] *Report of Committee of Council on Education 1862–3*, pp. xvii–xxviii.

repeated them,[35] but in fact general inspection was quite unable to prevent teachers practising a mechanical method of teaching in schools. The view of the Reverend F. Watkins, Her Majesty's Inspector in Yorkshire, Lincolnshire, Nottinghamshire and Derbyshire, was typical of many others.

There can, I think, be no doubt that the Revised Code has extended the area of elementary knowledge. But I cannot find that it has increased its depth, the contrary appears to be the case in this district. Indeed from the nature of the examination, which is entirely formal and mechanical, only mechanical results can be expected. I believe that I am only stating a fact of almost universal experience, when I speak of the want of intelligence shown by children in the subjects which they learn at school. I am aware that it is questionable whether under his present instructions, an inspector has any right to test this intelligence ... I have always taken what may be called the 'common-sense view' of this question, and have, whenever there has been time, examined the children in the subject-matter of the reading lesson, have considered the sense as well as the power of spelling shown by them in the dictation, and tested their real understanding of arithmetic, as well as its correctness. And I am obliged to say that there are very few schools which come out satisfactorily from such a trial ... [36]

In the end any solution to this problem lay with the teachers. Too many relied on rote-teaching. The Reverend R. Temple, Her Majesty's Inspector for Shropshire, Montgomery, Denbigh, Flint, Chester, Stafford, Worcestershire and Hereford, illustrated this in his report for 1869. He wrote:

It is, too, very amusing to watch the look of blank dismay which comes over a teacher's face when I tell some fluent urchin to shut his book and go on with his lesson by rote, and the scholar, proud of his accomplishment, obeys me ... I am frequently told by the teachers that 'the children have not gone beyond the 30th page in the book', and am evidently regarded as violating a sacred constitutional right when I direct the class to read the 40th page.[37]

That teachers should adopt such attitudes is easily understood. Lowe had put them in an impossible position, and had mistakenly devised an instrument of policy which defeated its own ends. Lowe made an error in expecting a system of individual examination to

[35] *Report of Committee of Council on Education 1867–8*, pp. xxx–xxxi.
[36] *Report of Committee of Council on Education 1869–70*, pp. 258–60.
[37] *Report of Committee of Council on Education 1869–70*, p. 239.

serve two purposes which tended in fact to be mutually contradictory. For on the one hand, individual examination was expected to act as a stimulus to teaching and learning and to the achievement of certain educational standards, while on the other it was made a basis for the assessment of a teacher's salary on the principle of a productivity award. As a result teachers tried to increase their salaries by using mechanical methods so that their pupils could display sufficient information to pass on the day of the examination and Inspectors were powerless to discourage this.

Lowe came to realise this and later expressed his opposition to the extension of the system to specific subjects in 1867 and class subjects in 1875. Matthew Arnold had suggested that the Minute of 20 February 1867 which introduced specific subjects would worsen the situation. He wrote in his general report for 1867:

> In the game of mechanical contrivances the teachers will in the end beat us; and it is now found possible, by ingenious preparation, to get children through the Revised Code examination in reading, writing and ciphering, without their really knowing how to read, write, or cipher, so it will with practice no doubt be found possible to get the three-fourths of the one-fifth of the children over six through the examination in grammar, geography and history, without their really knowing any one of these three subjects.[38]

Lowe could not help but agree with Arnold on this and his own views were reported by Lord George Hamilton:

> One day, when I was sitting next to him on a Committee, I asked him if he approved of the present methods of administration based on payment by results which were then in force. To my amazement he replied: 'If you will move for its total abolition in the House of Commons, I will second it.' I said to him: 'You are aware that you are supposed to have started and created the system?' 'Yes', he said, 'I know the fools say so. What happened was this: when I was at the Education Department, as my eyes hurt me a good deal, whenever I went into the country I used to send to the National School to let me have one or two boys or girls who could read well, and they used to come up and read to me in the evening. I found out that few, if any, of these boys or girls could really read. They got over words ... but five syllables completely stumped them. I therefore came to the conclusion that, as regards reading, writing and arithmetic, which are three subjects which can be definitely tested, each child should either read or write a passage, or do

[38] *Report of Committee of Council on Education 1867–8*, p. 297.

some simple sum of arithmetic to show that they were entitled to the grant which was given for reading, writing and arithmetic, and the idiots who succeeded me have piled up on the top of the three R's a mass of class and specific subjects which they propose to test in the same way. The result is wholesale cramming and superficiality, for the great majority of the children who pass through these class and specific subjects lose all knowledge of them a few months after they have left school.[39]

Lowe may not have intended to increase mechanical learning in the schools but this was the effect of the Code and Lowe ought to have foreseen it. Some teachers will always approach their task in a narrow way and use rote-learning. There were examples of this before the introduction of the Code and long after its decease too. It seems in fact to be a perennial outgrowth of the teaching process whatever the system of administration, examination or teacher-training. Lowe, however, unwittingly put a premium upon it. Some Inspectors took the view of the Reverend R. Temple that the Revised Code, if fairly worked, provided a 'solid framework of accurate elementary instruction, clothed with a fair and healthy growth of knowledge and intelligence'.[40] All too often, however, the Code led to an education which was a mere 'skeleton of dry bones'[41] and teachers never raised their eyes from the set tests and texts of the annual examination. The fault, the teachers claimed, lay with the Code and they bombarded the Cross Commission with evidence to this effect.[42] As a result, the Commission concluded that changes must be made in the payment of the parliamentary grant and that in particular the fixed grant given for attendance should be increased and the variable grants dependent upon results, reduced. This was eventually implemented in 1890.

## THE EFFECT ON RELIGIOUS EDUCATION

Many contemporaries feared that the Revised Code would squeeze religious education out of the curriculum by offering payments for secular education: 'just as intellectual progress would be sacrificed to physical training, if all the payments were

[39] Lord George Hamilton, *Parliamentary Reminiscences and Reflections 1868–1885*, London 1916, pp. 157–8.
[40] *Report of Committee of Council on Education 1869–70*, p. 238.
[41] *Ibid.*
[42] *Final Report of the Commissioners appointed to inquire into the Elementary Education Acts*, 1888, p. 180.

to depend on success in wrestling and gymnastic exercises alone', as the Reverend T. R. Birks put it in an open letter to Lord Granville.[43] This was not Lowe's intention, and he emphasised in his speeches that schools were still expected to provide religious education and that it was the job of Her Majesty's Inspectors to ensure that they did. As he told the House of Commons: 'If managers do neglect religious teaching in order to make money they will find themselves mistaken, because they must still satisfy the Inspectors as to their religious instruction, and if they do not do that they will lose their grants altogether.'[44] Lowe built this into the Revised Code and reminded Inspectors of their responsibility for this in additional instructions to them, issued in September 1862.[45]

There is no statistical evidence to show whether there was a decline in the amount of religious instruction during the period of the Code, and such evidence as there is comes mainly from Her Majesty's Inspectors' reports, though it is possible that local studies based on school records will, as they accumulate, provide additional evidence. The Committee of Council reviewed the evidence in 1868 and found that opinions among Inspectors differed so widely that it was impossible to arrive at any consensus.[46] If there was a decline then the responsibility for this lay more with the clergy than with Lowe and the Code; for the Code placed no restrictions upon religious education but rather obliged Inspectors of Church of England schools to report upon the instruction given, and certainly the Code did not hinder a clergyman from giving sound religious instruction in his local school every day or, as one Inspector put it, 'twice every day if he is disposed to do so'.[47]

## DECLINE IN THE NUMBER OF PUPIL-TEACHERS

A more easily recognised effect of the Revised Code was the decline in the number of pupil-teachers. In his efforts to economise,

[43] Reverend T. R. Birks, *The Revised Code: What would it do? And what should be done with it?*, London 1862, p. 8; see also Reverend John Menet, *The Revised Code. A Letter to a Friend*, London 1862, p. 27.

[44] *Parliamentary Debates*, CLXV, col. 223.

[45] *Report of Committee of Council on Education 1862–3*, p. xx; *ibid.* 1866–7, p. 17.

[46] *Report of Committee of Council on Education 1867–8*, pp. xxxvi–xli.

[47] Reverend J. J. Blandford's report, *Report of Committee of Council on Education 1867–8*, p. xxxviii.

Lowe made a reduction in the support given to teacher-training which amounted to a complete reversal of the Committee of Council's previous policy as initiated in the Minutes of 1846. The structure of the support for colleges was altered and subsidies for pupil-teachers swept away. Masters were no longer to receive payments for teaching them and the pupil-teachers no longer received a salary direct from public funds but were to receive them by agreement with the school managers. By this economy Lowe hoped to save annually £300,000.[48]

Lowe did not anticipate that his measures would reduce the number of pupil-teachers. He considered that if, as it seemed from the past, school managers found them a valuable addition to their certificated staff, then they would find the necessary cash to employ them from their income of voluntary subscriptions, fees and the capitation or results grants.[49] However, in fact, during the first few years of the operation of the Code most managers who faced a reduced grant income economised either by reducing their intake of pupil-teachers, or by lowering the wages that pupil-teachers formerly received so much that potential entrants sought other employment. Under the Minutes of 1846 schools had been encouraged to have one pupil-teacher to every twenty-five scholars[50] but under the Revised Code requirements were minimal. By Article 52 the grant was to be reduced if there was not a pupil-teacher to every forty scholars after the first fifty, and this meant, as Kay-Shuttleworth noted, that 'the first eighty-nine scholars might be taught by one principal teacher without help'.[51] Managers consequently appointed far fewer pupil-teachers than previously and also considerably undercut the previous rate of pupil-teachers' wages. The average payment under the Minutes of 1846 had been £15 for male and female alike; but from returns analysed by the Committee of Council in 1867 it appeared that on average £13 9*s.* 9*d.* was now being paid to a male pupil-teacher and £12 15*s.* 2*d.* for a female.[52] In such a situation it was not surprising that the number of pupil-teachers fell, as Table 10 shows.

The Committee of Council in their Report for 1869 noted that

[48] *Parliamentary Debates*, CLXV, col. 208.
[49] R. Lowe, in *The Times*, 13 February 1862, first leader.
[50] Minutes of 1846, Kay-Shuttleworth, *Four Periods of Public Education*, p. 535.
[51] Sir J. Kay-Shuttleworth, *Memorandum on Popular Education*, 1868, Reprint The Woburn Press 1969, p. 23.
[52] *Report of Committee of Council on Education 1867–8*, p. viii.

TABLE 10 *Number of pupil-teachers apprenticed, 1861–1869*

| | |
|---|---|
| 1861 | 2,984 |
| 1862 | 2,762 |
| 1863 | 2,971 |
| 1864 | 2,568 |
| 1865 | 2,631 |
| 1866 | 3,070 |
| 1867 | 3,742 |
| 1868 | 4,417 |
| 1869 | 4,557 |

Source: *Report of Committee of Council on Education 1869–70*, p. lxxxii.

the number of pupil-teachers throughout the country was steadily rising: but suggested that it would increase further if managers directly controlled the arrangements under which pupil-teachers were engaged. Too many, the Report maintained, left this matter to the principal teachers with the result that many pupil-teachers were engaged at a salary of only £5 a year to begin with, while principal teachers drew 'very liberal salaries'.[53] Under the Minute of 1846 all pupil-teachers were paid £10 in their first year, but a survey in 1869 revealed that 10 per cent of male pupil-teachers and 15.9 per cent of females were engaged at £5 or under, that 80.4 per cent males and 79.5 per cent females had wages beginning at between £5 and £10 and that 9.6 per cent males and 4.6 per cent females began with salaries of over £10. Similarly, the prospects of pupil-teachers had worsened under the Revised Code. Under the 1846 Minute the salaries of all pupil-teachers rose to £20, but the same survey showed that only 72.9 per cent male and 70.3 per cent female pupil-teachers had wages rising to between £15 and £20.[54] The Committee of Council commented upon this state of affairs as follows:

The Revised Code purposely leaves all matters of this kind to be settled in each case on the spot, according to the general rate of wages in the district; but the object of doing so is defeated if the local authorities do not interfere to prevent even the suspicion that any interested influence has affected too exclusively the scale of remuneration enjoyed by the various classes of teachers in their schools.[55]

It is obvious that Lowe's reliance upon the operation of

[53] *Report of Committee of Council on Education 1869–70*, p. xxiii.
[54] *Report of Committee of Council on Education 1869–70*, p. xxiv. [55] *Ibid.*

economical laws for the regulation of salaries had led to a depression of the condition of pupil-teachers, and this in turn had its effect on the diminishing number of candidates seeking admission to the training colleges.

Table 11 shows the effect which the Revised Code had on the total number of pupil-teachers in the schools in the first few years of its operation. The arrest, in 1867, of the previous decline was the beginning of a steady increase in the number of pupil-teachers in the following years, which was accelerated by the measure which the Committee of Council took by its Minute of 20 February 1867 to counteract the effect of Lowe's measures. The main reduction had been in the number and quality of male pupil-teachers, and it had been due not so much to a lack in the number admitted as to removals during the course of apprenticeships in the schools. As the Committee of Council reported: 'the boys, as they grow up, are tempted with higher wages in other employments, and the managers are disposed to let them go, as they become more expensive'.[56] To counteract this, the Committee of Council offered in February 1867 a grant to elementary schools of £10 for every male pupil-teacher who went on to a Normal School and gained there a first class in its examinations, and £5 for a student who gained a second class. If the students successfully completed their first years in the training college, then additional grants were paid to the schools which apprenticed them, at the rate of £8 for a student placed in the first division at the examination and £5 for a student placed in the second division.[57]

Lowe's measures, though they provided some pecuniary saving, would have had disastrous effects on the training of teachers had they been allowed to continue. While in theory it might seem possible that managers would still be able to afford to take on

TABLE 11 *Pupil-teachers in schools under inspection, 1863–1867**

| 1863 | 1864 | 1865 | 1866 | 1867 |
|---|---|---|---|---|
| 13,849 | 11,712 | 11,383 | 10,955 | 11,519 |

* Years ending 31 August.
Source: *Report of Committee of Council on Education 1867–8*, p. vii.

[56] *Report of Committee of Council on Education 1866–7*, p. ix.
[57] *Ibid.* p. xcviii.

pupil-teachers, in practice they could not. Many of Her Majesty's Inspectors insisted in their reports that pupil-teachers were the best source of suitable masters and mistresses and that if their number was allowed to decline then the nation's teaching force would be sadly depleted.[58] While it was true that pupil-teachers were not the only source from which training colleges could be filled, and though the colleges were encouraged 'to find excellent candidates for training among the voluntary teachers in Sunday Schools, or among young persons engaged in occupations implying a certain degree of instruction',[59] provided always that they were more than 18 years old, pupil-teachers remained the main source of teachers. Table 12 shows how successfully the Minute of 1867 counteracted the initial effects of Lowe's policy.

TABLE 12 *Pupil-teachers in public elementary day schools, 1870–1890*

| Year ending 31 August | Boys | Girls |
|---|---|---|
| 1870 | 6,384 | 8,228 |
| 1872 | 9,381 | 12,357 |
| 1874 | 10,503 | 16,713 |
| 1876 | 11,102 | 19,436 |
| 1878 | 10,835 | 20,439 |
| 1880 | 10,822 | 21,306 |
| 1882 | 8,983 | 19,616 |
| 1884 | 7,707 | 19,045 |
| 1886 | 8,162 | 21,636 |
| 1888 | 8,627 | 23,092 |
| 1890 | 7,695 | 23,467 |

Source: *Report of Committee of Council on Education 1898–9*, p. 120.

Apart from reducing teacher supply Lowe's measures would also have eventually increased the pupil–teacher ratio. In this way he would have defeated the very end he sought to achieve, for without an effective and adequate teaching force his campaign for a mass basic education could not have been fought. Lowe obviously miscalculated in this part of his policy.

58 *Report of Committee of Council on Education 1866–7*, pp. 142, 248–9, 288, 327.
59 *Report of Committee of Council on Education 1867–8*, p. xi.

## EFFECT ON TEACHER-TRAINING COLLEGES

The main effect of the Revised Code on the training colleges was to reduce their numbers. Table 13, compiled from the Reports of the Committee of Council, makes this clear.

TABLE 13 *Students resident in training colleges, 1861–1874*

| | Year | No. |
|---|---|---|
| December | 1861 | 2,869 |
| December | 1862 | 2,972 |
| December | 1863 | 3,109 |
| Michaelmas | 1864 | 2,633 |
| February | 1865 | 2,482 |
| February | 1866 | 2,403 |
| February | 1867 | 2,360 |
| February | 1868 | 2,257 |
| February | 1869 | 2,286 |
| February | 1870 | 2,600 |
| February | 1871 | 2,933 |
| February | 1872 | 3,347 |
| February | 1873 | 2,896 |
| February | 1874 | 2,982 |

This was partly the result of the effect which the Revised Code had in reducing the number of pupil-teachers, but also of Article 91 of the Code, by which pupil-teachers who had completed their apprenticeship with credit could take up posts as assistant teachers in schools without further training in a Normal School.[60] Assistants were left to make their own terms with school managers as to hours and wages[61] but often they could secure salaries as favourable as assistants with college training, and consequently they preferred to seek employment immediately after the completion of their apprenticeship. Article 91 also allowed pupil-teachers to be provisionally certificated for immediate service in charge of small rural schools. Such certification could last until the holder became 25 years of age, although then it would be cancelled if the teacher had not obtained a permanent certificate by passing the appropriate examination. As the Principal of St Mark's College, John Cromwell, complained, in a memorandum of 9 September 1869,

[60] *Report of Committee of Council on Education 1861–2*, arts. 90 and 91.
[61] *Ibid.* p. xxxv, Revised Code, art. 93.

'Articles 91, 132, 133, offer a direct premium to ex-pupil teachers to shun the colleges.'[62]

The fall in the number entering training colleges in the years immediately following the Revised Code is shown in Table 14. After 1867 the number of admissions began to rise following the Minute of 20 February 1867 which gave extra grants to schools from which pupil-teachers had entered training colleges.[63]

TABLE 14 *Entrants to training colleges, 1862–1870*

| | Males | Females | Total |
|---|---|---|---|
| January 1862 | 821 | 770 | 1,591 |
| January 1863 | 913 | 842 | 1,755 |
| January 1864 | 594 | 694 | 1,288 |
| January 1865 | 501 | 697 | 1,198 |
| January 1866 | 508 | 707 | 1,215 |
| January 1867 | 436 | 685 | 1,121 |
| January 1868 | 445 | 676 | 1,121 |
| January 1869 | 440 | 744 | 1,184 |
| January 1870 | 672 | 787 | 1,459 |

Source: *Report of Committee of Council on Education 1861–2*, p. lxxxii.

A second effect was the reduction in government grant to the colleges. This was an economy which Lowe had very much wanted to achieve, and in fact during his term of office he made two separate attempts to frame regulations under which it might be accomplished. Under the Revised Code of May 1862 no more grants were to be made for building, enlarging or improving the premises of training colleges. Annual grants were to be made, however, for certificated assistant teachers, for lecturers and for the tuition and board of Queen's Scholars. In addition, grants were to be made on the payment by results principle according to the examinations passed by Queen's Scholars at the end of each of two years in the college.[64] This was to operate according to the scale shown in Table 15. It should be remembered that there was nothing new about this in principle: under the Minutes of 1846 grants to Normal Schools had been awarded on the success of students in the annual examinations.

[62] *Ibid.* p. 427. 1869–70.
[63] *Report of Committee of Council 1869–70*, Revised Code 1870, art. 90.
[64] *Report of Committee of Council 1861–2*, pp. xxxv–xxxvii, Revised Code, arts. 95–111.

TABLE 15 *Grants paid to Queen's Scholars under Revised Code*

| At the end of: | For candidate placed by Examination in each Division | To be allowed to College (in the case of Females Two-thirds of these Sums) £ s. d. |
|---|---|---|
| First year's residence | 1 | 20 0 0 |
| | 2 | 16 0 0 |
| | 3 | 13 0 0 |
| | 4 | 13 0 0 |
| Second year's residence | 1 | 24 0 0 |
| | 2 | 20 0 0 |
| | 3 | 16 0 0 |
| | 4 | 16 0 0 |

Source: *Report of Committee of Council on Education 1861–2*, p. xxxix, Revised Code, art. 123.

However this scheme of payments was barely under way when it was cancelled by the Minute of 21 March 1863. This was Lowe's second attempt to prune public expenditure on training colleges, and, as the Minute said, the aim of the Committee of Council was to limit 'their support of Training (Normal) schools to the proved demand for trained teachers'.[65] The colleges were now forbidden to expand their numbers beyond those which they were able to accommodate in 1862, and future annual grants were not to exceed 75 per cent of the total expenditure of a college or £50 for each male student and £35 for each female student, resident in the college throughout the year in which the grant was being paid. Various provisional arrangements were made for the years from 1864 to 1867, but from 1868 onwards the grant was paid at the rate of £100 for each male and £70 for each female student who, in the previous five years, had trained over two years in the college, completed his or her probation and become employed in the schools.[66] No other grants were payable. The grant for lecturers was abolished and Queen's Scholarships also disappeared from the Revised Code for 1864, though the Inspectors continued to examine candidates for admission to the training colleges. The payment by results principle, however, still operated in that the

[65] *Report of Committee of Council 1862–3*, p. xliv. [66] *Ibid.* pp. xlv–xlvi.

first instalment of the total annual grant to a college was paid in January on the results gained by the resident students of a college in the certificate examinations of the previous December. This measure had the desired effect of reducing expenditure as Table 16 shows.

TABLE 16 *Annual grants to training colleges, 1859–1875*

| Year | £ | s. | d. | Year | £ | s. | d. |
|---|---|---|---|---|---|---|---|
| 1859 | 89,587 | 10 | 6 | 1868 | 69,886 | 6 | 7 |
| 1860 | 92,328 | 19 | 0 | 1869 | 70,807 | 17 | 2 |
| 1861 | 101,865 | 13 | 1 | 1870 | 73,442 | 12 | 7 |
| 1862 | 104,700 | 11 | 8 | 1871 | 81,583 | 15 | 0 |
| 1863 | 111,966 | 17 | 1 | 1872 | 93,881 | 16 | 1 |
| 1864 | 95,666 | 16 | 10 | 1873 | 86,412 | 15 | 10 |
| 1865 | 75,624 | 7 | 10 | 1874 | 92,187 | 5 | 11 |
| 1866 | 69,934 | 14 | 2 | 1875 | 94,376 | 19 | 4 |
| 1867 | 75,792 | 4 | 9 | | | | |

Source: *Reports of Committee of Council on Education 1859–75*.

The effect of the arrangements of 1863 on the colleges was to place them in the position of risking a loss of income from grants if their students did not enter the teaching profession.[67] This, together with the overall reduction in the number of students which had followed the introduction of the Revised Code and the limit of 75 per cent placed upon the amount of expenses to be paid out of public grants, enforced a period of retrenchment upon them.

Apart from making a financial saving Lowe had also hoped to make the course of training in Normal Schools more appropriate to the teaching that students would have to practise later. However, he had little effect on the colleges in this respect. Article 100 of the Revised Code, which provided for grants for lecturers, repeated the hope expressed in the Minute of 20 August 1853 that lecturers would have skill in adapting their attainments in the various academic subjects such as history, geography, English literature, physical science and applied mathematics, 'to elementary instruction'.[68] However it was little more than a hope and in any case it was cancelled by the Minute of 21 March 1863.

[67] See *Report of Committee of Council on Education 1869–70*, p. 427, for complaint of the Principal of St Mark's College, Chelsea, on this point.

[68] *Report of Committee of Council on Education 1861–2*, p. xxxvi.

The revised syllabus of 1863 attempted to reduce the subjects in the training-college curriculum and also make the curriculum more practical. Compared with the syllabus of 1856 the new syllabus was consequently more narrow but only marginally so. For example, the 1863 syllabus added 'Repetition from Memory' of at least 300 lines of poetry and a prose composition in both the first and second year's work. On the other hand it dropped mensuration problems from the arithmetic syllabus, omitted mechanics and algebra and limited the study of Euclid to two books in the first year. Similarly, it reduced the arithmetic syllabus for the second year, omitting logarithms and compound interest, and substituting a revision of the first year's work which concentrated on written and mental sums, addition, subtraction, multiplication and division of numbers, neat figure work and simple quadratic equations. A further notable change in 1863 was the omission of the alternative subjects, physical science, higher mathematics, English literature and Latin. This was obviously an attempt to reduce the academic content. Instead Euclid, Books I–IV, was added to the second year syllabus and 'economy' – 'elementary questions in sanitary and other practical science of common application, and in political economy' – was added to the work of both the first and second year. The introduction of 'economy' would seem to be the direct handwork of Lowe. Certainly it was a subject dear to his heart, and it gave an obviously utilitarian flavour to the training college syllabus.[69]

However, when all the changes are noted and comparisons made between the syllabus of 1856 and that of 1863, it does not seem that there was a severe narrowing of the curriculum for teacher-training. The reduction of the syllabus for the second year seems to be justified on the grounds that it was over-ambitious, and the general principle that the syllabus should in part be related to practice in the schools was a sound one. The syllabus did not of course reflect twentieth-century assumptions about the nature of a training-college curriculum, but it is unhistorical to expect it to do so. It seems fair to conclude that Lowe did not affect the training-college curriculum as much as might be imagined.

If Lowe had little effect on the curriculum, his use of payment by results in the colleges may have served to encourage mechanical

[69] *Minutes of Committee of Council on Education 1856–7*, pp. 9, 11, 12; *Report of Committee of Council on Education 1862–3*, pp. xxxiii–vii.

methods of teaching. The Minute of 21 March 1863 included that element in its arrangements for the payment of instalments of annual grants, and it is likely that this encouraged some mechanical teaching. However it is equally unlikely that these regulations began mechanical teaching. Under the Minutes of 1846 the existence of certificate examinations, upon the results of which grants were paid to the colleges, was just as likely to provoke mechanical teaching, and the Revised Code and the Minute of 1863 only made an existing situation slightly worse. To see the Revised Code as a great divide in this matter and argue that before 1862 the colleges were admirable institutions, whereas after the work of Lowe they were cramped in the curricula and riddled by mechanical teaching, is to fall into the fallacy of *post hoc ergo propter hoc*. Even after the Revised Code of 1871 which dropped the principle of payment by results in the award of annual grants to the colleges, mechanical teaching continued.[70] It seems that such teaching will always exist so long as some teachers persist in considering that it is the only way to achieve examination success for their students. The fault lies in the teaching, and it cannot be seriously maintained that it is wholly the result of administrative regulations. It may be convenient to generalise about the work of the training colleges between 1860 and 1890 as the result of Lowe's work in the Revised Code, but such explanations are too simple to do justice to all the relevant factors. R. W. Rich claimed that 'by exalting "payment by results" as the supreme principle in national education, "the Revised Code" lowered the standard of the education of the teacher, it paralysed the earlier enthusiasm of the training colleges, it restricted their curricula, and put a premium on mechanical methods of defeating the examiner'.[71] In another passage, the same writer described the results of the Revised Code on the training colleges, as 'disastrous', and continued: 'In spite of all their deficiencies, they (the colleges) had been reaching out towards a liberal cultivation of the teacher. For the next twenty years they were sullenly to restrict themselves to mechanical taskwork, narrow in scope and low in standard.'[72] All this is to take too rosy a view of the colleges in the days before

[70] *Report of Committee of Council on Education 1874–5*, pp. 233–4; *Report of the Board of Education 1912–13*, pp. 58–60.

[71] R. W. Rich, *The Training of Teachers in England and Wales during the Nineteenth Century*, Cambridge 1933, p. 193.

[72] *Ibid.* p. 179.

the Revised Code. It is true that there was some reduction in the requirements for certificates after the Revised Code, but this was mainly to meet the fall in the quality and quantity of the students.[73] The question of whether the Revised Code restricted the college curricula has already been discussed, and it does not seem to have changed the pre-Code curricula very much. It could be argued of course that the dominance of the three Rs in the school curriculum inhibited the colleges from changing their curricula during the next twenty years, and kept the college syllabus in line with what teachers would be expected to teach in the schools. There is some truth in this. The training college was then seen more as a place of professional training than an institution of general higher education. Thus the Reverend B. M. Cowie, Inspector of Church of England schools for schoolmasters, could complain in 1866 that the colleges were not preparing teachers adequately for their work in the schools under the Revised Code.[74] In this way the Revised Code did press for a greater vocational bias in teacher-training. However it did not cramp the syllabus too much and certainly it was not responsible for the 'mechanical character of our training school instruction'[75] which Matthew Arnold lamented. The syllabus, it is true, appears in the Minutes of the Committee of Council as distinctly factual and bare in outline.[76] However, it is how teachers and examiners 'practise' the syllabus which eventually determines the quality of the education a student undergoing it may receive. Unfortunately, some, though not all, training-college teachers chose to teach their own subjects in a mechanical way,[77] and at least one Inspector found that even the practical lessons which students gave were 'not the real work of the students themselves' but dictated in notes by the teacher of method.[78] On balance it seems that the Reverend B. M. Cowie, who inspected Church of England colleges for schoolmasters over a period of years, gave in his report for 1871 a clear and convincing answer to the complaint

[73] *Report of Committee of Council on Education 1866–7*, p. 394, report of Reverend B. M. Cowie.

[74] *Report of Committee of Council on Education 1866–7*, p. 397.

[75] *Report of Committee of Council on Education 1868–9*, p. 447.

[76] See for example *Report of Committee of Council on Education 1869–70*, pp. lxii–lxxiv.

[77] *Report of the Board of Education 1912–13*, pp. 58–9.

[78] *Report of Committee of Council on Education 1866–7*, p. 447.

that the teaching-college curriculum was confined. Having considered the spectrum of subjects offered – English language and literature, mathematics, geography, history and political economy – he concluded that there was no reason inherent in the subjects themselves which would prevent able teachers from making them 'vehicles of culture'.[79] Lowe and the Revised Code cannot be made the scapegoat for all the educational ills of the latter part of the nineteenth century.

## EFFECT ON THE STATUS OF TEACHERS

The Revised Code does seem to have affected the status which teachers held in society. Kay-Shuttleworth's intentions in the Minutes of 1846 had been to improve the status of teachers. He had concluded from the reports of Inspectors that there was a relation between the imperfections in schools and the condition of schoolmasters and that the most prominent cause of this was the fact that 'the master of an elementary school is commonly in a position which yields him neither honour nor emolument'.[80] He realised that if masters were not provided with suitable incomes and pensions they would be attracted to commerce rather than teaching, and consequently urged that a third of a teacher's income should be fixed and secure, regardless of all local sources such as 'school pence' and the contributions of the wealthy, and that a total of £90 per annum was a proper minimum income if consideration was given to the position a teacher ought to hold in society.[81] By the Minutes of 1846 the Council agreed to pay, direct to the masters, augmentation of pay according to the length of their training in a Normal School. A teacher who had completed one such year could have an addition of £15 to £20 per annum, a teacher with two years' training £20 to £25 per annum, and one with three years' training £25 to £30 per annum, provided that the school managers provided a rent-free house and a salary of at least twice the amount of the augmentation grant.[82] Under Lowe's Revised Code teachers were no longer to receive pay direct from the Education Department, but instead from their respective

[79] *Report of Committee of Council on Education 1871–2*, p. 155.
[80] Kay-Shuttleworth, *Four Periods of Public Education*, p. 474.
[81] *Ibid.* p. 477.
[82] Minutes of 1846, printed in Kay-Shuttleworth, *Four Periods of Public Education*, pp. 538–9.

school managers. In future, arrangements for salaries were to be agreed between teachers and managers, and Lowe made it clear that he preferred this to be regulated by the laws of supply and demand.[83]

Teachers lost status by this measure in two ways. First they could no longer assume the position of civil servants, for they were no longer in the direct pay of the Government. Secondly, they were reduced to a position of bargaining for their salaries. Since there was no shortage of teachers and since they offered a service which produced few benefits of obvious material worth, teachers found themselves with few counters to exploit across the bargaining table. In fact, the only bargaining factor which they did have was the results which their pupils obtained in the annual examinations. There is need for more local research before the effects of this change of the Revised Code can be fully assessed, but certainly teachers, both headteachers and assistants, had to bargain for their salaries.[84] Most headteachers in fact, especially in the Board Schools which came after 1870, were paid on a grant-share basis, in which they received a share, invariably in arrears, of the grant paid by the Education Department on the results of the annual examination.[85]

The Revised Code made no attempt then to improve either the status or salaries of teachers. However it is doubtful whether the teacher had much status prior to the Code. Certainly in evidence to the Newcastle Commission one schoolmaster complained that

> the man who studies human laws, he who understands the human frame and the healing art, the artist who can produce a picture, each has a recognised position and is esteemed; but the man who labours for the elevation of his fellow, who deals with the human intellect, who is entrusted to cut and polish the most precious jewel in creation, is a mere social nonentity.[86]

The Revised Code probably did little either to worsen or improve this situation. However, since salary is one of the factors in that

[83] *Parliamentary Debates*, CLXV, col. 234.

[84] See for example R. R. Sellman, *Devon Village Schools in the Nineteenth Century*, Newton Abbot 1967, pp. 94–101.

[85] *Ibid.* p. 125. In Devon it was found that 31% of headteachers in Board Schools and 19% of those in voluntary schools were paid on a grant-share basis up to 1903. Assistants were usually paid on a flat rate.

[86] *Report of Commission appointed to inquire into the State of Popular Education: Evidence*, II, p. 310.

complex which determines status in society, the Revised Code did have an effect, for it reduced teachers' salaries at least temporarily. Table 17, compiled from the Reports of the Committee of Council for the period 1859 to 1875, clearly shows this temporary fall in salary between 1861 and 1870. The relation between status and salary is a positive one and the reduction made the profession of schoolteacher appear less attractive than it might otherwise have been. In this respect the Revised Code did have a worsening effect upon the status of teachers.

TABLE 17 *Certificated teachers' salaries, 1859–1875*

| Year | Average salary of certificated masters | | | Average salary of certificated mistresses | | |
|---|---|---|---|---|---|---|
| | £ | *s.* | *d.* | £ | *s.* | *d.* |
| 1859–60 | 94 | 3 | 7 | 62 | 13 | 10 |
| 1861–62 | 94 | 10 | 3 | 62 | 15 | 5 |
| 1863–64 | 93 | 17 | 6 | 61 | 7 | 10 |
| 1864–65 | 90 | 4 | 6 | 58 | 8 | 9 |
| 1865–66 | 86 | 10 | 9 | 55 | 2 | 1 |
| 1866–67 | 87 | 3 | 0 | 55 | 0 | 2 |
| 1867–68 | 88 | 18 | 5 | 55 | 11 | 0 |
| 1868–69 | 91 | 5 | 11 | 56 | 1 | 7 |
| 1869–70 | 93 | 5 | 7 | 57 | 1 | 0 |
| 1870–71 | 95 | 12 | 9 | 57 | 16 | 5 |
| 1871–72 | 98 | 5 | 6 | 58 | 11 | 9 |
| 1872–73 | 100 | 0 | 9 | 59 | 4 | 10 |
| 1873–74 | 103 | 10 | 10 | 62 | 9 | 11 |
| 1874–75 | 106 | 18 | 4 | 64 | 6 | 4 |
| 1875–76 | 109 | 6 | 7 | 65 | 7 | 8 |

RELATIONS BETWEEN INSPECTORS AND TEACHERS

The Revised Code had one other effect which, though difficult to document, was nevertheless substantial. It worsened relations between teachers and Inspectors. It may not be true that prior to the Code, the Inspector had been regarded as the teachers' friend, but certainly after the Code, he became an opponent who was to be out-manoeuvred by every tactic possible. The Revised Code defined the Inspector's role more closely: he became an assessor for the central government, charged with the responsibility of ensuring that the schools gave value for money, and for the teachers he became an awarder with power to increase or decrease their salaries. As a result the Inspectors' annual visits to schools became occasions of crucial importance, causing anxiety to both teachers and pupils which must on occasions have come near to terror.

The date of the annual visit now dominated the whole work of the schools. The process of teaching went on in an atmosphere of tension, and teachers were strongly tempted to ensure good results at the Inspector's examination by encouraging rote-learning, by co-operating with each other in discovering and passing on to colleagues the questions which an Inspector might ask and even by assisting the children on the day of the examination in various ways.

For example, the following extract from a circular to Her Majesty's Inspectors from the Education Department dated 5 April 1889, shows how teachers had been helping children in needlework.

Sir, My Lords find that in the Children's Needlework, which has been examined by the Directress of Needlework at this Department, there are many instances of the materials having been prepared and fixed before they were distributed to children. The Table of Exercises, in the Instructions to Her Majesty's Inspectors, distinctly prescribes that, except in and below Standard I, no fixing or preparation of pieces is allowable; and you should impress this rule upon teachers. The children must themselves fold hems, draw threads for stitching, make bands, place tapes, fix buttons in position, cut buttonholes, cut holes before patching, place patches, trace patterns, etc.

Some teachers also used sign language to tell their class what the Inspector required of them; for example, hands in the teacher's pockets indicated multiplication, while hands behind his back meant subtraction.[87]

If teachers on the one hand approached Inspectors in a spirit of conspiracy and deceit, Inspectors for their part developed an attitude of distrust towards the teachers. The result was a state of cold war. Lowe had of course intended that the Revised Code should put pressure upon teachers. He rightly felt that idle teachers did not deserve to be protected and given a security of tenure and salary which people in other walks of life could not command. Unfortunately, his policy also injured the conscientious teacher

[87] Lowndes, p. 14.

who, coping with poor attendance and less able pupils, endeavoured to educate his children to the best of his ability and also secure a salary sufficient to keep his family at a decent, if modest, standard of living. School log-books provide the best evidence of this particular effect of the Revised Code. There the struggle and anxiety of many teachers to secure the regular attendance of pupils and some progress for their children in the mastering of the basic elementary subjects, is made clear. Similarly, they often show the disappointment which teachers felt when their efforts did not produce the required results.[88] On the other hand they also reveal the salutary effects of the system. For example, the following extract from the log-book of Penistone National School for 1873 shows the effect of an Inspector's visit and his report on the conduct of the previous schoolmaster in charge there, one Joseph Haines who had left the school on 5 June 1873, and also on the pupil-teacher, Lucy Child.

*1873, July 30*

SUMMARY OF H.M. INSPECTOR'S REPORT AND ACCOMPANYING REMARKS BY THE DEPARTMENT

I regret to say that the school appears to have been grossly neglected by its Master during the past year. The state of attainments is wretchedly poor. In Arithmetic only one child passed out of thirty-three presented, and the Second Standard Children were unable to do even First Standard sums. The contrast between these Results and those of previous years is very great. The Elder girls should learn Cutting out and more specimens of Needlework must be shown at next Inspection. The Pupil Teacher's Work has been greatly interfered with by her irregularity of attendance.

A deduction of one-tenth has been made for the Grant in consequence of the very unsatisfactory character of H.M. Inspector's Report. Larger deductions may be made next year unless great improvement be shown. (Article 32 (b).)

L. A. Child. Writing, Grammar and Arithmetic. She has passed an unsatisfactory Examination. If she fails to the same extent next year, the Grant will have to be reduced by £10, and thenceforth by £20, for every year at the end of which a similar failure is repeated. (Article 32 (c).)[89]

[88] Sellman, pp. 94–104, for a published account of this.

[89] Penistone St John the Baptist School Log-Book, p. 151: Univ. of Leeds Museum of the History of Education, catalogue no. A/LB/1537.

Another extract for the week ending 18 July 1873 shows the succeeding teacher's reactions at the magnitude of the task before him and his resolve to tackle the job conscientiously.

Numbers present at all this week = 86.
Have had a hard tough week's work.
The ignorance as well as the state of discipline is very discouraging, and a hard year's work is before me. On testing the whole school on Friday, only three boys in the I and II Standards could work a simple addition sum correctly and in the three upper Standards III, IV and V *not one* scholar could work a sum in addition of money consisting of eight lines in the space of half an hour. Plenty of work before me. Have commenced this week with drilling, the best aid to discipline.

Signed J. H. Collins[90]

The corollary of this was that children were also made to work hard, a side effect of the operation of the Revised Code which has often gone unnoticed. Edmond Holmes, who was a severe critic of the Revised Code, saw this as the 'one redeeming feature' of it, that 'the children were compelled to work, to exert themselves, to put their backs into it'.[91]

Despite the advantages of the new system of inspection which the Revised Code began there is no doubt that it widened the rift between teachers and Inspectors. The Inspector became a lonely figure in English education, feared and despised by teachers. The Revised Code effectively delayed the development of his role as a teacher-adviser and gave him an inquisitorial image which dies hard.

To sum up, Lowe was attempting to make an already existing system work more efficiently and, if possible, at reduced cost to public funds, in an attempt to achieve mass literacy and elementary numeracy. The Revised Code which he devised to achieve all this had the following effects: it made some immediate reduction in public expenditure; it helped to extend basic literacy and numeracy throughout a much wider section of the population; it produced a dominance of the three Rs in the elementary school curriculum; it was partly responsible for the growth of mechanical learning in schools; it encouraged a reduction in the number of pupil-teachers and depleted for a time the overall teaching force available in the schools; it had an adverse effect on the status of teachers in society; and by defining the role of Inspectors more

[90] Penistone National School Log-Book, p. 146. [91] Holmes, p. 109.

specifically as examiners, created a tension in the relationship between teachers and Inspectors. As a programme of mass education with limited objectives the Revised Code was appropriate and successful. Unfortunately it also had far-reaching side effects which hindered the development of a more liberal elementary education in schools. At best it was a mixed blessing.

As for Robert Lowe, the good that came out of the Revised Code he intended; the evil he failed to foresee. It is possible to hold that most of its most damaging effects arose from the subsequent operation of the Code by his successors and more particularly by those crucial additions to it of 1867 and 1875 which extended the Code to subjects other than the three Rs and by the introduction of the merit grant in 1882, which though devised to take into account an Inspector's view of a school as a whole, served mainly to intensify mechanical teaching and increase the tension.[92] Nevertheless, the substantial criticism must be made of Lowe that his policy was extremely shortsighted. Lowe himself came to realise that the extensions his successors made to the system brought regrettable disadvantages. It seems probable that he did not foresee these at the time of the Code's inception because he was too much blinkered by his all-consuming concern to effect an economy in public expenditure. After 1867 Lowe changed his views. He became increasingly concerned to found a more national system of education and accepted the increased public cost it would entail. Meanwhile, his Revised Code left its unmistakable mark on the history of English education.

[92] *Final Report of the Commissioners appointed to inquire into the Elementary Education Acts*, 1888, p. 185.

# 6
# THE 1870 ACT

Lowe resigned from his office as Vice-President of the Committee of Council on Education in April 1864. In the next two years he became increasingly concerned with the question of franchise reform and this culminated in his unswerving opposition to the various Reform Bills of 1866 and 1867. This opposition was, however, closely connected to his views on education since it was grounded in his adherence to the idea of meritocracy. If, as far as it was possible, government should be in the hands of the educated, then the extension of the franchise to those without education was a regrettable step. As Lowe told the House of Commons on 15 July 1867, the Representation of the People Bill was based on what he considered a most questionable principle: 'the principle of numbers as against wealth and intellect'.[1] Once the Bill was passed Lowe took his views to their logical conclusion. The new electorate must be educated, and to ensure this he began a campaign for a more 'national' system of education.

Lowe's activities in the next three years made a considerable contribution to the progress and pattern of the Education Act which eventually received the Royal Assent on 9 August 1870. In advocating new legislation he provided a framework of principles and a blueprint for administrative change which were incorporated into the Education Bill. In addition, at a critical moment, when the Bill was in danger of foundering amid a welter of disagreements, Lowe suggested a compromise course which ultimately secured general approval. Finally, as Chancellor of the Exchequer, Lowe was in a position to support the Education Department in its implementation of the Act of 1870 during the initial years from 1870 to 1873.

## ADVOCATE OF REFORM

The Reform Act of 1867 forced Lowe to clarify his views about the existing system of educational provision. He had always known

[1] *Parliamentary Debates*, CLXXXVIII, col. 1540.

that it was quite inadequate as a means of providing education for the nation as a whole. Lowe made this quite clear in his speeches on the Revised Code. The existing provision depended on local voluntary effort and this was not consistently forthcoming over the country as a whole and often notably absent in the areas of most need. Consequently the Privy Council with its grants assisted only those areas which already had some voluntary provision; those which had not, remained in want. Lowe had pointed this out to the House of Commons on 13 February 1862, quoting the situation in Oxfordshire where out of 339 parishes with populations of less than 600 only 24 were assisted by the Privy Council, in Herefordshire where only 5 were assisted out of 130, in Devon where only 2 were assisted out of 245, in Dorset where only 10 were assisted out of 71 and in Cornwall where only one parish was assisted.[2]

Nevertheless, despite this knowledge, from 1860 to July 1867 Lowe maintained that faulty though the system was, the difficulties in the way of change were too enormous and that consequently the only choice left was to administer the system as efficiently as possible. 'We must accept the situation', he concluded, 'and make the best of it.'[3] Lowe also took the view that given the situation as it was, the initiative for the extension of educational provision must come from individuals and all the Government could do was to follow their lead.[4] Having decided to make the system work as efficiently as possible and having devised the Revised Code for that very purpose, Lowe set his face against change. He told the House of Commons on 5 April 1867 that the Code had given the existing system a new lease of life and urged them not to sweep it away since in the process of change 'the education of one generation of Englishmen would be nearly lost'.[5] Perhaps in a few years time they would be in a better position to see whether the system could be moulded into a national system of education or whether it must 'give way to something more logical'[6] but for the present Lowe urged the maintenance of the *status quo*.

Lowe had already decided his 'logical' way to found a national system of education. He told the Select Committee on Education in 1865:

[2] *Parliamentary Debates*, CLXV, col. 199.
[3] *Parliamentary Debates*, CLXV, col. 198.
[4] *Report of Select Committee on Education 1865*, p. 37, Q. 643.
[5] *Parliamentary Debates*, CLXXXVI, cols. 1184–5. [6] *Ibid.*

If I had to start the thing afresh and had not to consider all the feelings and influences which are wrapped up in it, my idea is that education would certainly be better conducted by rates levied by local bodies, with some central inspection; but that is an abstract opinion, and I do not think that it would be possible, after all that has been done, to conduct it in that way.[7]

More particularly Lowe considered that 'denominational feeling' would be a great stumbling block to the establishment of any new system of rate-provided schools.[8] In the circumstances, however, Lowe felt no great concern to press for a more logical system of education.

The passage of the Reform Act which became law on 15 August 1867 seems to have changed Lowe's attitude of passive acquiescence in the existing state of affairs. On 15 July 1867 he told the House of Commons of his conversion to the need for a speedy implementation of a more national system of education. His speech on this occasion, so often summarised as 'we must educate our masters', is here given more fully so that the range of Lowe's explanation to the House may be seen more clearly.

One word I should like to say on the subject of education. I have been one who thought that our institutions in that respect were as efficient as they could well be. I shrink from the notion of pressing education on people. It seemed more in accordance with our institutions to allow the thing to work and freely to supplement the system. The whole question has now completely changed. All the opinions I held on that subject are scattered to the winds by this measure of the Government. Sir, it appears to me that before we had intrusted the masses – the great bulk of whom are uneducated – with the whole power of this country we should have taught them a little more how to use it, and not having done so, this rash and abrupt measure having been forced upon them, the only thing we can do is as far as possible to remedy the evil by the most universal measures of education that can be devised. I believe it will be absolutely necessary that you should prevail on our future masters to learn their letters . . . I was opposed to centralization, I am ready to accept centralization; I was opposed to an education rate, I am ready now to accept it; I objected to inspection, I am now willing to create crowds of inspectors. This question is no longer a religious question, it has become a political one. It is indeed the question of questions; it has become paramount to every other question that has been brought before us.

[7] *Report of Select Committee on Education 1865*, p. 39, Q. 671.

[8] *Ibid.* p. 39, Q. 673.

From the moment that you can intrust the masses with power their education becomes an absolute necessity, and our system of education, which – though not perfect, is far superior to the much vaunted system that prevails in America or any nation on the Continent as one system can be to another – must give way to a national system.[9]

Lowe's speech was a public declaration of his intent to concern himself once more with the education question. It was already becoming a live issue, and Lowe was only one among many who addressed themselves to it. On 28 February 1867 the House had already heard a plea from Colonel Sykes, the Member for Aberdeen, for a compulsory system of education 'as in Prussia'.[10] Granville was concerned with the question and indeed he and Lowe were discussing it, on Lowe's initiative, over dinner in February 1867[11] and again in November.[12] In October 1867 the Earl of Kimberley told farmers at a local agricultural chamber meeting that the imposition of an education rate to finance compulsory education was an inevitable development and in writing to Earl de Grey about the meeting added that though the farmers disagreed, he thought that there was 'a growing feeling everywhere in that direction'.[13]

Lowe's contribution to the current discussion, however, was not merely one among many and quite indistinguishable from the rest. Nor was it a case of 'what oft was thought, but ne'er so well expressed'. Lowe's contribution was definite and practical: it suggested a positive plan of campaign, and the fact that he published it no doubt contributed to its eventual acceptance as a basis for legislation. It was given its first public hearing in an address which Lowe delivered before the Philosophical Institution of Edinburgh on 1 November 1867, and entitled *Primary and Classical Education*.[14] In it Lowe advocated educational reform and suggested principles upon which a more national system might be founded for what he called 'the education of the poor, or primary education'.[15]

[9] *Parliamentary Debates*, CLXXXVIII, cols. 1548–9.
[10] *Parliamentary Debates*, CLXXXV, col. 1163.
[11] Gladstone Papers, B.M. Add. Mss. 44165, fol. 121, Granville to Gladstone, 11 February 1867.
[12] Gladstone Papers, B.M. Add. Mss. 44165, fol. 145, Granville to Gladstone, 21 November 1867.
[13] Ripon Papers, B.M. Add. Mss. 43522, fol. 116, Kimberley to de Grey, 27 October 1867.
[14] *Primary and Classical Education*, 1867, Edinburgh.
[15] *Ibid.* p. 4.

First he accepted quite categorically that the education of the people should be the duty of the State: it was as much a duty of the Government as the regulation of foreign affairs, the management of the army and navy, or the regulation of the police and the administration of justice.[16] Under the existing system the Government admitted its duty to educate the people but was not in a position to carry it out. It left it to private enterprise aided by government grant and consequently many parts of the country lacked adequate schools.[17] The Reform Act had brought a new situation and consequently the State could no longer shirk its duty. The new voters must be educated. Hitherto Lowe had never admitted the illogicality of his position as one who enjoyed the fruits of education in his own personal life and station but who made only limited efforts to ensure that the less fortunate in the nation received an adequate education. Now he realised not only the illogicality but also the moral shortcomings of his attitude. In his address he said:

> We cannot suffer any large number of our citizens, now that they have obtained the right of influencing the destinies of the country, to remain uneducated. It was a great evil that we did so before – it was an evil and a reproach, a moral stigma upon us. But now it is a question of self-preservation – it is a question of existence, even of the existence of our Constitution, and upon those who shall obstruct or prevent such a measure passing will rest a responsibility the heaviest that mortal man can possibly lie under.[18]

Lowe stressed this 'political' argument for a national system of education not only because it had been the clarifying factor in the development of his own thought on the question, but also because he felt that it was the only compelling argument which would make the various religious parties agree to changes in the system. He was enough of a realist to think that political battles were won more by arguments which appealed to men's fears and interests than those which appealed to their intellects. As a result he emphasised the cry of the 'preservation of the Constitution' rather than assert, as Lord Russell did, that 'every child has a moral Right to the Blessing of Education and it is the Duty of the State to guard and maintain that right'.[19] This was the first of four

[16] *Ibid.* p. 6. [17] *Ibid.* pp. 6–7. [18] *Ibid.* p. 9.
[19] *Parliamentary Debates*, CXC, col. 493.

resolutions which Russell was to put to the House of Commons on 2 December 1867 and though Lowe discussed it at a dinner party given by Russell for Lowe, Bruce, Granville, Baines, Jowett and J. D. Coleridge,[20] it was not the emphasis which he chose to make. Lowe's general view – that *a priori* assumptions were always suspect and the existence of 'natural rights' difficult to prove – led him to prefer to argue the case for greater state intervention in education on political rather than idealist grounds.

Secondly Lowe came to the conclusion that compulsion was necessary to establish a national system of education. This was no easy decision for one so strongly nurtured in the *laissez-faire* tradition as Lowe was. In discussions during this time with his friend Benjamin Jowett, Lowe toyed with various educational schemes such as the establishment of educational districts and the employment of an inspectorate devoid of its denominational character, but remained unsure about introducing compulsion.[21] However, he was eventually compelled to it by the logic of the situation and, having accepted it, Lowe preached it uncompromisingly. He told his Edinburgh audience that he was against any schemes for providing education which allowed people to tax themselves and build schools but did not compel them to do it. If a national 'universal' system was wanted then compulsion must operate from the central government.[22]

However, Lowe did not want a wholly centralised system of education. His third principle was that the best way of organising education was to combine local and central agencies.[23] Lowe distrusted a complete monopoly of power by the central government. He had a profound liberal faith in the importance of shared responsibilities between local and central bodies as the only guarantee that some measure of freedom would survive. His plan was to establish local bodies 'for carrying on the process of education' and leave to the central government the duty of superintending it.[24]

More particularly, and this was Lowe's fourth principle, the

[20] E. H. Coleridge, *Life and Correspondence of J. D. Lord Coleridge*, London 1904, II, p. 153. I am indebted for this reference to D. Rowland, 'The Struggle for the Education Act and its Implementation', unpublished B. Litt. thesis, Oxford 1957.

[21] E. Abbott and L. Campbell, *The Life and Letters of Benjamin Jowett*, I, London 1897, p. 393.

[22] *Primary and Classical Education*, p. 9.

[23] *Ibid.* pp. 4–5.

[24] *Ibid.* pp. 4–5.

main duty of the State was to test the nature of the education given in the schools established by the local bodies.[25] He stood firmly by the principle he had employed in establishing the Revised Code. In Lowe's view every educational system should be judged in terms of results since this was the only satisfactory measure of efficiency.

Finally, Lowe held that 'the State represents in the matter of education not the religious but the secular element'.[26] This was a long-standing conviction of Lowe's, forged almost thirty years previously in the heat of controversy about educational provision in New South Wales. Lowe had gone to Australia in 1842 partly for medical reasons and partly because there seemed to be better opportunities to establish himself as a barrister in Sydney, where there was much less competition than in England.[27] Within a year he had become a member of the Legislative Council and was soon involved in the controversy about the best system of providing schools. Two systems contended for adoption. The 'Irish' system, as introduced by Lord Stanley for Ireland in 1831, and the non-denominational system of the British and Foreign School Society. When Lowe took up the matter the Governor, Sir George Gipps, was hoping to shelve the educational issue, but Lowe saw it as his mission to educate the Australians and refused to let the matter drop. 'Nowhere in the world is education more required than it is here', he told the Legislative Council, pointing out that if they did not educate their children 'large drafts of criminals are coming over here and they will educate the children'.[28] Lowe also pressed the argument for an educated electorate, as he was later to do in England, pointing out that the property qualification of £20 in Australia was easily acquired by any hardworking illiterate.[29] As a result of his advocacy, Lowe became Chairman of a Select Committee of the Legislative Council appointed to inquire into education in the colony. In June 1844 it recommended the establishment of the Irish system[30] and for the next few years, in a series of speeches and newspaper articles, Lowe pressed for its adoption. It was eventually implemented in 1848.[31]

[25] *Primary and Classical Education*, p. 5. [26] *Ibid.* p. 4.
[27] Knight, pp. 21–3. [28] *Ibid.* p. 84. [29] *Ibid.* p. 85.
[30] See Patchett Martin, I, pp. 225–31, for a copy of the *Report of the Select Committee.*
[31] For a full account of Lowe's activities with regard to education in Australia see Knight, pp. 82–96.

Lowe's experience in Australia had made him a secularist in education. The Irish system provided for schools with a common literary and moral education for children of all sects and allowed time for their religious instruction in separate denominational groups. This seemed to Lowe in 1844 to be the best solution to the educational question in New South Wales, where Protestant and Catholic differences threatened to prevent the establishment of any system of education. Now in 1867 it seemed to provide the best basis for a national system of education in England, where the 'religious difficulty' was also likely to loom large in any discussion about a new system. There was of course no question of establishing in England a system of 'common' schools. Denominational schools existed and the State could not dispense with them. However, Lowe wanted to ensure firstly, that if they received assistance from the State then it should be for the secular instruction which they gave and not for their religious teaching; and secondly, that they should operate a 'conscience clause' so that dissenters could withdraw their children from dogmatic teaching.

During his tenure of office as Vice-President, Lowe had suggested that Anglican schools should be content to teach in school the Ten Commandments, the Lord's Prayer and the Apostles' Creed and leave the doctrinal parts of the Catechism and teaching about the Holy Sacraments to the time when children were prepared for Confirmation.[32] He had also refused building grants for Church of England schools unless they were prepared to operate a conscience clause for dissenters.[33] Now at Edinburgh in 1867 Lowe took these precedents further with his proposals firstly that the system of denominational inspection which had gone on since 1840 should be given up,[34] and secondly that denominational schools should not be given state assistance unless they had a conscience clause.[35] The Education Act of 1870, Lowe was later pleased to note, adopted both of these proposals.[36]

In fact, all the principles for action which Lowe enunciated at Edinburgh and repeated at Liverpool in January 1868[37] were in

[32] *Parliamentary Debates*, CLXIV, cols. 732–3.

[33] *Report of the Select Committee on Education 1865*, pp. 41–2, Qs. 699–713.

[34] *Primary and Classical Education*, p. 9. [35] *Ibid.* p. 10.

[36] *Parliamentary Debates*, CXCIX, col. 2061.

[37] *Middle Class and Primary Education.* Two speeches by Robert Lowe delivered at the annual dinner of the Liverpool Philomatic Society and at the conference on Education at the Town Hall, Liverpool, 22 and 23 January 1868.

some form or other incorporated in the Education Act of 1870. The State recognised its duty to provide education, and the need for compulsion to ensure the adequate provision of schools was accepted, though compulsory attendance at school by children was not as yet enforced. A system involving the establishment of local school boards and their co-operation with the central government was devised. The State continued to test and inspect the education given in schools. Finally, that the State's responsibility was primarily for secular education was implied in the arrangements made for inspection and for religious teaching, since inspection of religious knowledge was discontinued and religious teaching in local board schools had to be not only non-denominational[38] but also held at such a time that children could be withdrawn from it. It may well be that the English educational system would have evolved on the lines it did without Lowe's enunciation of these basic principles. However, it remains true that Lowe, more publicly than any other politician, suggested the lines of development upon which a new system was eventually built.

## PROVIDING THE ADMINISTRATIVE BLUEPRINT

Lowe may also be credited with having played a more definitive part in the genesis of the Education Act of 1870. In his Edinburgh speech Lowe outlined an administrative plan for establishing a new system of educational provision, which W. E. Forster, who designed the Education Bill, later used and implemented. Lowe's plan is here given in his own words.

> Commence an educational survey and report upon Great Britain parish by parish; report to the Privy Council in London the educational wants in each parish, the number of schools, the number of children, and what is wanted to be done in order to place within the reach of the people of that parish a sufficient amount of education. When that has been done, I think it should be the duty of the Privy Council to give notice to that parish that they should found a school, or whatever may be wanted for the purposes of that parish. If the parish found a school, then it would be the duty of the Privy Council to assist it, and that in the same way as it assists the schools already in existence. I would say in passing, that I do not think we should disturb the schools already existing, except that they must submit to undenominational inspection,

[38] 33 & 34 Vict. c. 75, s. 7.

and to a conscience clause. If the parish does not agree to what is done, then I think there ought to be power vested in the Privy Council, or the Secretary of State, or some other great responsible public officer, to make a compulsory rate on them to found that school. I think the schools they found should be entitled to the same inspection and examination as the schools already in existence, and receive the same grants on results. That simple machinery would, in a short time, alter the whole face of the question, and place education within the reach of every one of Her Majesty's subjects.[39]

Lowe delivered this when the Liberals were in opposition. In the following autumn Disraeli dissolved Parliament and at the ensuing election, the Liberals were returned with a majority of 112 seats. In December 1868 Gladstone formed his ministry and Lowe became Chancellor of the Exchequer. Earl de Grey became Lord President of the Council and the task of framing an Education Bill was given to W. E. Forster, the Vice-President. The immediate priority was, however, the Irish Church Bill and not until its passage had been secured in July 1869 did the Government allow the Education Bill to come to the fore. Forster had not been idle. He had successfully introduced the Endowed Schools Bill which became law on 2 August 1869 and he had done the initial spade-work for framing an Education Bill. On 21 October 1869 he produced for the Cabinet a memorandum[40] on this subject. In it Forster reviewed four plans which had been proposed to secure 'a complete national system', and among them was Lowe's plan from his Edinburgh speech of 1867.

Together these four plans were representative of a wide and divergent cross-section of opinions on the question of educational provision. At one extreme there was the plan of the National Education Union which wanted the Government to induce, by giving increased aid, greater voluntary efforts so that the whole country could be covered by schools raised by subscriptions and so make any compulsory provisions unnecessary. This Forster rejected as unacceptable because he doubted that it would meet the country's educational needs: it 'has been proved', he wrote, 'that educational volunteers will not supply national education'.[41] At the other extreme, the Birmingham League plan wanted local authorities to establish free schools to be built and maintained by

[39] Lowe, *Primary and Classical Education*, pp. 10–11.

[40] Gladstone Papers, B.M. Add. Mss. 44611, fols. 99–102.

[41] *Ibid.*

rates and taxes, the rates paying one third of the cost, the taxes the remainder. Such schools would teach no religious dogma, and would be managed by ratepayers though subject also to government inspection. Forster was critical of this plan on the grounds that its 'complete logical machinery' would quickly undermine the existing schools, relieve the parents of paying school fees, entail the country in enormous expense and drive all the voluntary agencies out of the field of education. The more moderate plan introduced by Bruce in his abortive Bill of 1868 proposed to make compulsory provision for schools by allowing districts to rate themselves for existing schools, and for the erection of new schools, and by reserving to the Government the right to compel them to levy such a rate where educational destitution was proved. Forster found this scheme unpractical since it would, he considered, prove impossible to compel ratepayers to provide rate aid for denominational schools. In the end, Forster concluded that Lowe's plan provided the most practicable basis for action. He wrote:

I, therefore, now look with most hope to the plan sketched out by Mr. Lowe, the ruling idea of which, I understand to be compulsory school provision, if and where necessary but not otherwise.

But it seems to me impossible to carry out this plan, unless we first, and without delay, divide the country into educational districts and make every district responsible to the central government for the elementary education of its inhabitants.[42]

Forster went on to suggest that Lowe's plan, for the parish to be the base for these educational districts, should be adopted rather than Bruce's suggestion of using the Poor Law unions.[43]

In short, it is clear from this memorandum that Forster was indebted to Lowe for the plan of administrative interference which he eventually built into the Act of 1870 to establish a system of national education. Sections 8 to 13 of the Act, which treat the powers of interference possessed by the Privy Council to compel the supply of education throughout the country, are detailed applications of the outline for action which Lowe gave in his Edinburgh speech and which is quoted above. The Cross Commission in its Report of 1888 pointed out how eclectic Forster's Bill was.[44] The Manchester and Salford Bill of 1851 and the 1867

[42] *Ibid.* [43] *Ibid.*

[44] *Final Report of the Commissioners appointed to inquire into the Elementary Education Acts*, 1888, p. 21.

Bill of Bruce, Egerton and Forster himself, covered many of the provisions of the 1870 Act. Both of these previous Bills had suggested locally-elected district committees with authority to levy local rates for education; both had adopted existing schools as the basis for operation to be supplemented only where there was need and with provision for the transference of these existing schools on agreed terms to the management of the local committees; both assumed that in schools under the district committees the reading of the Scriptures should be part of the daily instruction; both enforced a conscience clause; both provided for inspection under the authority of the Privy Council. However, neither provided a scheme for the administrative interference which the Government would need to establish national education. What they lacked Forster found elsewhere, in Lowe's blueprint for administrative action.[45]

## FOUNDER OF THE DUAL SYSTEM

On 17 February 1870 Forster presented his Education Bill to the Commons. Immediately the main point of contention emerged. The Bill gave the school boards the power either of providing schools themselves or of assisting the existing schools, and this raised what was called the 'religious difficulty'. If school rates were levied and then used to assist existing denominational schools, dissenters, for example, might find themselves not only paying for the upkeep of Church of England schools but also obliged to send their children to such schools. Similarly Roman Catholics might have to pay for and send their children to Protestant schools. Moreover, it would create sectarian strife at board elections, with the various denominations seeking to gain an ascendancy on the board so that they could control the use of school rates for their own particular and perhaps sectarian ends. It was this difficulty which led Mr G. Dixon, a Member of Parliament for Birmingham and spokesman of the Birmingham Education League, to move on 14 March 1870 an amendment which would take away from the school boards decisions about the religious question by making all rate-aided schools unsectarian and insisting that in other schools religious teaching should be given

[45] *Final Report of the Commissioners appointed to inquire into the Elementary Education Acts*, 1888, p. 21.

separately at a specific time on the time-table so that children could absent themselves from it.[46]

No one was more aware than Lowe that denominational feelings would be a bar to the easy passage of the Bill. He himself was in principle a staunch secularist but he knew that if there was to be legislation for a more national system of education, then only the spirit of compromise could achieve it. It was in this vein that he spoke at the end of a long debate on 15 March 1870. While admitting his own opposition to the voluntary system he contended that 'it is not by displaying a spirit of narrow dogmatism or by persisting in opinions we have once taken up that this great, this intricate, and this difficult question is to be settled'.[47] He reminded the House of the debt the nation owed to the voluntary system. It had done for the State what the latter was not prepared to do for itself and in undertaking the education of the people had carried out a duty which he 'had always thought was incumbent upon the Government'.[48] In such circumstances the voluntary schools could not be swept away. Some compromise must be reached and Lowe, now obviously speaking for the Government, ended by suggesting that the House should go into Committee on the Bill and argue out their differences until some compromise emerged. The Government had not 'nailed their colours to the mast'.[49] They were prepared to make changes in the Bill to meet the different opinions which had been advanced in debate and Lowe urged Members not to throw away the opportunity of founding a national system of education by bickering over difficulties which were small in comparison to the end in view. He said:

> This Bill for the first time . . . recognises the undoubted duty of the Government of England to provide for the education of the people. This is a great and noble object, that might stir any man's heart within him and raise him above any smaller considerations which are apt to interfere with the performance of the noblest acts. Do not let us be turned aside from that object by small difficulties and jealousies, which, if we will only meet each other in a spirit of consideration, I am perfectly satisfied will disappear.[50]

[46] *Parliamentary Debates*, CXCIX, col. 1927.
[47] *Parliamentary Debates*, CXCIX, cols. 2063–4.
[48] *Parliamentary Debates*, CXCIX, col. 2059.
[49] *Parliamentary Debates*, CXCIX, col. 2064.
[50] *Parliamentary Debates*, CXCIX, col. 2065.

Compromise did not come naturally to Lowe, but in this case a realistic appraisal of the situation and a sincere concern to see the Bill through made him, to the surprise of some members of the House, its most ardent advocate. The Bill went into Committee and the Cabinet agreed to modify the Bill in several respects, and it was during this stage in the proceedings that Lowe took positive action and suggested a compromise course which was eventually found acceptable to the majority.

On the same day that Lowe made his speech in favour of conciliation, 15 March, the Cabinet had agreed to modify the Bill and introduce a time-table clause[51] and during the next two months it continued to wrestle with modifications. On 13 May 1870 the Cabinet received the following draft amendments which Forster and de Grey submitted to meet the religious difficulty.[52] First, there was W. F. Cowper-Temple's clause that rate-founded schools should offer non-denominational religious instruction. Secondly, there was a time-table conscience clause to enable pupils to withdraw from periods of religious instruction in school. Thirdly, inspection of religious instruction was to be discontinued. Fourthly, under Clause 22 of the Bill, the school boards were to be allowed to give rate aid to denominational schools, though such aid was to be limited to secular instruction. On 14 June the Cabinet, with one exception, agreed to accept these amendments. The exception was Lowe, and his action at this point had a dramatic effect upon the eventual shape of the 1870 Act.

Gladstone's Cabinet Minute for 14 June shows that Lowe 'objected strongly' to the amendments agreed upon.[53] Others saw difficulties but in the end acquiesced and Lowe stood out alone in opposition. Lowe's particular objection was to the decision to go ahead with Clause 22, which would allow rate aid to denominational schools for 'secular instruction'. He considered that opposition to this was so great that the Bill would be lost if this clause was presented in Committee, and so the next day he wrote to Gladstone with a completely new and radical suggestion for overcoming the religious difficulty. He argued that the value of the rating system was that payment and control should go together. Gladstone's proposal would not secure this, for under Clause 22

[51] Gladstone Papers, B.M. Add. Mss. 44638, fol. 48, Cabinet Minute.

[52] Gladstone Papers, B.M. Add. Mss. 44086, fol. 146, Bruce to Gladstone, 13 May 1870.

[53] Gladstone Papers, B.M. Add. Mss. 44638, fol. 83.

rate money could be paid to schools where the managers were not answerable to the ratepayers. So Lowe suggested that the only satisfactory course was to take the money for denominational schools not out of rates, but out of General Exchequer funds. He told Gladstone:

Increase the Privy Council Grant by one half and the thing is done and done in the way most agreeable to the recipients. If this were done I should relieve the Board of ratepayers from any connection whatever with schools other than rate-supported schools. You would thus attain a double advantage i.e. circumscribe the functions of the dreaded local authority and relieve your proposal from the obloquy of a fresh burden on the rates.[54]

Lowe ended by suggesting further that, as a measure of economy to offset the increased expenditure from public funds which his proposal would entail, the Privy Council should discontinue the payment of building grants.[55]

Gladstone replied to Lowe the same day that his suggestion was 'so big in relation to the machinery of the Bill' that he must see Forster about it as soon as he could.[56] Gladstone acted swiftly and, still within the same day, managed to add to his own approval of Lowe's plan that of Forster, Cardwell, Bruce, Hatherley, Clarendon and Glyn, the Chief Whip, and Kimberley and Granville gave their approval later.[57]

At one stroke Lowe had in fact founded what has since been called the 'dual system' – a system in which voluntary schools have existed alongside, but separate from, the Board Schools, to provide a network of elementary schools throughout the country.[58] The rest of the Cabinet's ready acceptance of Lowe's proposal may be attributed mainly to the fact that it was seen to be obvious good sense and indeed the only viable solution. It had become clear that a Bill which allowed school boards to contribute to denominational schools would not be carried. However, another factor may also have contributed. Lowe indicated in his letter to Gladstone that much as he differed, he would abide by the decision of the majority

[54] Gladstone Papers, B.M. Add. Mss. 44301, fol. 146, Lowe to Gladstone, 15 June 1870. [55] *Ibid.*

[56] Gladstone Papers, B.M. Add. Mss. 44301, fol. 148, Gladstone to Lowe, 15 June 1870.

[57] Gladstone Papers, B.M. Add. Mss. 44759, fol. 131, Minute to Argyll.

[58] Morley was mistaken in attributing this proposal to Gladstone: see Morley, *Life of Gladstone*, I, p. 702.

in the Cabinet if they proceeded with the proposal to give rate aid to denominational schools. Nevertheless, he pointed out that he might be obliged to resign by his constituents. Lowe was then Member for the University of London and, as he claimed, 'if there is anything I am sent to represent it is the principle of undenominational Education'.[59] From this part of his letter it has been suggested that Lowe secured Cabinet acceptance of his proposal by threatening to resign.[60] This rather stretches the evidence however, and in the absence of other corroborative evidence, there is nothing conclusive to suggest that it was the possibility of Lowe's resignation rather than the good sense of his proposal which secured Cabinet agreement. On the other hand, it must be acknowledged that it would certainly have been embarrassing to the Government if the Chancellor of the Exchequer had left the Cabinet on this issue and this may have had its effect on Gladstone and the other ministers.

On 16 June 1870 the Bill went into Committee and Gladstone introduced what was in fact a new Bill to the House. He enumerated the following changes. First, the Cowper-Temple clause which provided that no religious catechism distinctive of any particular denomination should be taught in a Board School. Secondly a time-table conscience clause would operate in all schools. Thirdly, local boards would have no connection with voluntary schools and the latter would receive public aid directly from the Privy Council and for this purpose the existing grant from the Privy Council to the voluntary schools would be increased by up to 50 per cent. Finally, aid for building grants would cease.[61] On 22 July 1870 the Bill passed the Commons and received the Royal Assent on 9 August. Section 7 of the Act provided for the time-table conscience clause and the end of religious inspection, and Section 14 for the Cowper-Temple amendment.[62] Arrangements for the payment of public grants to schools, whether voluntary or rate-aided, were administered under Minutes of the Council and consequently were not provided for in the Act.

Though the Act embodied the major changes which Lowe had suggested, in Section 25 of the Act the principle of rate aid to denominational schools remained. Under this section school

[59] Gladstone Papers, B.M. Add. Mss. 44301, fol. 147.

[60] D. Roland, 'The Struggle for the Education Act and its Implementation 1870–73', unpublished B. Litt. thesis, Oxford 1957, p. xii.

[61] *Parliamentary Debates*, CCII, cols. 281–2.

[62] 33 & 34 Vict. c. 75.

boards could pay the school fees of children whose parents were too poor to afford them and this aid was available for all children regardless of the type of school, whether voluntary or Board, which they attended. Though it had not prevented the passing of the Act the existence of Section 25 subsequently aroused opposition. Some nonconformists refused to pay rates while this clause remained and there was pressure to withdraw it. Lowe supported the opposition to Section 25. Not only did he object to rate aid for denominational schools but he considered that they had already received a 'bonus' under the Act and thought it not 'unreasonable to require them to give in return education without fee to the children of parents who can't afford to pay'.[63] He suggested to Granville that such a step 'would stop the whole row'.[64] However in the Cabinet Ripon, the Lord President, and W. E. Forster, were supporters of the Established Church and against change, and on the matter of denominational schools Lowe considered that 'Gladstone was not quite sound either'.[65] Altogether Lowe, who was pressing for the logical completion of the 'dual system' by jettisoning Section 25, concluded that the Government were 'in bad hands' when it came to education. On 5 March 1872 Dixon moved a series of resolutions against the Act and in particular against Section 25.[66] On 23 April 1872 Mr J. Cavendish, the Member for Sunderland, moved for leave to bring in a Bill to repeal Section 25 of the 1870 Act[67] but the motion was lost by 115 votes to 316.[68] Lowe, perhaps significantly, did not vote in this division. On 30 November 1872, Forster circulated a draft bill to amend the Act[69] and this included the repeal of Section 25, but he would not support Lowe's plan to put upon church schools an obligation to receive poor children without fees or aid. The Bishop of Peterborough, William Connor Magee, had publicly suggested a proposal similar to that of Lowe, but Forster and Ripon decided 'to hold out against Lowe, Bishop and everyone'.[70] They did as they intended. The Act, although amended on 5 August 1873, kept Section 25.[71]

[63] Granville Papers, P.R.O. 30/29/66, Lowe to Granville, 29 Nov. 1871.
[64] *Ibid.* [65] *Ibid.* [66] *Parliamentary Debates*, CCIX, col. 1395.
[67] *Parliamentary Debates*, CCX, cols. 1714–18.
[68] *Parliamentary Debates*, CCX, col. 1744.
[69] Gladstone Papers, B.M. Add. Mss. 44619, fol. 109.
[70] Ripon Papers, B.M. Add. Mss. 43537, fol. 79, Ripon to Forster, 19 January 1873. [71] 36 & 37 Vict. c. 86.

Lowe had not had his way completely, but he had in large measure provided the pattern for the future.

In advocating a more national provision of elementary education Lowe had consistently adopted an empirical approach. Had he been starting 'carte blanche' he would have established a national system of rate-aided secular schools, and religious education would have been given elsewhere under the agency of the churches. However, accepting the historical situation as it was, he realised that the voluntary schools must remain. To replace them with a national secular system would not only be expensive but destroy much that was good and also upset many people. Similarly he accepted that for reasons of religious liberty, denominational schools could not be expected to accept either a secular curriculum or some form of non-denominational religious teaching. Nor could ratepayers who represented many different religious opinions be expected to agree to their rates being used to support denominational schools. In the circumstances the only practical solution was a compromise. As Lowe said of the Bill: it 'is founded not on any abstract dogma, not on any theory which we are anxious to cram down people's throats as to what will be the best system of national education, but it is based on English good sense; it appreciates what exists already and tries to supplement and to improve instead of to destroy'.[72] The compromise which was accepted was to all intents and purposes that suggested by Lowe. Rates were to be used to finance local Board Schools in which there would be non-denominational religious teaching, and voluntary schools would draw upon central funds raised from national taxes and continue their own particular forms of religious teaching. These two sets of schools could then operate independently, united only by a common acceptance of a time-table conscience clause. This dual system seemed to Lowe to be the only practical way 'to meet a pressing want of the people of England'.[73] It is significant that the majority of Lowe's contemporaries agreed with him. Whatever posterity has thought about the dual system, at the time it was the only practicable policy.

## IMPLEMENTING THE ACT 1870–1873

Under Sections 67 to 69 of the 1870 Act, Lowe, as head of the

[72] *Parliamentary Debates*, CXCIX, col. 2060.
[73] *Parliamentary Debates*, CXCIX, col. 2065.

Treasury, had the distinct duty of approving the expenses which local authorities incurred in making returns to the Education Department about the elementary schools and the children requiring elementary education in their areas.[74]

Apart from this, direct responsibility for the administration of the 1870 Education Act belonged to the Lord President and Vice-President of the Committee of Council for Education. However, Lowe, as Chancellor of the Exchequer, was indirectly in a position to influence the establishment and work of the Education Department because of his ultimate power over the purse-strings. Although he had pressed for a more effective national system of education and supported the 1870 Act at every stage, he never allowed this to deflect him from what he took to be the first duty of a Chancellor of the Exchequer, namely to economise wherever possible in public expenditure. Consequently Lowe, ably assisted by Lingen, constantly worked to make Treasury control over educational expenditure paramount. Lingen had formerly been at the Education Department with Lowe and his transference to the Treasury had recently been secured by Lowe. As in the early sixties the combination of Lowe and Lingen was once again in a position to decide policy about educational expenditure.

For example, on 27 January 1871 in a letter to the Vice-President, the Treasury pointed out that the Chancellor of the Exchequer was a member of the Education Committee which the Lord President should call to consider expenditure on education. It noted that the Committee 'meets less frequently than it used to do' and that as a result the Lord President of the Council and the Vice-President, by failing to summon the Committee, were in fact exercising its function themselves. Foreseeing that expenditure on education would steadily increase, the Treasury suggested that any Minutes involving additional expenditure should conform more nearly to the practice of other great spending departments, and be submitted formally to the Treasury before they passed beyond the draft stage, so that the Chancellor of the Exchequer could comment upon the finance involved.[75]

Just over a month later, on 3 March 1871, the Treasury again asserted itself, writing to the Vice-President to reprimand him politely but firmly about the inefficient way in which the Education

[74] 33 & 34 Vict. c. 75.

[75] Treasury Papers, Out Letters, P.R.O. T9/13, pp. 520–1, 27 January 1871.

Department prepared its estimates and raised questions about allowances. Too often the Department referred the Treasury to a long series of Minutes and letters which often related to many other points besides the one in question, and this made it impossible for the Treasury 'from sheer want of time to understand and therefore to control, as it is their duty to do by previous approval each class of expenditure'.[76] The Treasury suggested that the Committee of Council should look at the estimates of the Revenue departments and the Post Office as examples of large and complicated departments, where they would observe that without profuse notes and references every branch of service, however minute, was immediately capable of being identified in the estimates.[77]

Lowe also used his position as Chancellor to exert control over the various government departments, including the Education Department, through the Orders-in-Council of 4 June 1870 and 19 August 1871, which regulated Civil Service recruitment. It is not easy to separate the opinions of Lowe and Lingen, but generally they were so much in agreement on these issues that official Treasury pronouncements may be taken as indicative of the attitudes of both men. Typical of this was a letter which the Treasury sent on 30 July 1872 to the Vice-President of the Committee of Council, reminding him that no new head of expenditure could be opened by any department without the previous consent of the Treasury 'and that the observance of this consent is guarded by means of the review of all public payments which is exercised by the Comptroller and Auditor General'.[78] Under the same Orders-in-Council Lowe also tried to ensure that appointments in the Education Department were by open competitive examination under the regulations of the Civil Service Commission. Clerks for the Education Department were to be appointed under Regulation II of the Orders-in-Council and the Treasury suggested that to keep 'the high standard which it is necessary to maintain in the appointment of Examiners' they should come from open competition under Regulation I.[79] In May 1871 Lowe also suggested further that assistant Inspectors should be examined under the

[76] Treasury Papers, Out Letters, P.R.O. T9/14, pp. 4–6, 3 March 1871.
[77] *Ibid.*
[78] Treasury Papers, Out Letters, P.R.O. T9/14, pp. 403–4, 30 July 1872.
[79] Treasury Papers, Out Letters, P.R.O. T9/14, pp. 10–11, 13 March 1871.

Civil Service Commission before appointment: in reading, handwriting, orthography, arithmetic and English composition.[80] However, Lowe was not entirely successful in this and the Department continued to recruit its examiners and inspectors through the exercise of patronage until well into the present century.[81]

Lowe was certainly concerned to exert Treasury control over the Education Department but in general the effect of his interference was to support rather than hinder its work. There is no evidence in the Treasury papers that Lowe conducted an extensive campaign to cut educational services. What does emerge is that on occasions where he thought economy could be made, Lowe pressed for it unremittingly.

Lowe accepted that the 1870 Act would necessarily entail an increase in the establishment of the Education Department and he consistently allowed it to rise. On 11 August 1870 for example, two days after the passing of the Act, the Treasury approved the appointment of a third assistant secretary and intimated that it would approve a fourth as the business of the Department increased. It also approved the appointment of two permanent examiners with a promise of four more soon, and an increase of up to twelve copyists.[82] On 13 March 1871 the Treasury approved the increase of assistant secretaries from three to four, at salaries of £800 rising by annual increments of £50 to £1,000. It also agreed to an increase in examiners from sixteen to twenty. Six were to be in the senior class with salaries of £650 rising by increments of £25 to £775 and fourteen in the junior class with salaries of £300 rising by similar increments to £600. At the same time the Treasury also established the salary for the statistical clerk at £400, that for accountants at £500, and salaries of £300 for the assistant architect and the assistant counsel respectively.[83] A little later, on 24 March 1871, the recruitment of fifty assistant clerks in three classes was approved: there were to be ten class I clerks with salaries of £300 rising by increments of £15 to £400, twenty class II clerks with salaries of £210 rising by £10 increments to £275 and twenty class III clerks with salaries of £100 rising by £10 increments to

[80] Treasury Papers, In Letters and Files, P.R.O. T1/7986B/13195/1871, File No. 6603, 1 May 1871.

[81] *First Report of the Civil Service Inquiry Commission*, 1875, p. 213.

[82] Treasury Papers, Out Letters, P.R.O. T9/13, p. 413, 11 August 1870.

[83] Treasury Papers, Out Letters, P.R.O. T9/14, pp. 10–11.

£200.[84] Nine more class III assistant clerks were agreed to in 1872.[85]

This steady increase in the administrative staff of the Education Department was paralleled by the increase which Lowe allowed in the inspectorate. In a Treasury Minute of 5 February 1870 Lowe pointed out that 'an increase in the number of inspectors followed *necessarily* [Lowe's emphasis] from increase in the number of schools . . . because inspection is the condition of *every* grant'. He accordingly made no objection to the proposed appointment of three additional Inspectors and three more assistants, though he insisted that any future proposals for increase must be submitted to the Treasury.[86] In February 1871 the Education Department requested an increase in the estimates for 1871–2 to provide for sixteen more Inspectors, fifty Inspectors' assistants and sixty-three temporary Inspectors. Lowe was in favour. He no doubt approved Lingen's comment in a memorandum on the question that 'inspection regarded as an economic check repays its cost'. However he was also persuaded by Lingen that an economy could be made by refusing to appoint more full Inspectors and by requesting the Education Department to use more Inspectors' assistants on the grounds that the latter were 'a cheap machinery and very efficient'. Lingen also advised Lowe that with the abolition of denominational inspection, collective examinations in large towns and other centres were now possible and this would reduce the need for so many Inspectors.[87] Lowe accepted this advice and the Treasury informed the Education Department that it would need more explanation and information before appointing more Inspectors. It asked the Department to reconsider whether it could manage with assistant Inspectors if a system of collective examinations was put into operation.[88] Forster in reply objected to the charge that the Education Department had asked for more Inspectors than it required. An increase was needed not so much to meet the expansion in the number of children to be examined but because the schools 'seeking aid for the first time are increasing in number as rapidly as the children in those already under

[84] Treasury Papers, Out Letters, P.R.O. T9/14, pp. 23–4.
[85] Treasury Papers, Out Letters, P.R.O. T9/14, pp. 467–8.
[86] Treasury Papers, In Letters and Files, P.R.O. T1/6958B/1895/1870.
[87] Treasury Papers, In Letters and Files, P.R.O. T1/7086B/13195/1871, File No. 2795, 16 February 1871.
[88] Treasury Papers, Out Letters, P.R.O. T9/13, p. 547, 21 February 1871.

inspection – and this is a job inspectors must do for themselves'. Forster contended that in such a period of transition it would be unwise to delegate inspection to 'inexperienced hands'.[89] In the end Forster's arguments seem to have had their effect, for Lowe agreed to the increase and sixteen more Inspectors were appointed.[90]

Usually, then, Lowe appreciated the need for increases in the establishment of the Education Department and, as long as he could satisfy himself that there was no extravagant use of public money, he approved the appointment of extra staff. He was, however, a most conscientious Chancellor of the Exchequer and safeguarded the public finances with all the attributes of a superb watchdog. This was nowhere more apparent than in his dealings with the Education Department over the question of the appointment of a music Inspector. In January 1872 the Department had requested such an appointment at an estimated cost of £650. The Treasury agreed in principle though it insisted as a condition that the Committee of Council on Education should strictly confine the study of music in all the schools and colleges under their inspection 'to the practical object of teaching children, while they are at school, to sing from notes sufficiently to make vocal music a popular recreation'. On the other hand the Treasury resisted the payment of £650 and suggested £400 as a suitable salary for the Inspector with in addition an allowance of 21*s*. for every night spent away from home, and 'locomotion' expenses.[91] The Education Department persisted in its demand for £650, itemising the estimate as £400 in salary for the Inspector and some £200 for assistants, and pointing out that the Inspector would be advising the Department as to an expenditure for music in elementary schools of at least £60,000 under the Code of 1872.[92] Finally, on 20 March 1872, Lowe compromised and allowed a maximum expense of £650, but of this £200 was to be for assistants and expenses. Moreover, it was sanctioned in the first instance for one year only and Lowe insisted that the Education Department should be informed that the Lords of the Treasury 'desire to notice that there is apparently room for economy in this particular'. He went

[89] Treasury Papers, In Letters and Files, P.R.O. T1/7086B/13195/1871, File No. 3462, 27 February 1871.

[90] Treasury Papers, Out Letters, P.R.O. T9/14, p. 15, 15 March 1871.

[91] Treasury Papers, Out Letters, P.R.O. T9/14, pp. 216–17, 8 January 1872.

[92] Treasury Papers, In Letters and Files, P.R.O. T1/7174B/4796/1872, File No. 3327, 20 February 1872.

on to make a suggestion which was adopted that it might be made partly by not allowing payment for a second day's examining in teacher-training colleges where the remaining students were less than six and the remaining papers less than twenty.[93]

Lowe's ruthlessness in pursuing economy may be illustrated by two other episodes concerning salaries in the Education Department. First, on 21 June 1871, though approving a new salary scale for assistant clerks of £150 rising to £200, Lowe categorically refused to backdate this award to April 1871 for five assistant clerks who had reached their maximum on the old scale some months previously.[94] Secondly, two days later, despite Lingen's support for two assistant secretaries, Messrs Sykes and Cory, who felt that they had been overlooked in the recent salary rises, Lowe again refused to adjust their pay. In a petition which came by way of Forster to the Treasury, Sykes and Cory indicated that examiners had secured such large increases in the recent pay awards, on the grounds that they were taking on extra work under the 1870 Act, that the differential between examiners and assistant secretaries had been altered to the distinct disadvantage of the latter. The salaries of some examiners had risen from a scale of £650–£775 to one of £1,000–£1,192, while that of assistant secretaries had been increased only by £200 from £1,000 to £1,200. They drew attention to the fact that they also had taken on extra duties and that whereas in 1853 assistant secretaries for a salary of £1,000 had administered only 3,000 schools and a grant of £250,000, they now administered for their salary of £1,200 some 10,000 schools and a grant of about one million pounds. Lowe remained unmoved. 'I see no cause for increase', he wrote in a Minute. 'It is not our business to make everything pleasant all round but to spend money where the public service requires it.'[95] The Education Department raised the issue again in August but once more Lowe refused to consider it. 'There is nothing new in this – refuse' was his cold and final comment.[96]

Lowe also refused to allow a major increase in the salary of the

[93] Treasury Papers, In Letters and Files, P.R.O. T1/7174B/4796/1872, 20 March 1872.

[94] Treasury Papers, In Letters and Files, P.R.O. T1/7086B/13195/1871, File No. 9603, 21 June 1871.

[95] Treasury Papers, In Letters and Files, T1/7086B/13195/1871, File No. 9847, 23 June 1871.

[96] Treasury Papers, In Letters and Files, T1/7086B/13195/1871, 23 August 1871.

Secretary of the Education Department but there was more to this than a concern for economy. Rather it was a symptom of Lowe's ambivalent attitude towards the Education Department. While realising that its responsibilities had increased under the 1870 Act and while prepared to allow its establishment to grow, Lowe was strongly and illogically unwilling to give it full status as a major ministerial department. On 20 January 1871 in a Treasury Minute, Lowe, once more upon the advice of Lingen, decided that the Secretary of the Education Department should not rank as a permanent Under-Secretary of State. Accordingly he fixed the Secretary's salary at a figure of £1,600 – between that of an Under-Secretary who had a maximum of £1,800 and that of a class of officers whose salaries reached a maximum of £1,500. That his action in this was motivated more by questions of status than finance was underlined by his recognition that the duties of Sir Francis Sandford, who was then Secretary, had been 'enormous' since the implementation of the 1870 Act, and his authorisation for a backdating of Sandford's salary to be paid at the maximum of £1,600 from the date when the Act had come into operation.[97] Three months later, Lowe went further and increased the salary of the Secretary to a maximum of £2,000 on a scale rising from £1,500 by annual increments of £100, and Sir F. Sandford was established on the maximum.[98]

Lowe's attitude towards the status of the secretaryship was paralleled by his unwillingness to support the establishment of a Minister of Education. In 1865 he had opposed it on the grounds that there was not enough business to warrant the appointment of a Minister.[99] In 1867 it was notable that in his Edinburgh speech, when he suggested government compulsion to establish schools in localities where they were lacking, he vested it in 'the Privy Council, or the Secretary of State, or some other great responsible public officer',[100] but not in a separate ministry. In 1874 when the issue rose again, Lowe, while praising the Education Department to the limit – 'it had taken up education in a most elementary state

[97] Treasury Papers, In Letters and Files, P.R.O. T1/7086B/13195/1871, File No. 479, 20 January 1871; also Out Letters, P.R.O. T9/13, pp. 517–18, 25 January 1871.

[98] Treasury Papers, In Letters and Files, P.R.O. T1/7086B/13195/1871, File No. 5834, 19 April 1871.

[99] *Report of Select Committee on Education 1865*, p. 36, Qs. 629, 665.

[100] *Primary and Classical Education*, p. 10.

and had succeeded in bringing it to a very considerable point of perfection'[101] nevertheless persisted in opposing a Minister of Education on three grounds. Firstly, because it would make education a matter of party politics. He did not want matters of educational administration to be used to injure the government of the day and he thought that questions of education should be removed 'as far as possible from the arena of party politics'.[102] Secondly, he repeated his former argument that there was not enough business in the Education Department 'to occupy the whole of the time of a Minister of the first class'.[103] The Education Department administered public money on certain conditions, and although it might be difficult to lay down those conditions, once they were established, the duty of seeing that they were complied with belonged rather to the permanent officials than to a Minister. Thirdly, Lowe feared that a Minister of Education would ultimately limit freedom in education, and though he could see the need for government provision and control of the elementary education system, he wanted the universities, the public schools and other secondary schools for the middle classes to operate in a free market conditioned by the factors of supply and demand and not under the management of a Minister of Education.[104] The only possible argument Lowe would admit for a special Minister was that since the main difficulties in public debate on education were connected with religion, there 'should be a Minister of great authority in the House of Lords to fight the battles of education against the jealousies and prejudices of the Bishops in that assembly'.[105]

Lowe's opposition to a Minister of Education was not quite as illogical as it may seem to posterity. When Lowe said it was the duty of the State to provide education for the people, he meant to the limited extent of elementary education and not secondary education, which was to remain in independent hands. Consequently, it was feasible for him to suggest that the Government's business in education would not expand so much as to demand the full attention of a Minister. In fact the future proved him wrong. Not only did elementary education expand but by 1899 the

[101] *Parliamentary Debates*, CCXIX, col. 1619, 15 June 1874. [102] *Ibid.*
[103] *Parliamentary Debates*, CCXIX, cols. 1619–20.
[104] *Parliamentary Debates*, CCXIX, col. 1620.
[105] *Parliamentary Debates*, CCXIX, col. 1619.

Government had seen fit to establish a central authority to co-ordinate the work of the various bodies which were engaged in secondary education. On the other hand it might reasonably be expected that Lowe's experiences with the Education Department over the preparation of estimates in the period 1871–3 might have led him to see that the constitution of the Department was ill-equipped to deal with the rapid growth in business and expenditure with which it had to deal after 1870, and that a centralised board under a Minister would be more effective. That he did not come to such a conclusion was perhaps because at the time he was so concerned to make his own department, the Treasury, all-powerful in government, and exert control over education through the power of the purse.

Given that it was his duty as Chancellor of the Exchequer to keep the level of public expenditure as low as he could, it may be concluded that Lowe had supported the Education Department adequately, if not generously, in the first three years after the passing of the 1870 Act. Its establishment had grown, and though it had not achieved the status of a full ministry but indeed had become subject in some ways to Treasury control, this cannot be wholly attributed to Lowe. Though there had been many earlier suggestions, it was not until the Select Committee on Education of 1884 that there was a firm recommendation for the establishment of a Board of Education under a President with ministerial status[106] and this was not implemented until 1899.

In pointing out Lowe's part in the passage of the 1870 Education Act, Forster's is not diminished, but it does suggest that some re-valuation of Lowe's position in educational history is required. His concern for education did not stop in 1864 when he resigned as Vice-President of the Committee of Council on Education. He became a consistent, thoughtful and influential campaigner for a system of national elementary education. He was a firm supporter of Forster in the preparation of the Bill and further, by suggesting a compromise course, secured its passage and in so doing founded the 'dual system'. Finally, as Chancellor of the Exchequer until 1873, Lowe agreed – though on occasions reluctantly – to a steady increase in the establishment of the Education Department so that it could cope adequately with the expanded duties which its implementation of the 1870 Act entailed.

[106] *Report of Select Committee on Education 1884*, para. 3, p. iii.

Lowe now looked forward, with great hopes, to the moral and civilising effects that a national system of elementary education might bring to society. He was to say in 1877 – 'by a general system of education we have . . . offered an alternative to the public house which we may fairly expect that many will adopt, and increased civilisation will react upon those who grew up with fewer opportunities of learning'.[107]

[107] R. Lowe, 'The Birmingham Plan of Public House Reform', *Fortnightly Review*, N.S. XXI (18 January 1877), 9.

# 7
# SECONDARY EDUCATION

Any liberal radical bent upon reform in the second half of the nineteenth century found himself in a dilemma. On the one hand his *laissez-faire* philosophy cautioned him to preserve individual liberty and encourage self-help while on the other his utilitarian desire to achieve efficient reform pressed him to the conclusion that this could only be achieved by collective action and state interference. This conflict of principles is particularly apparent in Lowe's approach to the question of endowed schools and the whole field of what is now called secondary education.

Lowe had two aims in this connection. He wanted to improve the teaching efficiency of the endowed and private schools which provided secondary education at that time and he wanted to reform the predominantly classical curriculum. His undoubted adherence to the teachings of Adam Smith on this subject led him to the view that the operation of a free market in education might achieve most of what he wanted. Briefly it rested on the assumptions that education was a parental and not a state responsibility, and that the free competition of schools to provide the consumer-parent with the best education that they could at the lowest price would produce not only efficient teaching but also a relevant modern curriculum. However, Lowe was enough of a realist to see that Adam Smith's ideas did not on their own provide an adequate programme for effective reform. Consequently he added to them a touch of Benthamism and proposed a policy for secondary education of *private provision and public inspection.* It has been contended that Robert Lowe was 'the last true representative of Adam Smith on education' and that he favoured private education in the classical economist tradition of Smith, while other contemporaries such as J. S. Mill, Nassau Senior and Edwin Chadwick moved towards a system of state paternalism.[1] This seems, however, to draw the contrast between Lowe and his contemporaries

[1] E. G. West, 'Private versus Public Education. A Classical Economic Dispute', in *The Classical Economists and Economic Policy*, ed. A. W. Coats, London 1971, pp. 123–43.

too strongly and to ignore his expressed views in favour of government inspection and examination of secondary schools. Moreover it implies that there was a consensus of opinion among the classical economists about secondary education which it is difficult to substantiate. In the field of elementary education most of the classical economists held that *laissez-faire* had no place and that it was a proper area for government intervention.[2] There was no similar consensus about secondary education and Lowe took an independent line. He was certainly prepared to compromise his *laissez-faire* ideas and his views on secondary education put him amongst that not inconsiderable number of mid-Victorians[3] who were willing to consider sweeping state intervention to achieve what seemed to be needed.

Secondary education in the middle of the nineteenth century was confined mainly to those whose parents could afford to pay for it. There was no state aid for schools providing other than elementary education and although there were endowed schools with scholarships for the poor, secondary education was, with some exceptions, the preserve of the middle and upper classes. Lowe was convinced that the provision of secondary schools should remain in the private sector. It was always his view that education was primarily the responsibility of parents.[4] State aid was appropriate to provide elementary education for the lower classes who could not pay for it themselves but it was essentially 'a species of poor-law relief'.[5] Where parents could pay for education themselves, as was the case with the middle classes, then they must be allowed to do so. Otherwise all the advantages which Lowe considered came from self-help would be lost, as for example the incentive it gave to parents to take an interest in their children's education, and by transference the incentive it gave to the children themselves to acquire an education which their parents paid for directly in fees. Lowe's preference for the private sector was also reinforced by the desire for retrenchment in public expenditure which he shared with Gladstone and many other politicians of his day. State aid to secondary schools would be yet another burden on the taxpayer. More than this, it would be a great social injustice if taxes

[2] See Tu, 'The Classical Economists and Education', pp. 691–718 for a summary view. [3] See for example Matthew Arnold, *A French Eton*, 1864.

[4] Lowe, *Middle Class Education*, pp. 4, 23.

[5] S.I.C. IV, *Minutes of Evidence 1868*, p. 631, Q. 6565.

taken, either directly or indirectly, from the working man were used to help to provide an education for the children of what he called 'small capitalists'.[6] For philosophical and financial reasons, then, Lowe favoured the private provision of secondary education. In addition, he was strongly influenced by the arguments of classical economic theory, which also pointed towards private rather than public education.

The origin of Lowe's views on secondary education may be traced to those which Adam Smith expressed in *The Wealth of Nations*. Lowe acknowledged his debt to Smith[7] and the close similarity of many of their ideas proves the connection.[8] Smith's treatment of education in the *Wealth of Nations* was by no means systematic but upon most educational issues, elementary, secondary and university, he had said enough to provide Lowe with a foundation of ideas which could be applied to particular situations. For example, as has been seen, Lowe's insistence in the Revised Code that the three Rs were the essential core of elementary education came from Smith,[9] as did the view that state intervention was necessary to help to provide education for the labouring population.[10] Payment by results was a proposal which Smith had urged on the grounds that if a school teacher was paid otherwise 'he would soon learn to neglect his business'.[11] Lowe's concern after the 1867 Reform Act that the electorate must be educated was again a belated but nevertheless precise application of Smith's views.[12] In fact, throughout the 1860s, Lowe's adherence to the doctrines of Adam Smith became increasingly apparent. However, it was in his views about secondary education that Lowe followed Smith most closely.

Smith began his discussion of education by concentrating upon endowments and he asked two questions about them which in effect provided Lowe with all that he needed. The questions were: 'Have they contributed to encourage the diligence and to improve the abilities of the teachers? Have they directed the course of education towards objects more useful, both to the individual and to the public than those to which it would naturally have gone of its own accord?'[13] Lowe, like Smith, answered both these ques-

[6] R. Lowe, *The Times*, third leader, 8 January 1864.
[7] Lowe, *Middle Class Education*, p. 7.
[8] See West, 'Private versus Public Education', pp. 123–43.
[9] Adam Smith, pp. 605, 619. [10] *Ibid.* p. 616. [11] *Ibid.* p. 619.
[12] *Ibid.* p. 621. [13] *Ibid.* pp. 600–601.

tions in the negative, and in so doing provided an alternative policy for the achievement of his aims in secondary education. In place of endowments he argued on the one hand, that a policy of free private enterprise would offer the best means of providing and improving secondary schools, and on the other, that the application of utilitarian demands to the curriculum would produce the reform that he desired.

The question of 'endowments' was central to Lowe's thinking about secondary education. Smith had argued that endowments prevented the operation of a free educational market in the same way that bounties worked to the disadvantage of a free-trade market. They enabled endowed schools to undersell other private schools,[14] and by providing teachers with secure salaries independently of their success or ability in their profession they necessarily diminished their application to their job and the overall quality of the education they provided.[15] Endowed scholarships which funnelled a number of students to institutions regardless of the quality of teaching which they offered, produced a similar devaluation.[16] A free educational market and 'unrestrained competition' would, on the other hand, produce better teachers and schools.[17] Lowe in his *Middle Class Education: Endowment or Free Trade* argued the same points and came to a similar conclusion. He stressed in particular that teaching needed economic incentives since it was not a 'highly intellectual trade'. He concluded that 'to be perpetually saying the same things to different people, to explain the same difficulties, to use the same illustration, requires some extraordinary stimulus from without to prevent it from degenerating into something as useless to the learner as it is intolerable to the teacher'.[18]

There were, however, two objections to the principle of the free market in education. The first was philosophical and argued that the consumer – in this case the parent – was an incompetent judge of the product – that is, the teaching, the curriculum or the school. This was an objection which J. S. Mill raised in his *Principles of Political Economy*[19] and which, it has been argued, Smith answered by implication in his views about the competence of ordinary folk

[14] *Ibid.* p. 615. [15] *Ibid.* p. 601. [16] *Ibid.* p. 603. [17] *Ibid.* p. 614.

[18] Lowe, *Middle Class Education*, pp. 8–9.

[19] J. S. Mill, *Principles of Political Economy*, People's edn 1865, p. 575: 'The uncultivated cannot be competent judges of cultivation.'

to choose their doctors and so also the teachers of their children.[20] Lowe, following Smith, insisted in his evidence to the Schools Inquiry Commission that parents were the proper judges of educational matters[21] but he made a significant addition to Smith's viewpoint by urging that the State should help parents to discharge their function in this matter. He realised that parents would often 'judge very badly'[22] but there was no alternative between parental control and government control, and the latter was abhorrent to the feelings and principles of the country and warranted only if state grants actually provided secondary education. Lowe concluded that the only course possible was 'to make the parents of the children the ministers of education, and to do anything you can to give them the best information as to what is a good education, and where their children can be well taught, and to leave it to work itself out'.[23] The second objection was more practical. Endowments could not be swept away without infringing legal and property rights and Lowe accepted this. Though he had 'the poorest opinion' of endowments and would abolish them if he had the power, ultimately he knew that it was not a practical question. The alternative was to retain endowments and yet secure 'the merits of a free system'.[24]

Lowe proposed to do precisely this by making every secondary schoolmaster's income consist of three parts. Firstly, a permanent sum 'sufficient for his proper maintenance' which could come from endowed funds or from fees, secondly, a sum based on the number of the children under him and, thirdly, a sum related to the proficiency of his pupils. This last would be tested under the inspection of the Privy Council and by an examination in 'the subjects that the school professes to teach',[25] and payments made by results. By this scheme no master could expect an extensive income from endowed funds alone and teachers would be given an incentive to work hard. Further, the publication of examination results would 'enlighten the parents'[26] and encourage them to put pressure upon schools which produced poor results, even to the extent of withdrawing their children and sending them to other more successful schools. Endowed schools would be compelled by

[20] West, 'Private versus Public Education', pp. 127–8, 135.
[21] S.I.C. IV, *Minutes of Evidence 1868*, p. 625, Qs. 6539–40.
[22] *Ibid.* p. 632, Q. 6569. [23] *Ibid.* p. 625, Q. 6540.
[24] *Ibid.* pp. 625–6, Q. 6541. [25] *Ibid.* p. 633, Q. 6576.
[26] *Ibid.* p. 627, Q. 6543.

law to accept government inspection and examination,[27] and other private schools would, Lowe expected, submit to such inspection in order to satisfy their clients, the parents.[28] Lowe had thus produced a plan for a partially free market in which the parent-consumer had the ultimate power to choose its schools and in which the State had the duty to inspect and advise the consumer.

Lowe's scheme involved public grants for secondary education, and in this way he moved away from complete provision by the private sector towards partial state provision. It was a position very much like that expressed by Matthew Arnold in *A French Eton*, though Arnold suggested that the state contribution to secondary school provision should be in the form of scholarships.[29] Arnold also saw the need for public supervision of secondary schools[30] and hinted that government inspection was the only way to achieve this.[31] Lowe, if less eloquent than Arnold, was more forthright and practical. He spelt out a plan not only for state inspection but also for public examination.

Lowe, like many other mid-Victorians, put great value upon examinations.[32] Together with inspection they were amongst the most important of utilitarian tools for the improvement of society. They maintained academic standards and provided a continuing stimulus to raise them still further. They were an incentive to teacher effort. They tested candidates for clerical and professional posts and so contributed to that vision of efficient meritocratic government which Lowe in particular had in mind. The application of examinations to secondary schools was consequently an obvious rather than an original step for Lowe. In fact even his scheme of government examiners to improve middle-class education had been detailed as early as 1847 by J. Booth in *Examination the Province of the State: or the Outlines of a Practical System for the extension of National Education*.[33] However, no other contemporary politician pressed as strongly as Lowe for what amounted to considerable state intervention in secondary schools. Lowe wanted to compel endowed and private schools to have government inspection[34] and though he hoped that in endowed schools charity funds would pay the expenses of this, he thought it so necessary

[27] *Ibid.* p. 626, Q. 6542. [28] *Ibid.* p. 636, Qs. 6595–7.
[29] Arnold, p. 69. [30] *Ibid.* p. 43. [31] *Ibid.* pp. 58–9.
[32] See Roach, pp. 8–18, 41. [33] *Ibid.* p. 56.
[34] S.I.C. IV, *Minutes of Evidence 1868*, p. 636, Q. 6597.

that he was prepared to pay for it out of public taxation.[35] He acknowledged that the Oxford and Cambridge local examinations which had operated since 1858 were a good test for schools, but they were too limited in their effects for his purpose. Schools entered only their clever pupils so that the 'ordinary child' was not touched by these examinations, and they provided no incentive for schoolmasters to ensure that 'the great mass of the school' was well taught.[36] Lowe wanted in fact for secondary schools the kind of incentive he had provided for elementary schools in the Revised Code. Moreover, he thought that one central system of inspection and examination was the best because it was the only system which might be adjudged the fairest. He prophesied that the Oxford and Cambridge local examinations 'would get into trouble ultimately' because it was impossible to keep their standards level,[37] and the proliferation of school examining boards in the last hundred years and the recent attempts to provide a more homogeneous examining system gives Lowe's prophecy an obvious relevance. Lowe also wanted the Government to organise this inspection and examination rather than the universities because he doubted whether the latter could exert the necessary control over Inspectors. He inferred from the differences he himself had had with H.M. Inspectors while he had been Vice-President of the Committee of Council that if a liberal university control rather than a tight government one held the reins, the Inspectors would probably 'run riot'.[38] Lowe took care to point out, however, that he did not want a state-imposed uniformity in the schools. He would not allow the Government to prescribe what the schools should teach. It would merely examine schools in those subjects which they offered.[39] Lowe assumed that they would always give religious instruction[40] but he would not even prescribe the three Rs, leaving it rather to the results of the inspection and subsequent parent action to ensure that pupils were taught to read, write and cypher.[41]

For Lowe, as for other liberal utilitarians like J. S. Mill,[42] examinations provided in education a convenient bridge upon which they could cross the gulf which seemed to separate their

[35] *Ibid.* p. 635, Qs. 6584–6.
[36] *Ibid.* p. 636, Q. 6593.
[37] *Ibid.* p. 644, Qs. 6667–9.
[38] *Ibid.* p. 627, Q. 6545.
[39] *Ibid.* p. 633, Q. 6576.
[40] *Ibid.* p. 640, Q. 6637.
[41] *Ibid.* p. 640, Q. 6638.
[42] See Mill, *On Liberty*, pp. 191–2.

philosophy of individual and parental self-help and their awareness of the need for state action if their dreams of utilitarian efficiency were to be realised. Government control of examinations was one way of ensuring educational efficiency while leaving the initiative to provide education in the private sector. The State was merely enforcing education and not providing it, and this was, as Mill argued, perfectly justifiable.[43] Lowe argued more positively that the State had a right to know what was being done with 'those children upon whom the welfare of the State depends' and that it would be 'doing a great service to instruct the parents as to the sort of education the children are receiving and the efficiency of the school'.[44]

On similar grounds Lowe justified state interference with the funds which educational endowments provided. From one point of view they were a form of private property and consequently sacrosanct. Lowe however took the view that they were 'in the nature of donations to which the Government may be considered a party',[45] and it could therefore re-appropriate the funds which arose from endowments if it thought fit. Lowe wanted such funds to be used either to provide part of the salaries which teachers earned, or to pay the expenses of inspection,[46] or to establish exhibitions to enable children from poorer families to go to secondary schools.[47] The abolition of endowments might be impracticable but their reorganisation by the State seemed to Lowe to be imperative if the benefits of a system of private provision and public inspection for secondary education were to be fully realised. Finally, there was no doubt in Lowe's mind that the proper body to carry out this reorganisation was a strengthened Charity Commission.[48]

To express views in politics is one thing; to strive to put them into effect is another. It remains to be asked how energetic and successful Lowe was in seeking to realise his ideas in practical policies?

In the matter of charitable endowments Lowe was able to carry out effective reforms. Educational charities had been under scrutiny since 1818 when Lord Brougham's Commission on charities had begun its work. By 1830 it had published twenty-four

[43] *Ibid.* p. 190. [44] S.I.C. IV, *Minutes of Evidence 1868*, p. 626, Q. 6543.
[45] *Ibid.* pp. 632–3, Q. 6570. [46] *Ibid.* p. 635, Q. 6584.
[47] *Ibid.* p. 638, Q. 6612. [48] S.I.C. IV, Report, pp. 629–30, Qs. 6548–52.

Reports covering charities with a total income of £500,000.[49] The Select Committee of 1835 had recommended a board of three Commissioners to overlook charities and eventually, after various abortive Bills, the Charitable Trusts Act of 1853[50] set up a Charity Commission of three members. This Commission, however, could achieve little since it had powers of only limited inquiry into charities through their trustees. It could not seek information from third parties and any proposals it made for new schemes still had to go through Chancery or a County Court, a costly business which acted to inhibit change. Lowe was particularly aware of this since, as Vice-President he was virtually *ex officio* a fourth member of the Commission. In 1860 Lowe successfully introduced to the House of Commons the Charitable Trusts Act of 1860 which gave the Charity Commissioners powers beyond those of inquiry.[51] Under this Act the Charity Commissioners had scheme-making powers, and though these were applicable only to charities with an annual income of £50 or less, it was a significant step forward.[52] Too much should not be claimed for Lowe in this, since he did not initiate the Bill, but merely carried it forward from the House of Lords. Moreover the Act did not do as much as Lowe wanted it to do. Although there is no other evidence that Lowe introduced a more radical Bill which the House drastically amended, as the Select Committee of 1884 suggested,[53] on 11 June 1863 Lowe did suggest to the House that the Commission should be given stronger powers.[54] Lowe did in his evidence before the Schools Inquiry Commission enumerate several features of the 1860 Act which were done, he claimed, against his will, and which he would repeal if he had the power. He objected to Section 4 of the Act which prevented the Commissioners from having jurisdiction over any school which had an endowment of more than £50 a year. He would have allowed the Commissioners the power of direct action to remove a trustee without prior application from one of the local inhabitants. He wanted Section 14 of the Act, which allowed the dismissal of masters 'admitted after the passing of this Act' on the majority

[49] *Report of Select Committee on Public Charities*, 1835, p. v.
[50] 16 & 17 Vict. c. 137.
[51] *Parliamentary Debates*, CLX, cols. 334–5.
[52] 23 & 24 Vict. c. 136, s. 4.
[53] *Select Committee on Charitable Trusts Acts*, 1884, p. iv; see also D. Owen, *English Philanthropy 1660–1960*, Oxford 1965, p. 207, n. 106.
[54] *Parliamentary Debates*, CLXXI, col. 723.

decision of trustees, to apply to 'all masters' and to all grammar schools. He would also repeal the limits of *cy-près* which the Act imposed upon the Commissioners allowing them to specify new purposes for a trust only if they were as near as possible (cy-près) to the testator's original intention.[55] Lowe never had the opportunity to amend the 1860 Act further and though by the Endowed Schools Act of 1874 the Charity Commission absorbed the Endowed Schools Commission, it received no further powers. However, by 1880 the Commission had framed over 4,000 new schemes, and Lowe's part in carrying the Act which enabled this work to proceed was an essential one.[56]

Strangely enough for one with declared interests in endowment reform, Lowe declined to serve on the Schools Inquiry Commission which began in 1865. He gave as his reason a lack of confidence in his prospective colleagues.[57] Headed by Lord Taunton, the Commission eventually included Lord Stanley, Lord Lyttelton, Sir Stafford Northcote, W. F. Hook, Dean of Chichester, Frederick Temple, Headmaster of Rugby, A. W. Thorold Clerk, T. D. Acland, Edwin Baines, W. E. Forster, Peter Erle, a Charity Commissioner and John Storrar. Whether or not the reason given was the real one, Lowe's refusal seems decidedly perverse and ineffective.

In contrast, his evidence before the Commission was forthright and uncompromising and seems to have had its effect on the recommendations which the Commission finally produced. Obviously the Commission was influenced by the views of many besides Lowe but it is significant that it recommended several courses of action which Lowe had suggested. For example, the Commission took the view that the endowments were in a sense public property[58] and consequently subject to state reorganisation. They agreed with Lowe that the provision of exhibitions to enable the poor to go either to secondary schools[59] or to universities[60] was one of the most useful ways of employing endowment funds. They urged the abolition of fixed salaries and freehold tenure for masters.[61] They admitted the need to widen the school curriculum.[62] They had less faith than Lowe in the ability of parents

[55] S.I.C. IV, p. 627, Q. 6547.
[56] *Select Committee on Charitable Trusts Acts*, 1884, p. vi.
[57] See Lord Fitzmaurice, I, p. 433. [58] S.I.C. I, Report, 1868, p. 571.
[59] *Ibid.* p. 582. (cf. Lowe's evidence, S.I.C. IV, p. 636, Qs. 6603–5.)
[60] *Ibid.* p. 601. [61] *Ibid.* pp. 598–9. [62] *Ibid.* pp. 576–8.

to choose the proper education for their children[63] but they accepted that secondary schools would be financed by school fees.[64] It was in this context that they devised three grades of schools specially tailored to meet the needs, wishes and pockets of the parents who were to finance them: first grade schools continuing education up to the age of 18 or 19, and offering a curriculum of classical languages, with the addition of mathematics, modern languages and natural science; second grade schools offering a practical business education to the age of 16 in English, arithmetic, additional mathematics and science, with perhaps a modern language and some classics; and third grade schools providing education up to the age of 14 with a sound education in the three Rs.[65] The Commission also went further and adopted Lowe's view that inspection and examinations were essential for the efficiency of secondary schools[66] claiming that 'the examination of the schools is the pivot of all the improvements that we have recommended'.[67] Moreover, Lowe's particular view that it was not enough to leave examinations to the local boards of the universities of Oxford and Cambridge in some measure prevailed, for the Commission proposed a Council for examinations which would include six Crown nominees as well as six university representatives.[68] Finally the Commission's recommendation that a new central authority should be set up, rather like that of the Charity Commission but with enlarged powers, echoed the suggestion Lowe had made in his evidence.[69]

Despite the similarity between Lowe's ideas and many of the Taunton Commission's recommendations, Lowe's attitude to the Report was lukewarm and his *Middle Class: Endowment or Free Trade* was in a sense published as a challenge to it. Nevertheless, Lowe now found himself, in December 1868, a member of Gladstone's first ministry which had the task of implementing the Report. In fact as Chancellor of the Exchequer Lowe had oversight of the machinery for the drafting of the Bill and on 18 February 1869 the Treasury authorised the counsel to the Home Office to draft the Endowed Schools Bill.[70] Unfortunately, there is little evidence from which we may reconstruct the part Lowe played in Cabinet discussions on the Bill, and he had little to say

[63] *Ibid.* p. 307. [64] *Ibid.* pp. 14–15. [65] *Ibid.* pp. 16–21, 577–8.
[66] *Ibid.* pp. 619–22. [67] *Ibid.* pp. 629–49. [68] *Ibid.* p. 648.
[69] *Ibid.* p. 628. [70] Treasury Papers, Out Letters, P.R.O. T/9/13, p. 89.

on the subject in the House of Commons. It would seem from a letter he wrote to the Lord President, Earl de Grey, in January 1869 that he was opposing the establishment of any new central authority and insisting that 'the Central Authority should be the Committee of Council on Education without any foreign element'.[71] Apart from this there is little to indicate Lowe's precise attitudes.

The Report had suggested three important administrative institutions. First, provincial authorities to grade the schools in any one area and to suggest schemes for the reorganisation of educational trusts. Secondly, and above these, a permanent Central Authority to approve schemes from the local authorities before submitting them to Parliament, and to organise the inspection and examination of schools. Thirdly, 'some different Central Authority' to preside over school examinations organised by county courts of examiners, and teacher-certification examinations.[72] The Endowed Schools Act of 1869,[73] however, established none of these institutions. Instead a temporary central agency, an Endowed Schools Commission of three members, was set up to reorganise the schools in a period of three or four years. This Commission had considerable powers. It was stronger than the Charity Commission in that it did not have to pay regard to the principle of *cy-près* in remodelling endowments, and it could make new trusts and divide and group endowments as it thought fit.[74] No provincial authorities were established mainly because, as Forster explained, no suitable 'constituency' for them could be found.[75] Similarly, no central council for the conduct of examinations was set up, though it was proposed originally in part II of the Bill.[76] This council was to consist of twelve members, six from the universities of Oxford, Cambridge and London, and six nominated by the Government, but in the end part II of the Bill was dropped, mainly because of the opposition from headmasters – organised by Thring of Uppingham[77] – who objected to being controlled by a central examination system when other public schools, which

[71] Ripon Papers, B.M. Add. Mss. 43532, fols. 1–3, 25 January 1869.
[72] S.I.C. I, pp. 627–9.
[73] 32 & 33 Vict. c. 56. It received the Royal Assent on 2 August 1869.
[74] 32 & 33 Vict. c. 56, s. 30. [75] *Parliamentary Debates*, CXCIV, col. 1371.
[76] *Parliamentary Debates*, CXCIV, col. 1378.
[77] G. R. Parkin, *Life and Letters of Edward Thring*, 1898, I, pp. 172–4; also G. Baron, 'The Origins and Early History of the Headmaster's Conference 1869–1914', *Educational Review*, June 1955.

came under the Public Schools Act of 1868, were exempt. Forster explained to the House that this part of the Bill was postponed to allow time for its further consideration by the country at large,[78] but in fact dropping part II was the end of this particular Taunton Report recommendation.

It is difficult to know Lowe's precise attitude towards the Endowed Schools Act. It seems likely that he was pleased that no permanent central authority had been set up in addition to the Committee of Council.[79] On the other hand he probably regretted that no central examination system for the endowed schools had been established. As for the Endowed Schools Commission itself, he seems to have taken the view that it was unnecessary and that the Committee of Council or a strengthened Charity Commission could do all that the Act required. In January 1869 Lowe had suggested to de Grey that in fact most of the work could be done by the Vice-President of the Committee of Council with help from one Commissioner 'and one Examiner to act as Secretary'. He boasted that he would have done the work without fear of being over-borne by it with the help and advice of two others.[80] With this attitude and his ministerial concern to keep down public expenditure, it is not surprising that Lowe's support for the Commission was invariably grudging and at best only lukewarm.

Under the Endowed Schools Act the Treasury was given the power to assign salaries to the Commissioners and to control the appointment of assistant commissioners.[81] Lowe was thus in a position to encourage the work of the Commission. Lord Lyttelton, a brother-in-law of Gladstone, was appointed Chief Commissioner and the others were Canon H. G. Robinson, a barrister and former training college principal, and Arthur Hobhouse, another barrister and committed opponent of the 'dead hand' of the past which *cy-près* and endowment deeds put upon the present.[82] In theory Lowe was in agreement with the sentiments of the Commissioners and the purpose they had in hand, but in practice his support for them was decidedly restrained. The main reason for this was Lowe's determination as Chancellor of the Exchequer to save money. Rightly, he now saw economy as his first priority, and

[78] *Parliamentary Debates*, CXCVIII, col. 1466.
[79] Ripon Papers, B.M. Add. Mss. 43532, fols. 1–3, 25 January 1869.
[80] *Ibid.* [81] 32 & 33 Vict. c. 56, s. 31.
[82] See A. Hobhouse, *The Dead Hand*, London 1880.

so he kept the expenses of the Endowed Schools Commission to a minimum. Before the Act was passed the Treasury submitted an estimate of £8,000 for the Commission's annual costs[83] and on 21 August 1869 finally sanctioned the salaries and establishment of the Commission as follows: first Commissioner at £1,500 p.a., a junior legal Commissioner (Hobhouse) at £2,000 and another at £1,200; a Secretary at £1,000, an assistant secretary at £600, a senior clerk at £300, two junior clerks at £200, other clerks whose salaries were not to exceed £300 p.a. in total and a messenger at £65; and of all these only the Commissioners were to be allowed entitlement under the Superannuation Act of 1859.[84] Four months later the Treasury tried hard to resist an increase in the Commission's establishment of assistant commissioners and clerks, claiming that even if more assistants were appointed clerks could not be allowed 'as such officers are supposed to carry out their own business and to keep a record of their proceedings without clerical assistance'.[85] However, by January 1870, Lowe had relented from this position and Treasury approval was given for not more than four more assistant commissioners at salaries of £700 p.a. together with clerks at £150 p.a., plus expenses of 15*s*. a day for the Commissioners and 6*s*. a day for clerks.[86]

During the following year Lowe agreed to a steady increase in the numbers of the Commission. Approval was given for the temporary appointment of two of Her Majesty's Inspectors to the Commission as assistants, namely Mr D. R. Fearson on 31 January 1870 and Mr Fitch on 8 February.[87] On 22 March provision was made for the appointment of more assistant commissioners[88] and on 10 May approval given to employ Mr Hawkins, the Education Department's architect, to supervise plans of new school buildings submitted under schemes for the Endowed Schools Commissioners, though his payment for this was not to exceed £200 a year since, as the Treasury noted, his salary for his other work was already £400 a year.[89] However by September

[83] Treasury Papers, Out Letters, P.R.O. T/9/13, p. 196.
[84] Treasury Papers, Out Letters, P.R.O. T/9/13, pp. 208–9.
[85] Treasury Papers, Out Letters, P.R.O. T/9/13, p. 264.
[86] Treasury Papers, Out Letters, P.R.O. T/9/13, p. 278.
[87] Treasury Papers, In Letters and Files, T1/6981A/11643/1870 File 1937; and Out Letters, T/9/13, pp. 294, 300.
[88] Treasury Papers, Out Letters, P.R.O. T/9/13, p. 339.
[89] Treasury Papers, In Letters and Files, P.R.O. T1/6891A/11643/1870 File 9433; and Out Letters, T/9/13, p. 362.

1870, while approving the appointment of two more assistant commissioners and supporting clerks, the Treasury made clear its anxiety to curb the Endowed Schools Commission, asking it to refrain from further appointments 'until they have satisfied themselves by experience that the existing staff cannot by a more expeditious course of administration be made to suffice for the duty'.[90] At the same time it asked that Commissioners should keep diaries of their work and journeys so that a closer check could be made of expenses.[91]

In all this Lowe might seem to be doing no more than any Chancellor of the Exchequer would do to curb expenditure. There was, however, more to it than this. Lowe was also critical of the efficiency of the Endowed Schools Commission and impatient for results.

In their Report of 21 February 1872 the Commissioners reviewed their work, pointing out the difficulties which prevented them from producing results more quickly. To construct all the schemes that were necessary to realise the recommendations of the Schools Inquiry Commission would, they claimed, take years:[92] governing bodies had to be reconstructed, schools graded, school fees established, headteachers' powers of control agreed, the curriculum modified to introduce English and physical science amongst other subjects, and free places and scholarships provided.[93] A start had been made in the West Riding, Somerset and Dorset and to these had been added North Wales, Essex, Staffordshire, Devon, South Lincolnshire, Rutland, Warwickshire and Worcestershire.[94] They had tackled 1,089 schemes, and of these 24 were already law, 34 submitted to the Education Department but not yet law, 84 in draft and 214 in process of being drafted. In particular, the Commission felt that a speedy completion of their work was impossible in the absence of provincial authorities, and later in 1873, in his evidence before the Select Committee on the Endowed Schools Act, Lord Lyttelton pleaded for a speedy implementation of the principle of local organisation as envisaged by the Schools Inquiry Commission.[95] There was, however, little chance of this. As Forster had explained in 1869 there was no

[90] Treasury Papers, Out Letters, T/9/13, p. 437. [91] *Ibid.* pp. 438–9.
[92] *Report of Endowed Schools Commissioners*, 1872, pp. 4–5. [93] *Ibid.* p. 10.
[94] *Ibid.* p. 7.
[95] *Report of Select Committee on Endowed Schools Act (1869)*, 17 June 1873, p. 254, Q. 1254.

obvious 'constituency' for local provisional boards and this was still the position, although the establishment of school boards under the 1870 Education Act had at least given some experience of locally-elected educational bodies.

The Report did not allay Lowe's feelings against the Commission, and meanwhile a considerable body of opposition had grown against it. Headmasters of schools other than those exempted under the Public Schools Act were still antagonistic towards it. Some ratepayers in school board areas were annoyed by the insistence of the Commissioners that endowments could not be used to reduce education rates or to assist in the daily running expenses of schools, but only be used for new buildings, sites and equipment.[96] Others opposed the Commission on the grounds that it was taking money from the poor to subsidise the middle class, a view with which Lowe had always had sympathy.[97] On 10 March 1872 in a letter to Gladstone, Lowe's hostility towards the Endowed Schools Commission was clearly expressed. Gladstone had reprimanded Lowe for going beyond his office in suggesting appointments to the Endowed Schools Commission office.[98] Lowe replied that he had been trying to save Gladstone trouble, but he went on to suggest that the Endowed Schools Commission should be disbanded. 'I think it is within my province', he wrote, 'to say that this Commission from the impossibility of giving effect to its decisions is a useless waste of public money and ought not to be renewed.'[99] In January 1873 the Commission exasperated him further by referring to the Attorney and Solicitor-General, and ultimately to the Judicial Committee of the Privy Council, a question under Section 17 of the Act as to whether an Anglican clergyman could be appointed an *ex-officio* school governor. Lowe felt that the Treasury should have been consulted before the expense of taking legal opinion was incurred.[100] The law officers contended that the clergy should not be *ex-officio* governors, but

[96] *Report of the Endowed Schools Commissioners*, 1872, p. 28 and appendix 7.

[97] Ripon Papers, B.M. Add. Mss. 43532, fols. 1–3, Lowe to Ripon, 25 January 1869.

[98] Gladstone Papers, B.M. Add. Mss. 44302, fol. 24, Gladstone to Lowe, 9 March 1872.

[99] Gladstone Papers, B.M. Add. Mss. 44302, fol. 26, Lowe to Gladstone, 10 March 1872.

[100] Treasury Papers, In Letters and Files, P.R.O. T1/7279A/1616/1873, 29 January 1873.

the Commissioners refused to accept this,[101] and they eventually had their way in the Endowed Schools Amending Act of 1873 which stated that nothing in Section 17 of the original Act should be held to prevent 'the holder of any particular office' from being a governor.[102]

The days of the Commission were, however, numbered. In 1873 their powers were extended for one year only and on 7 August 1874 a further Amending Act transferred the Commission's powers to the Charity Commissioners with power to appoint two additional Commissioners and a Secretary in addition to the three existing under previous Charitable Trust Acts.[103] By this time Lowe was out of office but he now had the satisfaction of seeing endowed schools under the surveillance of a strengthened Charity Commission, just as he had suggested in his evidence to the Schools Inquiry Commission almost ten years previously.

In conclusion, three general points may be made about Lowe's attitudes towards secondary education. First, his view that such education should be provided by the private sector coincided with that of most of his contemporaries and was largely confirmed in the government legislation of his time. He would have preferred the abolition of educational endowments but since there was little support for this, he compromised and was content that they should be reconstituted under the Charity Commissioners, though it is arguable that if he had given greater support to the Endowed Schools Commission the reform of endowments would have been more thorough. On the other hand his view that there should be state inspection and centralised examination of secondary schools was both too forward looking and too foreign to the English tradition of freedom to gain acceptance. Lowe's plan for a national central examination system on conventional lines was too much of a move towards collectivism for most of his contemporaries and, indeed, it is still feared as a measure harmful to individuality and as essentially opposed to the existence of a free society. The future lay with the Oxford and Cambridge local examinations and the other university examining boards which joined them to provide school-leaving certificates and so indirectly promote efficiency in

[101] The Commission's case is argued in *Report of the Endowed Schools Commissioners*, 1872, pp. 34–5, 76–8 and appendix 9.

[102] 36 & 37 Vict. c. 87, s. 6, 5 August 1873.

[103] 37 & 38 Vict. c. 87, ss. 1–2.

the secondary schools. Finally, there is a notable similarity between Lowe's policies for elementary and secondary education. On the question of provision and administration he was for decentralisation in both. However, to ensure quality in the education which schools gave, he insisted that there must be centralised examinations. Lowe's support for such apparently opposed principles was a reflection of the mid-nineteenth-century dilemma in which radical liberals found themselves.

# 8
# CURRICULUM REFORM

There was a streak of utilitarianism in Lowe which had to come out, and it emerged most noticeably in his concern for curriculum reform. The content of the secondary school curriculum was antiquated, and irrelevant to the needs of the new scientific society in which he perceived himself. Starting from this basic premiss he became an ardent advocate of curriculum reform.

Lowe was in no way a prophet crying in the wilderness. In fact the 1860s saw a notable acceleration in the production of books on the nature of education. Newman's lectures on *The Scope and Nature of University Education* appeared in a revised edition in 1859, following their original delivery in 1852. Herbert Spencer's *Education* was published in 1861. In 1867 John Stuart Mill delivered his *Inaugural Address* as Rector of St Andrews University, and in the same year *Essays on a Liberal Education* edited by F. W. Farrar appeared, followed in 1868 by T. H. Huxley's *A Liberal Education: and where to find it*. Other writers related their thoughts more directly to the school situation. Earl Fortescue's *Public Schools for the Middle Classes* and Matthew Arnold's *A French Eton* were both published in 1864. The sixties also produced two Royal Commissions on secondary education. The Clarendon Commission reported on the public schools in 1864 and the Schools Inquiry Commission on the endowed schools in 1868. This was the context in which Lowe made his contributions. His address *Primary and Classical Education*, delivered in Edinburgh on 1 November 1867, his speeches on *Middle Class and Primary Education*, delivered at Liverpool to a conference on education on 22 and 23 January 1868, and his *Middle Class Education: Endowment or Free Trade*, published in 1869, put forward his views with a brilliance and vigour which challenged much contemporary opinion. Some were appalled[1] but as the Reverend S. Hawtrey, an assistant master at Eton pointed out, none could safely ignore

[1] See for example L. Campbell, *The End of a Liberal Education*, Edinburgh 1868.

'those brilliant speeches of Mr. Lowe, with which he is shaking the country's traditional opinions about Education'.[2]

Lowe's approach to the question was initially historical. He attempted to explain the cultural lag apparent in the school curriculum of his day. Once again he seems to have found a starting point in Adam Smith's views, but to these he also added his own historical explanation which centred on the influence of the Eldon judgment of 1805. With Smith, Lowe located the prime cause in endowments.[3] They were 'a great evil', Lowe told the Schools Inquiry Commission, primarily because they served to freeze the curriculum.[4] The statutes of an endowed school often prescribed classical studies, and it was difficult to deviate from this. Lowe had very much in mind the case of Leeds Grammar School. There since 1779 the Governors had tried to introduce into the curriculum, as additions to Latin and Greek, more utilitarian subjects such as algebra, mathematics, French and German. Two successive masters had opposed this and the case went to the Court of Chancery. In 1805, Lord Eldon had given judgment that the classical languages were the fundamental subjects in the curriculum, taking his definition from Dr Johnson's Dictionary that a 'grammar school' was 'a school where learned languages are taught grammatically', and as a result Leeds Grammar School was prevented from making major curriculum changes at that time. Lowe opposed Lord Eldon's interpretation[5] and regarded the case as a particular historical example of his general theory that endowments weighed upon the present as the dead hand of the past.

Lowe's knowledge of the precise influence of Eldon's judgment was incomplete. It has been shown[6] that curriculum change was not completely prevented at Leeds: by 1818 the school had a third master, mathematical instruction began and certainly by 1868 there had been considerable change and Leeds Grammar School was then notable for its science teaching.[7] Nevertheless, Lowe was not wholly mistaken in his view of the influence of Eldon's judgment, for though there was curriculum change in certain schools in the

[2] Reverend S. Hawtrey, *A Narrative Essay on a Liberal Education*, London 1868, p. 25. [3] Adam Smith, *Wealth of Nations*, pp. 615–16.

[4] S.I.C. IV, *Minutes of Evidence 1868*, p. 637, Q. 6603.

[5] S.I.C. IV, *Minutes of Evidence 1868*, p. 629, Q. 6548.

[6] R. S. Tompson, 'The Leeds Grammar School Case of 1805', *Journal of Educational Administration and History*, III, 1 (Dec. 1970), 1–6.

[7] S.I.C. I, Report, p. 133, n. 1.

years following it, Eldon's decision was absorbed into subsequent legal cases and law commentaries.[8] Certainly Eldon's decision was a causal factor in the genesis of Lowe's mind on the subject. He told the Schools Inquiry Commission that he thought that one of the great evils of endowments was that they had almost always been given for particular studies, and then things had expanded and the endowment had remained contracted. They had been 'a premium upon obsolete knowledge'.[9] For similar reasons he urged that the Charity Commission rather than the Court of Chancery should be the proper body to deal with questions of endowed schools' management. It could more easily gauge local and public opinion and 'would not go on as Lord Eldon did for years injuring in the most fearful manner the endowed charities of the country by that perverse interpretation of his about grammar schools'.[10]

If endowments from the past were not to be allowed to decide the curriculum, how was it to be determined? Lowe immediately ruled out the teacher as a competent judge of such matters. He said:

> It is the nature of teachers to recommend that which they know best themselves. To recommend anything else is to impose on themselves the trouble of going to school again. Nor was there anything in the occupation of a teacher which gave him a large acquaintance with man and things and enabled him either to discover the wants of society or to decide how best education could supply them.[11]

Lowe's perceptive comments on the built-in conservatism which teachers at all levels acquire, became increasingly apparent as the teaching profession expanded over the next century. The recent developments in in-service training are in the process of undermining the complacency of teachers, but in his day Lowe could see no such remedy for this acquired characteristic of theirs. If teachers were unfit to decide the curriculum, the alternatives were the State, school trustees or parents. Direct state control was in this connection neither desirable nor possible, Lowe contended.[12] School trustees had no particular qualifications for this function, and in the absence of other alternatives Lowe was prepared to entrust it to parents.[13]

8 Tompson, 'The Leeds Grammar School Case', pp. 4–6.
9 S.I.C. IV, p. 641, Q. 6639. 10 *Ibid.* p. 629, Q. 6548.
11 Lowe, *Middle Class Education*, p. 13.
12 S.I.C. IV, *Minutes of Evidence 1868*, p. 625, Q. 6540.
13 Lowe, *Middle Class Education*, pp. 11–13.

To help parents perform this function responsibly Lowe had two suggestions. First he wanted all endowed and private schools to accept government inspection and examination so that parents would have some guide as to their efficiency and quality.[14] Secondly Lowe suggested, in anticipation of many later developments, that there should be more parental participation in the educational process, and co-operation with schools in discussion meetings. Further he wanted 'to generate a healthy public opinion' by public lectures and by discussion in the press of curriculum and other educational matters.[15] His speeches in the years 1867–8 were an attempt to begin this process. If there was to be curriculum reform, some public discussion of curriculum theory would be necessary, and this he attempted to provide.

Lowe has some claims to be called the father of curriculum theory. At Edinburgh in 1867 he heralded its birth in the following terms:

> We must invent for ourselves a sort of new science – a science of weights and measures; of ponderation, if I may coin a word – in which we shall put into the scales all the different objects of human knowledge, and decide upon their relative importance. All knowledge is valuable, and there is nothing that it is not worth while to know; but it is a question of relative importance – not decrying this branch of knowledge and praising and puffing that – but of taking as far as possible the whole sense of human knowledge, and deciding what should have priority, which should be taught first and to which our attention should be most urgently directed.[16]

'Ponderation' did not catch on but it was a plea for the kind of curriculum study which has grown so rapidly as an educational subject in the sixties of this century. However, Lowe's approach to this subject was notably different from most current ones. He did not begin with an attempt to categorise educational objectives in terms of skills nor with discussions about the structure of the various disciplines of knowledge. Rather he began by suggesting principles for curriculum-building in terms of useful content.

Lowe suggested four basic principles. First, 'as we live in a universe of things and not of words, the knowledge of things is more important to us than the knowledge of words'.[17] This was

[14] S.I.C. IV, p. 636, Qs. 6595–7. [15] Lowe, *Middle Class Education*, p. 11.
[16] Lowe, *Primary and Classical Education*, p. 13. [17] *Ibid.* p. 14.

partly a plea for environmental and scientific studies rather than the study of ancient languages, as Lowe's subsequent explanation makes clear. It was also, however, a methodological principle as much as a description of content. Lowe noted that young children make their earliest essays in learning through contact with objects, and by language related to objects, and he stressed this as a sound pedagogic principle. Lowe was merely restating the principle Comenius had advanced two centuries earlier, but in the context of much nineteenth-century schooling it needed re-emphasis. Secondly, Lowe suggested that 'it was more important to know what is true than false'. Again Lowe was attacking the concentration upon classical studies in schools, and in particular its mythological content. Lowe wanted pupils to study knowledge that could be seen to be relevant. 'It is more important', Lowe said, 'to know the history of England than the mythologies of Greece and Rome. I think it more important that we should know those transactions out of which the present state of our political and social relations have arisen, than that we should know all the lives and loves of all the gods and goddesses.'[18] Thirdly, Lowe asserted that utility should be one of the main criteria for selecting curriculum content. 'As we cannot teach people everything', he said, 'it is more important that we should teach them practical things than speculative things.'[19] Lowe's fourth principle was that 'the present is more important to us than the past'.[20] He was appalled, for example, that pupils could be taught the geography of ancient Greece and yet not know where Australia was.[21]

These four principles obviously overlap, and Lowe's discussion of them is not very logical or clear. Together they add up to an indictment of the education provided by the public and endowed schools of his day and present a plea for a school curriculum to be practical, useful and relevant to its own times. There is no sophisticated philosophical discussion of the meanings of 'relevance' or 'utility'. Lowe's approach is severely empirical and his case rests mainly upon his description of current curriculum practice in the schools and its obvious deficiencies in terms of what he takes to be self-evident principles of utility and relevance. For example, he made a catalogue of the things which 'one who may have received the best education at the highest public schools or at Oxford' will not know. It included the anatomy of his own

[18] *Ibid.* p. 14. [19] *Ibid.* p. 14. [20] *Ibid.* p. 15. [21] *Ibid.* p. 23.

body, elementary physics (as for example how a thermometer works), biology, arithmetic and accounts, the geography of the modern world, modern history, English literature, modern languages, chemistry and geology. In addition, Lowe suggested, the public school product would probably be deficient in spelling and write an 'execrable hand'.[22] However, he would be well versed in the classical languages and ancient history. 'Every man is expected', Lowe said, 'to know how many Archons there were at Athens though he does not know how many Lords of the Treasury there are in London: he must know all the forms of their courts though he knows hardly the names of our own.'[23] It annoyed Lowe that the classes who by wealth and tradition held superior positions in society should be less well educated in practical matters than those who held inferior ones.[24] This offended his adherence to the principle of meritocracy as much as the unlimited extensions of the franchise did, and curriculum reform would at least ensure that those who ruled had an education which informed them about the society in which they lived.

In stating the case for more relevant modern studies Lowe might seem to be on the side of the Philistines. Such a view would be mistaken. Lowe was not calling for the complete overthrow of ancient and historical studies. All he wanted was a redress of the balance in the curriculum which at that time was heavily weighted towards the classics. The extent of this imbalance obliged Lowe to express his case for modern studies in extreme terms.

Although Lowe was primarily interested in changing the content of the curriculum he was also concerned that the curriculum should 'discipline the mind'.[25] Lowe made little attempt to analyse this concept but he wanted the pupil to be equipped with 'qualities of caution, of observation and of reflection'[26] and added that the most useful lesson a man could learn was 'the estimation of probabilities and sifting of evidence'.[27] Whether such skills acquired in particular fields were capable of transfer to other situations, Lowe did not trouble to inquire. He assumed that they were. Recent psychological studies are hesitant in their conclusions

[22] *Ibid.* p. 25. [23] *Ibid.* p. 23. [24] *Ibid.* p. 32.
[25] Lowe, *Primary and Classical Education*, p. 13.
[26] *Ibid.* p. 6. [27] *Ibid.* p. 16.

about transfer in thinking, but Lowe's common-sense position is by no means invalidated.[28]

Lowe wanted schools and universities to produce in their students an ability to think about human problems in a balanced way, so that the complexity of causes behind events were appreciated and solutions urged by weighing possibilities rather than imposing the conclusions of abstract deduction.[29] In this he seems to have argued for those balanced powers of reasoning which, it has been suggested, historical studies can best encourage.[30] However, in fact, Lowe considered that history as a school subject was as incapable of teaching the powers of reasoning he wanted as mathematics[31] and logic were.[32] Lowe's suggestion was that the physical sciences could best serve his purpose.[33] He hastened to point out, however, that the sciences should not be studied by rote, as a matter of memory, but as a study which produced 'a scientific habit of mind' which could then be applied to everyday affairs. It would give pupils, Lowe hoped,

> a habit of mind which enables a man, when dealing with practical affairs, in the first place to correct by careful observation and earnest enquiry all the materials for judgment, to weigh with caution the difficulties of the case, to estimate carefully the probabilities on either side, but assisting himself by adding little circumstances one upon another, each of which may seem trivial, but the aggregate of which produces an overpowering conviction.[34]

Whether or not the study of science could actually achieve all this is irrelevant to Lowe's conviction that it could. Lowe was a child of his time in that he was impressed and excited by science. 'There was no logic so subtle, so refined and so improving to the mind as that of nature.'[35] He had, for example, met Charles Darwin in 1831 in Wales, and becoming immediately attached to him as a superior person had followed him in 'canine' fashion twenty-two miles over the mountains, while Darwin continued his geological tour.[36] In 1859 Lowe read *The Origin of Species* avidly[37]

[28] See for example R. Thomson, *The Psychology of Thinking*, Penguin Books 1959, pp. 133–47.
[29] Lowe, *Primary and Classical Education*, p. 16.
[30] See G. R. Elton, 'Second Thoughts on History at the Universities', *History*, LIV, 180 (February 1969), 66.
[31] Lowe, *Primary and Classical Education*, p. 16.
[32] Lowe, *Middle Class and Primary Education*, p. 9.
[33] *Ibid.* p. 12.
[34] *Ibid.* p. 13.
[35] S.I.C. IV p. 641, Q. 6647.
[36] Patchett Martin, I, pp. 19–20.
[37] *Ibid.* II, pp. 201–7.

and wrote about it repeatedly in his correspondence. Benjamin Jowett, the Master of Balliol, in a personal memoir of Lowe noted the great fascination which natural science held for him, a man who had 'had the misfortune to be born in the pre-scientific age'.[38] For himself Lowe waxed eloquent about science. 'There is nothing in the *Arabian Nights* so extravagant' he said and, reflecting upon the classics he knew so well, went on 'we have got to the end of it. A scrap of Tacitus, a page of Licinanus, a mutilated essay of Cicero . . . have become inestimable treasures . . . But nature is boundless and inexhaustible.'[39]

Lowe was obviously optimistic in the claims he made for scientific study but it needs to be emphasised that he pressed them as much for the mental discipline he supposed science to engender as for the utility of its content. Lowe's approach to the curriculum was characterised by his attempt to balance on the one hand the utility and relevance of the content with, on the other, the need to produce in pupils lasting habits of thought.

This can be clearly seen in his discussion of the place of languages in the curriculum. He doubted the value of languages as a training for the mind[40] and in doing so struck at the main contemporary justification for the classics in the curriculum. If languages were to be taught then it should be for their utility value, and consequently English (as the native language of the pupils) had a prior claim over Latin and Greek, and similarly French and German had obvious uses as living languages. French enabled one to be understood in Paris[41] and German was, Lowe argued with partial prophetic insight 'the language of a people who are already great, and . . . are destined to become greater; with whom we have very close relations, which unless I am much mistaken are destined to become closer'.[42] To emphasise his point Lowe told the following story: 'I have been with a party of half-a-dozen first class Oxford gentlemen on the Continent, and not one spoke a word of French or German, and if the waiter had not been better educated than we, and known some other language than his own, we might all have starved.'[43] Lowe of course overstated his case against the classics. As one who had narrowly missed the Chair of Greek at

[38] *Ibid.* II, p. 497. [39] Lowe, *Primary and Classical Education*, p. 15.
[40] *Ibid.* p. 17. [41] *Ibid.* pp. 18–19.
[42] Lowe, *Middle Class and Primary Education*, p. 11.
[43] Lowe, *Primary and Classical Education*, p. 26.

Glasgow University in 1838 he was fully aware of their worth. It was for the average pupil that Lowe questioned the amount of time spent upon Latin in school. Those intended for the learned professions might still learn classical Latin. For others he thought 'modern Latin' was very desirable – 'such Latin as a person would speak with a Catholic priest on the Continent'.[44]

This prescription of Latin as a living language typifies Lowe's view of language study. Languages are vehicles of communication and consequently they are to be taught by the direct method. Grammar is not the way to begin language teaching. Oral work reinforced by simple, amusing and interesting readers, should lead by progression to a study of weightier works of literature.[45] Lowe wanted languages learned as Montaigne says he learned them – colloquially.[46] Lowe came close in all this to some twentieth-century approaches to language teaching. Beginning with a consideration of the actual origins of language, he contended that linguistics and the study of usage rather than grammatical analysis was the best way to acquire a command of them.[47] Looking askance at the way in which the classical languages were taught in his day, he concluded:

> if Aeschylus came to life again he would be easily plucked in one of his own choruses; and as for Homer, I am quite certain he did not know the difference between the nominative and accusative case; and yet the best hours of our lives are spent in this profitless analysis of works produced by men utterly unconscious of the rules we are endeavouring to draw from them.[48]

Languages for Lowe were a means to an end, not an end in themselves. They were a means of communicating knowledge either by conversation or by reading the literatures of the respective languages.[49] Thus they might help to inform the mind, but Lowe was extremely doubtful of their ability to discipline the mind in the sense of providing it with balanced habits of thought. His views upon this were in notable contradiction to those of many of his contemporaries. Their position was voiced by J. S. Mill in his inaugural address at St Andrews, when he supported Greek and

[44] S.I.C. IV, p. 631, Q. 6558.
[45] Lowe, *Middle Class and Primary Education*, p. 12.
[46] S.I.C. IV, p. 631, Q. 6559.
[47] Lowe, *Primary and Classical Education*, p. 19.
[48] *Ibid.* p. 20. [49] *Ibid.* p. 16.

Latin not only as agents of mental discipline but also as more valuable than any modern European language as a 'discipline of the intellect'.[50]

Lowe's demand for a modernisation of the curriculum on the grounds of utility and relevance had its foundation in the more basic argument that the curriculum should draw attention to the nature of the human condition as seen in the perspective of history. This could not be done if the minds of the young were exclusively directed towards studies of the ancient world. As Lowe saw it, modern society acted upon a concept of its position which was quite foreign to antiquity. 'Their conception of knowledge', said Lowe' 'wants entirely that which is our leading conception in the present day. I do not think you will find anywhere in the study of antiquity that which is now, in everybody's mouth – the idea of progress.'[51] Lowe did not mean by this that progress was inevitable, but he did mean that change and development were, and he urged that youth should be educated to accept this. He never developed his view in any detail, but underlying all his thought on the curriculum was this basic idea that an education which continually looked back to a golden age in the past was no good foundation for either the present or the future. In his opinion:

> It is no small fault of the modern system of education that it withholds that conception, the key of modern society – that is, not to look at things as stationary, but to look at the human race as, like a glacier, always advancing, always going on from good to better, from better to worse, as the case may be – an endless change and development that never ceases, although we may not be able to mark it every day.[52]

'Education for change' is a concept which needs much examination. In the context of Lowe's thought not only upon education but also on other subjects, it can be assumed that he would not support change for its own sake or on *a priori* grounds. He was too much of an empiricist for that. In the context of his times, Lowe's argument has an obvious relevance. With industrialisation, society was undergoing change more rapidly than at any previous time and yet secondary education – so far as it existed – was limited by statutes and endowments framed often three hundred years earlier and purveying a curriculum of even more ancient lineage. Lowe

[50] F. A. Cavenagh (ed.), *James and John Stuart Mill on Education*, Cambridge 1931, p. 150. [51] Lowe, *Primary and Classical Education*, p. 22.
[52] *Ibid.* pp. 22–3.

wanted the young to be educated for the rapidly changing society which he saw emerging.

Lowe was only one of several voices raised for curriculum reform in the 1860s, and how far his views were more influential than others it is impossible to say. Nevertheless, his contribution to curriculum reform was distinctively individual. In the first place his position as a prominent politician gave his utterances a certain notoriety which made them potentially influential and ensured them an immediate hearing.[53] Secondly, his programme for reform was a balanced, forward-looking and practical one which compares well with those produced by his contemporaries. For example, John Stuart Mill, like Lowe, wanted a curriculum in which both literature and science figured[54] but Mill's support for science was never very positive, his scheme had no place for modern languages, geography or history, and the defence of classical studies as agents of mental discipline remained the core of his views on the curriculum.[55] On the other hand, Herbert Spencer pressed for an exclusively scientific curriculum and regarded science as the subject of most 'intrinsic' worth.[56] Lowe was nearer to Spencer's position but he did modify the latter's stress on science and wanted schools to offer as wide a curriculum as possible, teaching, as he put it: 'anything that is proper to be taught to youth including physical science and the learned languages – the two poles, as I may call them – and all that lies between, any species of knowledge'.[57] Lowe's views were in fact very close to those advanced by Henry Sidgwick, in his essay on *The Theory of Classical Education*, for Sidgwick wanted a curriculum which included languages, literature and the natural sciences.[58] Finally Lowe questioned, in a way that was far from common at the time, the distinction between a 'useful' and a 'liberal' education. In his view it was too often assumed that a subject could not enlarge the mind unless it was utterly useless in future life. Lowe had no time for this 'worship of inutility'.[59] He was, however, equally opposed to an education which concentrated too much upon the acquisition of vocational skills. As has

[53] Patchett Martin, II, pp. 330, 336. [54] Cavenagh, p. 138. [55] *Ibid.* p. 150.
[56] Herbert Spencer, *Education. Intellectual, Moral, Physical*, London 1919, p. 14.
[57] S.I.C. IV, p. 625, Q. 6538.
[58] H. Sidgwick, 'The Theory of Classical Education', in F. W. Farrar (ed.), *Essays on a Liberal Education*, London 1868, pp. 81–143.
[59] Lowe, *Primary and Classical Education*, p. 18.

been shown, he felt strongly that education should offer a mental discipline, but he could not agree that this was more likely to be achieved through a 'literary' than a 'scientific' education. On the whole he favoured an education in science because it seemed to offer not only a mental discipline but also a better preparation for life – a view, it is interesting to note, which Henry Sidgwick advanced in terms which very much echoed those of Lowe.[60]

Lowe provided the most convenient summary of his views in the curriculum he suggested for the children of the middle class of his day. By middle class, Lowe meant those who would not think of sending their children to state elementary schools and yet had insufficient money to send them to the public schools.[61] Lowe criticised this class for its limited view of education. In his view, their concentration upon a vocational education, geared to book-keeping and acquired in the commercial academies, was reflected in their general apathy and inability to contribute to the cultural and political life of the nation.[62] In particular, Lowe regretted that they had played no part in his campaign against the extension of the franchise in 1867; the middle-class man was thinking 'too much . . . of his till and his counting house and too little of the great events passing around him'.[63] Their education lacked culture and mental discipline and Lowe prescribed the following curriculum as a remedy. There should be a basic study in English composition: a letter asking for employment was, Lowe suggested, beyond the capabilities of too many.[64] There should be studies in English literature, French and German, mathematics and, above all, in one of the physical sciences, to discipline the mind.[65]

Apart from talking about reform Lowe made one notable attempt to reform those most conservative of all educational institutions, the seven great public schools covered in the Public Schools Act of 1868. On 30 April of that year he wrote to his friend Lady Salisbury that he would move a clause in the Public Schools Bill requiring every boy to be examined annually by a government Inspector in reading, writing, arithmetic, geography, English grammar and English history, the results of the examination to be laid before Parliament. Lowe knew that he would not carry the clause 'but it would be amusing to see the reasons that will be

[60] Sidgwick, 'The Theory of Classical Education', pp. 133–4.
[61] Lowe, *Middle Class and Primary Education*, p. 3. [62] *Ibid.* p. 4.
[63] *Ibid.* p. 4. [64] *Ibid.* p. 11. [65] *Ibid.* pp. 11–13.

given against it'.[66] Lowe was as good as his word, and proposed a clause for annual examination by Inspectors to show parents 'the deficiences in the education given'.[67] He pointed out to the House that if the subjects which his clause enumerated were taught in the public schools then he could not understand why they should shrink from the proposed examination; if not, he could not see why the House of Commons 'should shrink from making the fact known to the world'.[68] As he had anticipated, opposition was immediate. It was argued that such a step would 'degrade the great public schools of England down to the level of village schools'.[69] However, there was some support for Lowe. W. E. Forster agreed with him, though he did not think that Inspectors would be the proper examiners, and others, including J. S. Mill, supported such an examination as an appropriate entrance qualification for the public schools.[70] In the end Lowe withdrew his clause, claiming that it stood *pro confesso* that the subjects he had listed were not taught at the schools but 'he would not expose the remedy proposed in the clause to the disadvantage of a division in the existing temper of the House'.

Lowe had at least tried to arouse his contemporaries from their complacency about secondary education. Once again, however, as with the Schools Inquiry Commission, Lowe had the opportunity to do more than raise issues. He could have been one of the Commissioners appointed under the Public Schools Act[71] but he declined. It might appear that Lowe was unwilling to work hard enough to realise his ideas, but his refusal to serve was in fact the triumph of his pragmatism. As he explained to Lady Salisbury, it would have been hopeless to set to work upon the same Commission as Lord Cranborne – Robert Cecil, Marquis of Salisbury – when their views were so opposed. 'It would have been one long duel between us in which the majority of the Commission would have been with him', Lowe concluded.[72]

In the last resort, Lowe was always a realist. The abolition of endowments and the adoption by schools of a modern curriculum

[66] Lady Burchlere, pp. 184–5.
[67] *Parliamentary Debates*, CXCIII, cols. 817–19.
[68] *Ibid.* col. 819.
[69] *Ibid.* col. 819, Mr Darby Griffith, MP for Devizes.
[70] *Ibid.* col. 823.
[71] *Parliamentary Debates*, CXCII, col. 1939; H. Labouchere, MP for Middlesex, pressed Lowe to serve.
[72] Lady Burchlere, p. 189, 26 June 1868.

were not immediate practical possibilities. The realisation of his ideas about secondary education lay in the future. That he could stand outside his time and against most of his contemporaries was a measure of his intellect. His lack of achievement was an example of the fate which often awaits the intellectual in politics.

# 9
# UNIVERSITY EDUCATION

Robert Lowe's views on university education were forged in the middle decades of the nineteenth century when the existing universities became increasingly the object of criticism and change. Since the beginning of the century there had been attacks on the ancient universities of Oxford and Cambridge and they had in some measure reformed themselves, but not enough to silence their critics. In 1850 Royal Commissions were set up to consider their situation and the debate intensified.

Exception was taken to the expense of education at Oxford and Cambridge, which effectively prevented its extension to a larger section of the nation. The existence of religious tests and the use of 'close' scholarships and endowments, both of which limited entrance to the universities, were similarly attacked. The constitutions of the universities, their method of government, the relationships between the colleges and the university, all came under scrutiny. The function of university teachers was analysed and contrasted with that of university teachers abroad, particularly in Germany, and the consequent discussion centred on the relation between teaching and research in the academic life of a university. Finally the whole nature and purpose of university studies was questioned: should a university concern itself with the diffusion of useful knowledge or with the enlargement of individual minds?[1]

The debate centred on the universities of Oxford and Cambridge though there were two other universities also in existence in England by 1850. The university of London had been incorporated in 1836, and at first conferred degrees on successful students from University College, London, which had opened in 1828 on a non-denominational basis, and King's College, London, which opened in 1831 as an Anglican college. The university of Durham had also been founded as a Church of England institution in 1833. More significantly, in 1851 Owens College had been

[1] The most notable contemporary discussions were: J. H. Newman, *On the Scope and Nature of University Education*, London 1859; Mark Pattison, *Suggestions on Academical Organisation*, Edinburgh 1868.

founded in Manchester, and this particular institution was to be the beginning of a series of 'modern' universities which were eventually to coexist with the 'ancient' universities of Oxford and Cambridge.

Lowe's thinking about universities was essentially *ad hoc.* It arose as a response to particular problems which came to his notice, and he never philosophised about the university either at length or in general. However, in contributing to the discussion about particular issues, such as the reform of Oxford University, the reorganisation of Durham University, the future of Owens College, Manchester, and the provision of university education in Ireland, he presented a coherent viewpoint.

In general terms this amounted to a utilitarian demand that the universities should be made to serve society more specifically. Echoing once again Adam Smith, Lowe wanted the universities to be effective teaching institutions, existing for the benefit of students rather than 'the ease of the masters'[2] and ready to alter their curriculum to meet changing ideas and the expansion of knowledge.[3] Lowe was also concerned to apply the criteria of economic productivity to the universities. This led him to advocate more productivity in terms of student teaching, a cut in the vacations allowed to university staff and shorter degree courses. Finally, Lowe conceived the universities as the most important tool in the fashioning of the meritocratic State which he wanted. They were to educate the intellectual elite of society to as high a standard as possible. Utilitarianism, the application of a kind of costs-benefit analysis, and the concern for a meritocracy, comprised the general framework in which Lowe approached questions of university policy. More specifically his views focused upon five issues: the opening of the universities to the nation; the achievement of better standards of learning; the improvement of university teaching; the widening of the university curriculum; and the role of the universities as the nurseries of civil servants.

## OPENING THE UNIVERSITIES TO THE 'NATION'

Lowe pressed his view that 'the university should be thrown open to admit the whole nation'[4] in various ways but, before these are discussed, it is important to stress that this view needs to be

[2] Adam Smith, p. 604. [3] *Ibid.* p. 615.
[4] *Parliamentary Debates,* CLXXXII, cols. 697–8.

interpreted in the context of Lowe's general ideas and with reference to the university provision which existed in the middle of the nineteenth century. Lowe was not envisaging the mass-universities which are developing in the twentieth century. Rather he was asserting the principle that the universities should be open to all students regardless of the class or creed to which they might belong, provided that they had the ability and merit to profit from the courses of study which the universities offered.

On the one hand, the principle of the open university which Lowe upheld might indeed lead to more and larger universities than those which existed in his day. However, his view that universities should be places of academic quality was always likely to be a factor which would limit any opening of the universities to the nation at large. The foundation of all Lowe's educational thought was his belief that primarily education was concerned with the achievement of quality. He assumed that there could be some general agreement about what constituted quality, and once having made that assumption he developed his other ideas without questioning it further. Thus there was no hypocrisy in his assertion that the university should be open to the 'whole nation'. It did, however, rest upon his assumption that only the nation's most able would attend an institution which in his view demanded qualities which the mass were unlikely to display. In short, Lowe wanted the universities to be open to the intellectual elite of the nation.

Looking particularly at the university of Oxford, the university of which he had most experience, Lowe considered that in four ways it inhibited the entrance of students from the nation as a whole. Firstly, the Test Acts confined full membership of the university to members of the Church of England. Secondly, the existence of 'close' scholarships limited entrance to students with certain kinship or local connections. Thirdly, the collegiate system served to keep down numbers; and fourthly, the expense of attending the university also prevented wider entrance. Lowe pressed for changes which would eliminate all of these limiting factors. He supported the series of abortive bills which finally in 1871 proved successful in abolishing the Test Acts.[5] He proposed that all fellowships and scholarships should be opened to competition by merit,[6] though he had in his own career once been

[5] *Parliamentary Debates*, CLXXXII, col. 697.
[6] *Parliamentary Debates*, CXXXIV, cols. 902–4.

grateful for the award of a 'close' fellowship, confined to candidates from his home county of Nottinghamshire.[7] He stated his opposition to scholarships which relied upon kinship, attendance at a particular school, or the voice of influential friends for their award, and upheld merit as the proper criterion for the award of both school and university places.[8] He suggested to the Royal Commission on Oxford University in 1852 an extension of the existing collegiate provision for the entrance of students. While accepting that, in order to maintain academic discipline and surveillance of the studies of undergraduates, attachment to some hall or college was necessary, he could see no reason to limit university provision to the existing colleges. Lowe thought that any Master of Arts 'of good character' who wanted to open a hall should be allowed to do so, subject to such general rules as the university might authorise. The provision of buildings and accommodation would be left to the principal concerned and the advantage, in Lowe's view, would be that competition might then serve to lower the expense of college education to a level which more of the nation could afford.[9] Alternatively, Lowe suggested that if the collegiate system was made more elastic so as to allow students to live in lodgings, as he noted Balliol College was proposing to do, then this would also be a means of opening the university to more of the nation by obviating the expense which collegiate residence entailed. This alternative suggestion had the advantage, to Lowe's mind, of allowing the colleges to indulge in that expensive style of living which many of the sons of the richer gentry could afford and enjoyed, while allowing the less well-off members of the nation to have at least the academic, if not the social, experience of a university education.[10]

As an Oxford man, Lowe regretted that Oxford could not reform itself but he conceded that the university did need government pressure to force it to take action.[11] Consequently, apart from his evidence to the Commission on Oxford University he also pressed upon Gladstone privately his ideas about reform. On the question of university government he advocated an elected Hebdomadal Council to head the university, and opposed the

[7] Patchett Martin, I, p. 24. [8] *Parliamentary Debates*, CXXXIV, col. 904.

[9] *Report of Royal Commission on Oxford*, 1852, Evidence, p. 13.

[10] *Parliamentary Debates*, CLXXXVII, cols. 1633–4.

[11] Gladstone Papers, B.M. Add. Mss. 44301, fol. 2, Lowe to Gladstone, 21 January 1854.

leaving of any authority to Convocation, which at that time consisted of every MA who had his name on college books. Such an assembly was in Lowe's opinion 'the most unsatisfactory tribunal possible . . . with half the gentry and clergy in England liable to the grossest delusions and to be put in motion by a few tutors of the large colleges'.[12] Lowe preferred a Convocation to consist of resident MA's who, following the pattern of municipal corporations, would elect the smaller executive body of the Hebdomadal Council, in which members would retire on rotation for election every three years. Congregation, that is the existing body of resident MA's, would in this way become superfluous.[13]

The University Act of 1854 only partially satisfied Lowe. The old Hebdomadal Board of heads of houses was replaced by an elected Hebdomadal Council but Congregation remained as a rather inefficient debating body and Convocation still had the ultimate legislative power.[14] The Act abolished local claims for fellowships and also partially for scholarships[15] and this was in tune with Lowe's ideas. The Act also allowed members of Convocation to open, under university licence, private halls of student residence.[16] This enabled Nonconformists to become members of a hall, and since no oaths could be exacted from students either at matriculation[17] or graduation it also enabled them to take the degree of BA, though they were still prevented from obtaining a college fellowship. Thus, whatever Lowe might think of the Act's constitutional provisions it did at least incorporate some of his ideas for opening up the universities more to the nation at large.

The changes which Lowe wanted at Oxford he would presumably have welcomed also at Cambridge and in fact the University of Cambridge Act of 1856 was very similar to the University of Oxford Act[18] of 1854. At Durham University Lowe had a more direct opportunity to press his views, when in 1862 he became one of the members of the Royal Commission for Durham University.[19] Ordinances were suggested to open the university without limit of age, to abolish religious tests, except for students taking a degree in theology, and to stop the requirements which

[12] Gladstone Papers, B.M. Add. Mss. 44301, fol. 3. [13] *Ibid.* fols. 5–6.
[14] 17 & 18 Vict. c. 81, ss. 5, 6, 8 and 16. [15] *Ibid.* s. 31. [16] *Ibid.* s. 25.
[17] *Ibid.* s. 24. [18] 19 & 20 Vict. c. 88, 29 July 1856.
[19] An Act for making Provision for the good Government and Extension of the University of Durham, 6 August 1861, 24 & 25 Vict. c. 82.

compelled Dissenters to attend services of the Church of England.[20] Further, all 'close' scholarships and fellowships were to be re-appropriated to found open scholarships which, as Lowe put it, 'may enable a diligent student to pursue his studies at very small expense to his parents'.[21] These ordinances were not immediately implemented by the university of Durham[22] but that they represented Lowe's views on the need for university reform is made clear by a leading article which he wrote for *The Times* regretting the action of the Dean and Chapter of the university of Durham, who successfully petitioned against the ordinances.[23]

The problem of providing university education in Ireland led Lowe to define his views further. He came out strongly against denominational institutions, for these served, in effect, to diminish rather than increase the opportunity for a university education available to the youth of that nation. In 1867 he spoke in defence of Peel's Queen's Colleges at Belfast, Cork and Galway as attempts to implement a 'noble idea of a united education for all classes in Ireland'[24] and objected to the proposal, which Gladstone had previously made, that students who had been to other colleges, as for example a Roman Catholic college, should be able to qualify for a Queen's University degree. However, by 1873, Lowe was prepared to support Gladstone's proposal to abolish Queen's University and set up a new national and non-sectarian university in Dublin which would teach and examine and to which sectarian and non-sectarian colleges might be affiliated.[25] In fact, the Bill proved abortive, arousing opposition from the supporters of Queen's University, which was to be abolished, from supporters of Trinity College, Dublin, which was to come under the umbrella of the proposed new university, and from the Catholics who found that their Catholic University, established in 1854 under John Henry Newman, was not to be endowed. On 26 July 1877 Lowe strongly opposed the suggestion that a Catholic college be endowed at Dublin; public money, he maintained, should not be

[20] *Report of the Commissioners appointed for the Purposes of the Durham University Act of 1861*, 1863, pp. 7–8.

[21] *The Times*, third leader, 4 April 1863.

[22] *Report of the Commissioners appointed for the Purposes of the Durham University Act of 1861*, 1863, pp. 13–14; also C. E. Whiting, *The University of Durham 1832–1932*, London 1932, pp. 109–17.

[23] *The Times*, third leader, 4 April 1863.

[24] *Parliamentary Debates*, CLXXXVI, cols. 1454–5.

[25] *Parliamentary Debates*, CCXIV, cols. 1481–92.

given for a strictly denominational institution.[26] By 1879, however, despite his preference for a system of mixed education in Ireland which would unite both Catholics and Protestants, Lowe had come to the conclusion that it was unwise to persist in trying to reconcile irreconcilables. 'If we cannot unite them, the best thing we can do is to give them separately the best education in our power', said Lowe.[27] Accordingly he supported Disraeli's Bill to leave the various colleges in Ireland untouched and to establish the Royal University of Ireland which would give degrees to all who passed its examinations regardless of where they had received their tuition. Nevertheless, in principle, Lowe's viewpoint was clear: university education should be non-sectarian. In 1873 Lowe had strongly supported a proposal which would have given the new university of Dublin power to suspend a professor or lecturer who wilfully gave offence to the religious convictions of any members of the university.[28] This opposition to sectarianism Lowe always maintained.

## HIGHER UNIVERSITY STANDARDS

By opening university scholarships to public competition, Lowe hoped not only to widen university entrance to the nation as a whole, but also to improve the standards of university learning. It was, Lowe contended, the decision of Balliol College, Oxford, to make its awards open which accounted for its success and pre-eminence as an academic institution,[29] and for further evidence on the beneficial effects of open competition, he pointed to the opening of examinations for writerships in the East India Company, which had been effected while he had been at the Board of Control in 1853.[30] The reward of merit through open competition and the consequent increase in the number of more able and more academically interested students would enable the universities to become places of better academic achievement and worthwhile standards. Lowe's concern for this went back to his own experience as a private tutor at Oxford and it remained consistently strong throughout his lifetime. For example, during his last year

[26] *Parliamentary Debates*, CCXXXV, cols. 1890–91.
[27] *Parliamentary Debates*, CCXLVI, col. 994.
[28] *Parliamentary Debates*, CCXIV, col. 1481.
[29] *Parliamentary Debates*, CXXXIV, col. 903.
[30] *Parliamentary Debates*, CXXXIV, col. 904.

in Australia in 1849, he was involved in the debates about the foundation of the university of Sydney and there he had objected to the proposal of the Constitution that when the number of graduates amounted to fifty, these should then elect their own Senate. This, in Lowe's view, would encourage 'a narrow and provincial standard of excellence'[31] quite unrelated to what might properly constitute university standards, for these could only be appreciated by those with a wider experience of universities. Back in England this concern for university standards became increasingly apparent. In particular, he repeatedly criticised the low standard of Oxford degrees.[32] He had had experience as an examiner for the pass degree at Oxford in 1837 and he had felt then that he had to resist the tendency of the university 'to keep down the standard of examinations in order to fill the colleges'.[33] James Bryce later told a story of Lowe as an examiner at Oxford for 'Responsions' – an examination often referred to as 'little-go'. According to the story a friend came in while the *viva voce* was in progress and asked Lowe how he was getting on. 'Excellently', said Lowe, 'five men plucked already and the sixth very shaky.'[34] Bryce told the story to suggest that Lowe had a character which delighted in failing people in examinations, but it is at least open to the alternative interpretation that Lowe was genuinely concerned about standards.

Lowe's suggestion for improving the quality of university education was to make examinations more effective. Like many of his contemporaries, Lowe placed great trust in the value of examinations. In the first place, he thought that the universities should insist upon stricter admission examinations so that they should no longer continue to be places where 'men of eminent learning were engaged in imparting knowledge which ought to have been given in elementary schools'.[35] Then, throughout the degree course, Lowe wanted the number of examinations increased, 'so that the student should never feel himself free from this stimulus'.[36] In this way he hoped to require more of students than the 'very moderate quantum' which then formed the standard of the university, and which was admitted on all sides to be utterly

[31] Patchett Martin, I, p. 398.
[32] See for example, *Parliamentary Debates*, CCXXXIII, col. 1982.
[33] Patchett Martin, I, p. 29. [34] Bryce, p. 301, n. 2.
[35] *Parliamentary Debates*, CCXXXIII, col. 1982.
[36] *Report of Royal Commission on Oxford*, 1852, Evidence, p. 13.

inadequate.[37] Finally, Lowe wanted to make examinations more effective by making them more impartial, and in Lowe's view the best way to do this was to take examinations out of the hands of the teachers who had taught the students who were to be examined.[38]

This particular viewpoint of Lowe's rested upon a precise and legalistic definition as to the nature of a university. For Lowe, a university was primarily a 'body for the granting of degrees', and it was this characteristic rather than its teaching function which distinguished a university from a college.[39] Both college and university might teach but only a university could grant degrees: a charter to this effect from the Crown was, in the British Isles at any rate, the distinctive mark of a university.[40] Thus the university of London did not provide teaching, but it was by charter a university. The university of London granted moreover, in Lowe's view, a degree which, unlike those of Oxford and Cambridge, was a fair and impartial degree because it was awarded by a body of men who were not concerned with the teaching of students. In this way, Lowe claimed, London University was concerned to keep up standards and not just fill its colleges as at Oxford,[41] where the temptation was to adapt university examinations to the amount of instruction which the colleges saw fit to give their undergraduates.[42] Examining was for Lowe a judicial function 'requiring just as much care and impartiality and as much disinterestedness as the distribution of punishments'.[43] This led him to consider that perhaps the best way to achieve impartial examinations both at university and school level might be to put it into the hands of a body like the Civil Service Commission which would be responsible to Parliament.[44] However, in the absence of such a body, Lowe's advice in 1877 to Owens College, Manchester, which at that time was petitioning to have a Royal Charter, was to be content to be a teaching institution and to have its degrees awarded by the university of London.[45] This would at least ensure that the degrees conferred would have the same value and standing, whereas if Owens College conferred its own degrees then they would have no

[37] *Ibid.*

[38] R. Lowe, 'Shall we create a New University?', *Fortnightly Review*, XXI, N.S. No. CXXII (1 February 1877), 170.

[39] *Parliamentary Debates*, CCXIV, col. 1483.

[40] Lowe, 'Shall we create a New University?', p. 160.

[41] *Ibid.* p. 170.

[42] *Ibid.* p. 163.

[43] *Parliamentary Debates*, CCXIV, col. 1483.

[44] Patchett Martin, I, p. 30.

[45] Lowe, 'Shall we create a New University?', p. 171.

more value than those given by Oxford and Cambridge and these, Lowe perversely suggested, were of little worth.[46] Indeed, Lowe even suggested that it would be better for the cause of learning and culture if the power of examining for degrees was taken away from Oxford and Cambridge and given – he would not say to London University – but to some committee of independent learned persons, who were 'totally free from the influences which have so long made the teaching of the vast majority of the students of Oxford and Cambridge a shame and a reproach'.[47]

Lowe's trust in the value of a central degree-granting, examining university, to which teaching colleges would be affiliated, motivated his opposition not only to the power of the colleges at Oxford and Cambridge but also to the proliferation of universities elsewhere. Thus, in England, he opposed a charter for Owens College, Manchester, and in Ireland he supported the proposal of Gladstone in 1873 for a university of Dublin, as a single degree-granting university, with teaching colleges affiliated to it, such as Trinity College, Dublin, the Queen's Colleges at Belfast and Cork and the Catholic University in Dublin.[48] Lowe supported this scheme because it would give power to the university as the ultimate examining authority over the colleges which entered their students for the university's examinations. He pointed out that the universities of Oxford and Cambridge had been at their lowest ebb in the period between Archbishop Laud's reforms and the beginning of the nineteenth century when the colleges had dominated and given 'degrees away without examinations'[49] merely because students had eaten the requisite number of dinners in the college Hall. Since then the university element had revived and the colleges had been put under stricter rule so that Oxford had risen by 1873 to what Lowe called 'her present eminence and glory'.[50] Lowe was glad that no longer, either at the universities or the Inns of Court, could a man get his degree or his qualification without examination; no longer could 'a man eat his way to the Bar like a rat through cheese'.[51] Gladstone's scheme failed, but in 1879 it was in some measure implemented when Disraeli set up the Royal University of Ireland to perform a function very much

[46] *Ibid.* p. 171. [47] *Ibid.* p. 164.
[48] *Parliamentary Debates*, CCXIV, col. 1484.
[49] *Parliamentary Debates*, CCXIV, col. 1494.
[50] *Parliamentary Debates*, CCXIV, col. 1495. [51] *Ibid.*

like that of London University and give degrees to all who matriculated and passed its examinations, regardless of the place where they had been taught.[52]

It needs to be emphasised that Lowe was not against the spread of university education. He wanted university teaching institutions to multiply until the supply equalled the demand,[53] but he considered that it would be better for the upholding of standards if these institutions were not full universities in the legal sense of degree-granting bodies. The multiplication of universities in itself was not an evil but

> any university which allows its own teachers actually or virtually to examine their own pupils is in that respect an evil, in as much as it palms off upon the public a biassed for an unbiassed tribunal. In a State that really gave attention to the subject such a practice would not be allowed at least in the distribution of degrees given by the Crown.[54]

Lowe resisted the plea that self-government and independence were necessary conditions for university work. 'We know', he wrote, 'what the self-government of Oxford and Cambridge means',[55] and so in the context of the universities of his day, Lowe was very much in favour of some state interference in the universities. Here, as in other matters, Lowe was prepared to admit that a completely *laissez-faire* philosophy was an inadequate means for securing the good society. In this particular case, and in order to achieve what Lowe considered to be acceptable standards of university education, some governmental supervision seemed necessary.

It is noticeable that Lowe's views on the universities were similar to those he held about secondary schools.[56] He was prepared for colleges offering university teaching to multiply under private endowment and in open competition for students' fees. If they then entered their students for the examinations of some independent body, their relative merits as university teaching institutions would be made clear by the results their students obtained. This was in Lowe's view the most efficient way of securing good standards of university education. Thus he opposed the charter for Owens College, since it would make teachers the

[52] T. W. Moody, J. C. Beckett, *Queen's Belfast 1845–1949: The History of a University*, London 1959, I, pp. 286–7.

[53] Lowe, 'Shall we create a New University?', p. 166.

[54] *Ibid.*

[55] *Ibid.* p. 165.

[56] S.I.C. IV, *Minutes of Evidence 1867–8*, pp. 635–6.

judge of their own work,[57] and Lowe considered that this was how a dilution in standards would come to pass. Lowe summarised his position as follows:

Instead of petitions to Government where the object is more or less adroitly veiled, but the real meaning of which is 'give us, as Queen Elizabeth used to say, the right to tar our own sheep', we should have petitions to Government to appoint some-body in whom the public at large might have confidence, to examine their students and to certify the quality and quantity of the teaching they had received. When this is the state of education, we shall have no reason to object to any number of colleges or universities.[58]

Lowe was in fact suggesting a national council for academic awards in which men drawn from the universities would combine to examine and award degrees. It is unlikely that it would ever have been possible to deny university teachers some part in this process, but Lowe's main point was that the award of degrees should be administered by an independent board consisting of university men and public servants combining in a national council.

Lowe's views were not followed in the foundation of universities which occurred in England in the late nineteenth and early twentieth centuries. The group of universities founded then and which may best be collectively described as the 'modern universities',[59] as opposed to the ancient universities of Oxford and Cambridge, did however, serve an apprenticeship under the tutelage of the London external degree system before being granted full self-governing and independent degree-granting charters. Owens College became the first constituent college of the Victoria University to which the college at Liverpool was admitted in 1884, and the Yorkshire College at Leeds in 1887. This federal university began to break up in 1901 and Manchester became an independent university in 1903, Liverpool in the same year and Leeds in 1904. Other university colleges, as for example, Reading, Nottingham and Leicester, continued to take university of London examinations until they received their own charters in 1926, 1948 and 1957 respectively. The universities founded after the Second World

[57] Lowe, 'Shall we create a New University?', p. 166. [58] *Ibid.* p. 166.
[59] A. W. Chapman called his history of Sheffield University *The Story of a Modern University*, Oxford Univ. Press 1955.

War, beginning with the University College of North Staffordshire at Keele in 1950, might well be called 'new' universities to distinguish them from the 'modern' universities, for certainly they have had different origins, having been granted charters from the start, with powers to grant their own degrees under the sponsorship of older universities. Keele, for example, began under the sponsorship of Oxford, Manchester and Birmingham. However, though Lowe's particular suggestions in this respect have never been adopted, the principle behind them remains as relevant for consideration now as then. Lowe was anxious to improve standards of university education and sceptical about the value of proliferating independent degree-awarding institutions. He was afraid that a process of inflation in the award of degrees might lead to academic devaluation.

## IMPROVED UNIVERSITY TEACHING

Concurrent with his concern for high academic standards at the universities, Lowe was also critical of the prevailing standards of university teaching. His criticism in this direction was primarily related to his experience and knowledge of Oxford University. Lowe had entered University College, Oxford, in 1829 and after taking his degree in 1833 with a first class in classics and a second in mathematics he went on to become a private tutor there for seven years between 1833 and 1840. His experience, combined with later reflection, caused him to be critical of the university as a whole. In his autobiographical memoir he wrote that at Oxford students were governed academically and socially by what he could only describe as a 'clerical gerontocracy'.[60] However, it was the college tutorial system which provoked his greatest criticism. Lowe considered that the root of this particular evil was the absence of incentive for college tutors to exert themselves.[61] Secure in the possession of their college emoluments, they waited for a college ecclesiastical living which would give them release from their enforced celibate life and establish them in some country rectory.[62] Lowe's argument here was in line with his opposition to educational endowments in general, whether at school or university, and it echoed the criticisms which Adam Smith had made of university

[60] Patchett Martin, I, p. 27.
[61] *Report of Royal Commission on Oxford*, 1852, Evidence, p. 12. [62] *Ibid.*

teachers.[63] Smith had pointed out that where a university teacher's salary was derived partly from pupils' fees there was then at least some incentive to teach well, and Lowe claimed that his experience as a private tutor at Oxford confirmed this.[64] Since the establishment of public examinations at Oxford in 1800 the private tutor, though he held no official position in the university, became increasingly indispensable for any student who wished to secure a place in the class lists, for the college tutors were often inefficient and the professorial lectures quite unrelated to the examinations set in the 'schools'.[65] Lowe wanted this system of private tuition to be recognised officially in the university, and the college monopoly broken, leaving a free choice of tutor to the individual student.[66]

Lowe was in fact suggesting that private enterprise was as acceptable in university education as it was in business as a means of securing efficiency and consumer – or in this case student – satisfaction. His viewpoint here was also identical with that he had advanced when suggesting some 'free trade' in secondary education. However, Lowe was not prepared to leave the young undergraduate entirely at the mercy of a free market. He wanted some system which would ensure that private tutors were fit persons to discharge the task of educating the young. This existing system allowed anyone to set up as a tutor. Lowe wanted a system of registration and recognition by which tutors would be accredited as morally, religiously and intellectually fit to assume their task. Their intellectual fitness could be ascertained by the unerring test of competition in examinations,[67] but Lowe did not suggest how their moral and religious fitness could be judged. Nevertheless, he was concerned lest the university should, by neglect, leave the task of forming the minds of undergraduates to men of whom they knew nothing save that their names had successfully appeared in previous university examination class lists.[68] The university should, in Lowe's view, accept the system of private tuition and control it at least in certain respects. A system of accrediting private tutors by registration was one method of control, and Lowe suggested in addition that the number of hours which a tutor

[63] Adam Smith, *Wealth of Nations*, p. 601.
[64] *Report of Royal Commission on Oxford*, 1852, Evidence, p. 12.
[65] Mark Pattison, *Memoirs*, Centaur Press, Sussex 1969, pp. 138–9.
[66] *Report of Royal Commission on Oxford*, 1852, Evidence, p. 13.
[67] *Ibid.* [68] *Ibid.*

taught ought to be limited. Lowe himself confessed to having taken ten different pupils in ten successive hours, term after term, and contended that this was 'neither fitting for the tutor, nor just to the pupil'.[69] Lowe obviously did not consider that university teaching was in any way similar to work upon a factory assembly line, where the process could go on hour after hour without any appreciable diminution of efficiency.

Lowe's plan for an efficient system of university tuition was in effect a system of payment by results, for only tutors who could show themselves capable of helping their pupils to secure good examination results would be likely to find themselves approached by new generations of pupils. It is notable that some ten years before Lowe established a payment by results system for elementary education he was pursuing the idea of pecuniary incentive and competition as an appropriate measure to apply to teaching. Moreover, he continued to press the idea and apply it more generally. Thus in discussing the future of Owens College, Manchester, he repeated his conviction that to ensure good teaching, especially at university level, some 'pecuniary incentive' was necessary.[70] Teaching was, he suggested, an honourable but also an irksome kind of labour, and an employment to which more than to any other the basic doctrine of political economy applied in the strictest sense, namely that all labour was an evil, of which every one wants to have as little as possible.[71] Consequently, teachers needed some incentive and because at the university the 'pecuniary interest' was absent, since students paid a block fee for tuition, 'and no exertion on the part of the teacher can increase and no remissness can diminish it',[72] Lowe suggested that some externally-administered examination system might be the best form of incentive.[73]

Lowe also felt strongly that the universities of Oxford and Cambridge would obtain better quality teachers if they opened their fellowships to merit following the example of the Indian and Civil Service. 'For fellowships to be effective', Lowe wrote from the India Office in 1854 to Gladstone, 'they must be made free from all restrictions as to residence, orders, celibacy or study.'[74]

[69] *Ibid.* [70] Lowe, 'Shall we create a New University?', p. 163.
[71] *Ibid.* [72] *Ibid.* [73] *Ibid.* p. 164.
[74] Gladstone Papers, B.M. Add. Mss. 44301, fol. 7, Lowe to Gladstone, April 1854.

Moreover, they should be limited appointments tenable for no more than ten years. In Lowe's view, this would provide a stimulus to fellows to exert themselves by writing and study and so qualify themselves for a chair or perhaps re-appointment as a fellow. Lowe would not accept that security of tenure produced good teachers; on the contrary, life fellowships were likely to have 'enervating' effects on their holders and become, rather than the reward for industry, 'it's most fatal antagonist'. His view implied the creation of more chairs to which worthy teaching fellows could move after some ten years, and Lowe accepted this as a necessary development. Such chairs should be open to laymen; and clerics, he asserted, would have no cause for complaint since after their ten years tenure of a fellowship they could easily obtain preferment in the Church.[75] In fact the opening up of fellowships to merit under the University of Oxford Act of 1854 was not as effective as Lowe hoped in producing better quality fellows. As Mark Pattison pointed out later, the abolition of old statutes and the opening to merit of fellowships was not enough. New regulations to cover the tenure of fellowships were also needed to ensure that fellows continued to study after their appointment. The old college statutes had usually insisted that fellows followed further courses of study, and though these courses were by now obsolete the intention of the original statutes was much to be admired. After 1854 old statutes were abolished but no new regulations framed, and consequently 'the ordinances of the Commission of 1854 converted the fellowships into sinecures. The Commissioners found an enormous abuse subsisting illegally, and they legalised it.'[76] It was the fear that unsupervised, the colleges might prove incapable of real reform, which led Lowe to suggest to Gladstone that some system of effective inspection should be built into the 1854 Act since colleges 'hampered as many of them are by oaths and corrupted by a long course of favouritism and nepotism' would prove unable to reform themselves without it.[77] Had it been possible to implement this there might then have been some insistence that new college regulations prescribed more closely the duties attaching to fellowships.

[75] *Ibid.* fol. 8.

[76] Mark Pattison, *Suggestions on Academical Reorganisation*, Edinburgh 1868, pp. 90–1.

[77] Gladstone Papers, B.M. Add. Mss. 44301, fol. 3, Lowe to Gladstone, 21 January 1854.

Apart from concerning himself with the improvement of university teaching, Lowe also pressed for increased productivity. He considered that university academics could teach nine months in the year instead of six[78] and his judgment had some justice in it for in England the university had not yet embraced research as one of its major functions and consequently the vacation periods were, on the face of it, unproductive months. As one of the Commissioners for Durham University, Lowe tried to implement his view by supporting the ordinance that Durham should have a two-year degree course, of two terms every year, the two terms covering nine months residence in each year. In this way eighteen months of university residence was still achieved, though over two years instead of the former practice of six months residence in each of three years.[79] Lowe's attitude in this was distinctly narrow, as Benjamin Jowett pointed out in evidence before Lowe during the investigation held by the Commission on Durham University. Jowett contended that education was essentially a slow process employing a 'certain growth of mind, as well as certain learning' and that by no device could you cram into two years what was really the work of three.[80] However, this scheme was, in Lowe's mind, devised mainly to cut down the cost of a university education to students[81] and was meant as an alternative to, rather than a replacement of, the three-year course. Nevertheless the scheme would also increase the university teachers' productivity. Lowe was convinced that university academics could do more work. On 30 April 1877 he supported a proposal in the Universities of Oxford and Cambridge Bill which would give power to the Commissioners to provide instruction during vacations. Lowe contended that 'it was a monstrous abuse that the Universities should teach only half the year as the other half was wasted in vacations'[82] though he admitted that some teaching did go on in the vacations and reflected that he himself had done this during his own period as a university teacher.

Lowe expressed views about one other aspect of university teaching, namely the place and function of the professoriate. In his evidence to the Royal Commission on Oxford University in 1852

[78] *The Times*, third leader, 4 April 1863. [79] *Ibid.*

[80] *Report of the Commissioners appointed for the Purposes of the Durham University Act of 1861*, 1863, p. 79, Q. 1898. [81] *Ibid.*

[82] *Parliamentary Debates*, CCXXXIV, col. 124.

he suggested that the university must have professorial appointments and indeed increase their number so that those who had distinguished themselves as teachers in the university could have their 'natural and appropriate reward', but his experience of it 'as a means of university education', that is to say, as a means of teaching, did not lead him to have great faith in it in that respect.[83] Later in a speech on the Universities of Oxford and Cambridge Bill, 26 April 1877, he pointed out that most of the teaching at those universities was done by college tutors, and consequently he would rather that college money be employed to establish fellowships so that the meritorious in examinations and teaching could succeed and have some reward, than that it should be handed over to the 'University' to establish chairs.[84] Lowe questioned the value of professors who had no teaching responsibilities in a university, as was so often then the case at Oxford and Cambridge. He was not against a learned professoriate. Indeed, he had himself competed – though unsuccessfully – for election to the Chair of Greek at Glasgow University in 1838, and as a Commissioner for Durham University he had been instrumental in suggesting the establishment of three new professorial chairs in chemistry, geology and mining.[85] Lowe's main point about the professoriate was a hope that it would contribute to the teaching of a university as well as serve that other function of encouraging and forwarding the pursuit of knowledge for its own sake. However, Lowe by no means underrated the benefits of this latter function, which he thought essential particularly for those who 'after having passed their examinations, are commencing the task, which every intellectual person must achieve for himself of self-education'.[86]

## WIDENING THE UNIVERSITY CURRICULUM

Lowe's view of the nature of university studies was wider than that of most of his contemporaries. Like Newman, Lowe held that 'universality'[87] was the ultimate criterion for the definition of university studies, and he told the House of Commons in a speech

[83] *Report of Royal Commission on Oxford*, 1852, Evidence, p. 13.
[84] *Parliamentary Debates*, CCXXXIII, cols. 1880–2. [85] Whiting, pp. 108–9.
[86] *Report of Royal Commission on Oxford*, 1852, Evidence, p. 13.
[87] Lowe, 'Shall we create a New University?', p. 169; cf. Newman, *On The Scope and Nature of University Education*, p. 9: 'A university . . . by its very nature professes to teach universal knowledge.'

on the Bill for the Abolition of Tests at Oxford University that the university should be 'co-extensive with the domain of human intellect itself'.[88]

Relating this general principle to the university curriculum, Lowe wanted the universities to continue the classical and mathematical studies which had for so long formed their staple diet and he also hoped that the door should, as it were, be kept constantly open for any future extensions of human knowledge to be included. In his evidence in 1852 to the Royal Commission on Oxford he expressed his hope 'that the Physical Sciences will be brought much more prominently forward in the scheme of University Education'.[89] The reasons he then advanced for this seemed on the face of it utilitarian. He wrote:

I have seen in Australia Oxford men placed in positions in which they had reason bitterly to regret that their costly education, while making them intimately acquainted with remote events and distant nations, had left them in utter ignorance of the laws of Nature and placed them under immense disadvantages in that struggle with her which they had to maintain.[90]

Yet apart from the utilitarian attractions of scientific studies Lowe was genuinely excited by the new realms of knowledge which recent scientific discoveries had opened up, and he wanted the nation's youth to have the opportunity to explore and delight in them. Benjamin Jowett testified to Lowe's fascination and concern for science in a memoir which he wrote on Lowe's death:

He [Lowe] hardly knew anything of it [natural science] but it seemed to him to have the promise of the future. It was the only knowledge in the world which was both certain and also progressive. Of Charles Darwin he spoke in a strain of respect which he would not have employed towards any other living person. Though a scholar and a man of various learning, he felt that from this greater world of Science he had been unfortunately shut out.[91]

What Lowe had missed he hoped future generations of university students would have the opportunity to study and, apart from exhortation to this effect, Lowe tried to practise what he preached. Thus, he used his position as Commissioner of Durham University

[88] *Parliamentary Debates*, CLXXXII, cols. 697–8.
[89] *Report of Royal Commission on Oxford*, 1852, Evidence, p. 13.
[90] *Ibid.* [91] Patchett Martin, II, p. 497.

to press for the establishment of a new school of physical science there and so widen the horizons of a university which had been little more than a school for clergy. He also supported the scheme which would divide scholarships at the university of Durham among the three faculties of arts, theology and science in proportion to the number of students in each, and not confine them to the study of Latin and Greek as had been the practice hitherto.[92] However, in pressing the claims of science, Lowe did not want the universities to neglect studies in the humanities. He wanted the university curriculum to be wide and if, on the one hand, he urged Oxford to establish studies in physical science, on the other, he advocated that it should include such an obviously 'useless' subject as Sanskrit among the subjects for the award of an honours degree.[93]

Lowe was also in agreement with Newman's general philosophy of a university education when he made it clear that the knowledge a university purveyed should not only be wide but also have a general rather than a particular significance and aim to enlarge the mind and understanding rather than teach a trade. As one of the Commissioners for Durham University he asserted in the course of examining the Rev. H. Jenkins, Professor of Divinity, that a university should embrace the whole course of knowledge and that in this it was distinguished from a 'college' by which he meant 'a place more devoted to instruction . . . and more narrow in its scope than a university'.[94] 'No university, really worthy of the name', Lowe wrote, 'will stoop to make its teaching a school for the learning of a particular trade, such as calico printing for instance, or put Pegasus in harness to draw the wheel of a cotton mill.'[95] Lowe hoped therefore that Owens College, Manchester, would

[92] *The Times*, third leader, 4 April 1863.

[93] *Report of Royal Commission on Oxford*, 1852, Evidence, p. 13.

[94] *Report of the Commissioners appointed for the Purposes of the Durham University Act of 1861*, 1863, p. 34, Q. 835.

[95] Lowe, 'Shall we create a New University?', p. 169; cf. Newman, *On the Scope and Nature of University Education*, p. 92: 'Let me not be thought to deny the necessity, or to decry the benefit, of such attention to what is particular and practical in the useful or mechanical arts; life could not go on without them . . . I only say that knowledge, in proportion as it tends more and more to be particular, ceases to be knowledge . . . When I speak of knowledge, I mean something intellectual, something which grasps what it perceives through the senses; something which takes a view of things; which sees more than the senses convey; which reasons upon what it sees, and while it sees; which invests it with an idea.'

not become too subservient to the needs of its local industries and develop a curriculum that was too vocational. The trustees of Owens College, in a report in 1850, referred to the idea that a university should adapt itself to the 'wants of the community' and this principle became basic in the development of Manchester University,[96] where studies in economic history, the social sciences, education, law and commerce and modern languages were soon established. Other universities followed this lead and in addition founded faculties of technology.[97] Lowe was not opposed to such developments. Indeed at Durham he had supported the scheme to found chairs in chemistry, geology and mining, with the express intention that the university of Durham should become 'useful to the mining and manufacturing industry of the North'.[98] Lowe's views on the function of a university were wide enough to include a wide range of studies not traditionally associated with the universities, but ultimately he was very clear about what constituted genuine university study and he was opposed to any subject which was not, in Newman's sense, 'liberal', which did not enlarge the mind and establish general principles of understanding and which was tailored too narrowly to vocational needs.

## NURSERIES OF CIVIL SERVANTS

Lowe's concern that the universities should continue to offer a liberal education rested upon his conviction that a liberal education was ultimately the most useful of all. It fitted men for the most responsible posts in society. The universities were to be the nurseries of civil servants and educate the men who would eventually hold the leading posts in all the professions. If there was to be a meritocracy then the universities should provide it. The logical conclusion of this train of thought was that the highest posts in the public administration should be made open to the best university graduates and this implied Civil Service reform. Lowe had considered this for a long time and in 1868 when he became Chancellor of the Exchequer he was at last in a position to put his ideas into practice.

[96] H. B. Charlton, *Portrait of a University 1851–1951*, Manchester University Press, 1951, pp. 36–7.
[97] See list in M. Argles, *South Kensington to Robbins*, London 1964, p. 77.
[98] *The Times*, third leader, 4 April 1863.

Lowe's interest in Civil Service reform went back, as he told the House of Commons on 9 April 1869, to his 'share in founding the system of Indian competition in 1854'.[99] Lowe had been Secretary to the Board of Control under Sir Charles Wood when in 1853 the latter's India Bill had introduced open competition by examination into the Indian Civil Service. Lowe had supported it wholeheartedly[100] and at the same time he had been drawn into the campaign for open competition in the home Civil Service which accompanied the Report of Sir Stafford Northcote and Sir Charles Trevelyan. Their Report on the organisation of the Civil Service, published in February 1854,[101] recommended the introduction of a competitive literary examination at a level comparable to that of the best university education as a means of recruiting able administrators. There was pressure for reform on these lines from various quarters and notably from Benjamin Jowett, then Fellow of Balliol College, Oxford, who was supported in this by Lowe.[102] However, there was so much opposition from the heads of Civil Service departments that the Government abandoned its proposed bill for reform.[103] Instead it contented itself with the Order-in-Council of 21 May 1855, establishing a Civil Service Commission of three members to regulate Civil Service examinations and recruitment.[104]

The Order-in-Council of 1855 in no way established open competition, and for the next fifteen years the prospect of its eventual realisation receded. It was the function of the Commission to conduct examinations for Civil Service entrants and to issue certificates giving pension rights to new civil servants. However, the Commissioners did not insist upon a necessary connection between these two functions and over 70 per cent of the certificates issued by them between 1855 and 1868 were awarded without competition and 'open competition had been applied to only twenty-eight

[99] *Parliamentary Debates*, CXCV, col. 487.

[100] *Parliamentary Debates*, CXXVIII, cols. 638–41.

[101] *Report of the Committee of Inquiry into the Organisation of the Civil Service*, 23 November 1853, P.P. 1854, XXVII.

[102] Granville Papers, P.R.O. 30/29/66, Lowe to Granville, 28 December 1869; Granville to Lowe 29 December 1869; see also E. Abbot and L. Campbell, *The Life and Letters of Benjamin Jowett*, 2 vols. London 1897, I, pp. 408–9.

[103] *Parliamentary Debates*, CXXXII, cols. 1305–7. Gladstone informed the House of Commons of this on 5 May 1854.

[104] For a detailed account of this see Wright, *Treasury Control of the Civil Service*, pp. 58–63.

situations on twelve separate occasions by no more than six departments'.[105] Heads of Civil Service departments were not obliged to fill vacancies with candidates who had passed the examinations, and so long as they could obtain pension certificates from the Commissioners for those they appointed, there was no need for them to change from the time-honoured methods of recruitment by nominations, recommendations and interviews.

In 1868 there was no campaign from public opinion to introduce open competition in the Civil Service and Lowe raised the issue acting upon his own convictions. He then proceeded to pursue the matter with his own inimitable tenacity of purpose until he had achieved his ends. On 10 November 1869 Lowe wrote to Gladstone to press him into action:

> As I have so often tried in vain will you bring the question of the Civil Service before the Cabinet today. Something must be decided. We cannot keep matters in this discreditable state of abeyance. If the Cabinet will not entertain the idea of open competition might we not at any rate require a larger number of competitors for each vacancy, five or seven or ten?[106]

Twelve days later Lowe suggested to Gladstone that the Treasury – Lowe's own department – should take the lead in making all its appointments by open competition and that other heads of departments should be asked to do the same.[107] Gladstone agreed but insisted that each department should have the right to adopt or reject the principle of open competition, and this was the position eventually approved in the Cabinet on 7 December 1869. On the next day Lowe sent the various departments a Treasury Minute to this effect[108] and with the exception of the Home and Foreign Offices all departments agreed to implement open competition,[109] though in practice some departments, including the Education department, failed to honour their agreement. Lowe and R. R. W. Lingen, with whom Lowe had worked at the Education Department and whom he now brought to the Treasury as Permanent Secretary, proceeded to draft an Order-in-Council to make this

[105] *Ibid.* p. 75.
[106] Gladstone Papers, B.M. Add. Mss. 44301, fol. 104.
[107] *Ibid.* fol. 106.
[108] Treasury Papers, P.R.O. T1/6971A/7615, 8 December 1869.
[109] Wright, pp. 81–2.

effective, and it was approved by the Cabinet on 25 May 1870 and issued on 4 June.[110]

The most important part of Lowe's work in this connection was, however, yet to come. By the Order-in-Council the work of the Civil Service Commission became subject to Treasury approval and in the years following 1870 Lowe and Lingen used all the power at their command to force government departments to implement the Order as fully and as quickly as possible. Their main weapon was their ability to refuse superannuation entitlement unless posts were filled by open competition and they exploited this to the full. By September 1873 only Granville at the Foreign Office, Bruce at the Home Office, and ironically Sandford at the Education Department, resisted Lowe. On several occasions Lowe tried to persuade Granville to change his attitude[111] but the latter, though sympathetic, pleaded that too many permanent officials in the Foreign Office were opposed to it. Lowe also pressed Gladstone to convert Granville though without effect,[112] and the Foreign Office held out against open competition until the end of the First World War. Lowe's own move to the Home Office in September 1873 ended the resistance in that department but appointments were still made by nomination in the Education Department as late as 1911.

Lowe's influence upon Civil Service recruitment was not limited to a mere insistence upon open competition. He also influenced in a most significant way the regulations of the Civil Service Commission under which departments might set open competitive examinations.[113] There were three schemes for such examinations under regulations I, II and III. Regulation I was designed to select those who would be employed in the most responsible and intellectual work of the Civil Service. Regulation II was for those who would be employed on more mechanical routine work and regulation III for writers.

Before candidates could take the examinations under regulations

[110] There is a copy of the Order-in-Council in the Granville Papers, P.R.O. 30/29/66.

[111] Granville Papers, P.R.O. 30/29/66, Lowe to Granville, 5 December 1870; Lowe to Granville, 8 May 1871.

[112] *Ibid.* Lowe to Gladstone, 5 December 1870.

[113] A copy of these Regulations may be found in the Granville Papers, P.R.O. 30/29/66; also in *P.P.* 1871, XVII, *Civil Service Commissioners 16th Report*, appendix 1, pp. 7–18.

I and II they had to take a preliminary test and satisfy the Civil Service Commissioners of their competence in handwriting, orthography and simple arithmetic. Then under regulation I candidates had to take some or all of the subjects listed in the following table, being placed in an order of merit according to the total of marks achieved.

*Examination subjects for open competitions under regulation I. 1870*

| | *Marks* |
|---|---|
| English Composition, including precis | 500 |
| History of England, including that of the Laws and Constitution | 500 |
| English Language and Literature | 500 |
| Language, Literature and History of Greece | 750 |
| ,, ,, ,, of Rome | 750 |
| ,, ,, ,, of France | 375 |
| ,, ,, ,, of Germany | 375 |
| ,, ,, ,, of Italy | 375 |
| Mathematics (pure and mixed) | 1,250 |
| Natural Science: that is (i) Chemistry including Heat | 1,000 |
| (ii) Electricity and Magnetism | |
| (iii) Geology and Mineralogy | |
| (iv) Zoology | |
| (v) Botany | |
| [The total of 1,000 marks could be obtained by proficiency in any two or more of the five branches.] | |
| Moral Sciences: that is, Logic, Mental and Moral Philosophy | 500 |
| Jurisprudence | 375 |
| Political Economy | 375 |
| Additional Subjects | 500 |

Under Regulation II candidates had to offer some or all of the following subjects.

*Examination subjects for open competitions under regulation II. 1870.*

| | *Marks* |
|---|---|
| Handwriting | 400 |
| Orthography | 400 |
| Arithmetic | 400 |
| Copying MS (to test accuracy) | 200 |
| Indexing and docketing | 200 |
| Digesting returns into Summaries | 200 |
| English Composition | 200 |
| Geography | 200 |

| | |
|---|---|
| English History | 200 |
| Book-Keeping | 200 |

Regulation III was for writers, and examinations for such posts were supplied to departments by the Civil Service Commissioners as need arose.

The significant point about these tables is the great gulf that existed between the syllabus under regulation I and that under regulation II. The subjects listed under regulation I approximated to the subjects which the universities offered in their degree courses, and since promotion to the highest posts in the Civil Service was open only to those who had competed successfully under regulation I, the overall effect was to ensure that only men with a public school and university education could obtain the most responsible positions. In this way Lowe successfully achieved what he had intended, namely the establishment of a university-educated meritocracy of public servants.

It has been pointed out that one effect of Lowe's work was to make the Civil Service 'open but socially and educationally stratified'.[114] This is true, but it is difficult to see what alternative Lowe had. Given that he wanted to ensure that the State was administered by those who had received the best education which society then offered, it was natural that he should look to the universities. It is obviously true that in the absence of a national system of secondary schools and with no educational ladder which the children of the poor might ascend, there were many of potential merit in the nation whom the Civil Service would never consider, but Lowe was in no position to change this. What he was in a position to do, he did. He opened up the Civil Service to competitive recruitment and by insisting upon the written examination as the main factor in selection, he created an avenue of educational and social mobility which, in later generations, children of the poor could and did follow.[115]

Lowe also had another consideration in mind when framing his policy. In his opinion candidates for the highest administrative posts should possess not only high educational achievements but also the relevant social and personal qualities. It was not enough

[114] Wright, p. 109.

[115] Between 1948 and 1956 40% of the entrants to the Administrative Class were from L.E.A. schools: *Recruitment to the Administrative Class*, Cmd. 232, July 1957, p. 25.

for a top civil servant to be intelligent and intellectually competent; he must also possess the cultural background and social grace which would enable him to act for the administration in both private and public negotiations. In Lowe's view candidates who had all these qualities were more likely to have been educated in the public schools and universities then elsewhere. Consequently, supplementary clerks admitted under regulation II had no opportunity for promotion to the higher posts since their education was not likely to have equipped them with the necessary qualities. Lowe expressed his views on this to the Select Committee on Civil Services Expenditure in 1873.

The education of public schools and colleges and such things, which gives a sort of freemasonry among men which is not very easy to describe but which everybody feels: I think that is extremely desirable: there are a number of persons in those offices who are brought into contact with the upper classes of this country and they should be of that class in order that they may hold their own on behalf of the Government, and not be overcrowded by other people . . . Supplementary Clerks might be found wanting in the very things to which I attach great value in the upper class; perhaps he might not pronounce his 'h's' or commit some similar solecism, which might be a most serious damage to a department in case of negotiation.[116]

Two points may be made about Lowe's views on this question. Firstly, they were the result of a realistic appraisal of the situation. Government did work in the way Lowe suggested. Secondly, and undeniably, Lowe's views were elitist, but given his premiss that government should be meritocratic, his policy was understandable. His belief in the value of a meritocracy was the key to his policy on the Civil Service. His claim was that regulation I, 'by attracting the elite of the Universities would supply the best ability in the country' and he consequently could not understand the attitude of recalcitrants like Lord Clarendon and Lord Granville at the Foreign Office, who refused competition and threw upon it 'the stigma of being unfit for the most important situations in the Civil Service'.[117]

Another effect of Lowe's reforms was to maintain the tradition

[116] Quoted in Wright, p. 353. (*Report from the Select Committee on Civil Services Expenditure*, 1873, Qs. 4544, 4548.)

[117] Granville Papers, P.R.O. 30/29/66, letter of Lowe, 5 December 1870. Addressee not indicated, but possibly Lingen.

in the Civil Service that a good 'liberal' education equipped men to rule better than a specialist education. Lowe valued a university education because, he would have contended, it produced men with trained minds which could then be applied to the solution of any particular problems which might arise. For this reason he wanted university men in the Civil Service and, as a corollary to this, he insisted that Civil Service entrance examinations should test a general rather than a specific education[118] and should guarantee that candidates had what he called 'the education of a gentleman'.[119] Lowe's policy established rule by highly educated amateurs rather than professional specialists, and this has become increasingly open to criticism as the problems which rulers face have become more technical in context. Nevertheless, Lowe's policy brought a considerable improvement on the previous situation when the administration had been in the hands of mere amateurs. He at least ensured that in the future the top civil servants would be intelligent and highly educated.[120]

Finally, Lowe's Civil Service reforms had a buoyant effect on the universities. It gave a new stimulus to their process of teaching and learning and it provided a new field of employment for their graduates. In so doing it restored to them their medieval function of serving society by supplying it with administrative and public servants.

In conclusion, Lowe's approach to university questions implied considerable changes in the social and intellectual functions of the universities of his day. In retrospect he can be seen to be pushing the universities into the twentieth century. There is an air of modernity about many of Lowe's views. The university-educated meritocracy which he advocated has been partially achieved and two-year degree courses, shorter vacations, more student teaching, a national council for the award of degrees, more courses in applied studies and the public accountability of universities are all current issues. Lowe's views provide no ready answers to contemporary questions about the structure and purposes of higher education. They do, however, provide provocative points for

[118] *Ibid.*

[119] Granville Papers, P.R.O. 30/29/66, Lowe to Granville, 29 September 1871.

[120] For an account of the subsequent development of Lowe's policy see R. K. Kelsall, 'Intellectual merit and higher Civil Service recruitment: the rise and fall of an idea', in *History, Sociology and Education*, published by History of Education Society, 1971, pp. 23–32.

comparison. They also suggest that solutions will most happily be found if universities can be made to respond to current needs. Lowe's attitude towards the universities would suggest that above all else, he was concerned that they did not become what Adam Smith called 'the sanctuaries in which exploded systems and obsolete prejudices found shelter and protection'.[121]

[121] Adam Smith, p. 610.

# 10

# LOWE AND THE SCIENCE AND ART DEPARTMENT

In his speeches on *Middle Class and Primary Education* Lowe had argued for more science in the school curriculum. He never publicly advocated technical or art education but, by virtue of his office during two periods in his career, he was in a position to develop both scientific and art instruction. When Lowe became Vice-President of the Committee of Council on Education in 1859 he had overall responsibility for the Department of Science and Art, and again as Chancellor of the Exchequer from 1868 to 1873 he had power to influence the Department's development. In both of these periods, however, certain constraints obliged Lowe to temper the enthusiasm for science which had emerged in his speeches.

Some of these constraints were matters of principle; others were practical. First, his *laissez-faire* principle that secondary education should be provided privately and administered independently, prevented him from forcing science into the secondary school curriculum. He could only state the case for science; he was powerless to enforce it. Similarly, his view that the expenditure of the Department of Science and Art ought to be for the 'poor' only and not for the middle classes, precluded him from giving public grants to private schools.[1] Thirdly, the hierarchy of educational objectives which he held put foremost the teaching of the three Rs and, consequently, he was reluctant to foster science teaching in elementary schools. Finally, as always with Lowe, his concern for public economy was a constant brake upon any desire to expand science or art education.

Within the limitations imposed by these constraints Lowe's policy towards the Science and Art Department varied from periods of fulsome support to periods when he was determined to cramp its activities all he could. When he first became concerned with its affairs in 1859, the Department had three main functions:

[1] Cole Diaries, 4 November 1859.

the administration of parliamentary grants in aid of art education, the administration of grants for science education and the development of a growing complex of museum buildings at South Kensington. Lowe supported all sides of the Department's work, but each one felt the force, at some time, of Lowe's restraining hand. Ultimately Lowe's concern for public economy emerged as a limitation on all the Department's functions. Consequently, it is not surprising that Lowe was more sympathetic to the Department as Vice-President of the Committee of Council than ever he was as Chancellor of the Exchequer, when his priority was the saving of public money.

Lowe's support for the museum side of the Department's activities illustrates this point particularly well. In the period from 1859 to 1864 he was a notable supporter of its expansion, and tried all he could to gain extra finance for additional buildings and for the expansion of museum collections. Ten years later, when as Chancellor of the Exchequer he was trying to reduce public expenditure, his former enthusiasm for the museum evaporated and he was obstructive in the extreme. As Henry Cole, the Museum Director, wrote in his diary on 25 June 1869, 'Lowe of '69 abused Lowe of '60'. It is a terse and accurate summary of Lowe's ambivalent attitude to the South Kensington Museum's affairs.

In 1859 the museum at South Kensington had been in existence for two years, though its origins had been much earlier. In 1835 the Select Committee on Arts and Manufacturers had suggested that one way of extending a knowledge of the arts and of the principles of design among the manufacturing population was the opening of public galleries. In 1851 the Great Exhibition provided an opportunity to begin this. The Exhibition made a profit of £186,000, and at the direction of Prince Albert, this was used to purchase the South Kensington site for the erection of museums and other educational buildings. In 1852 the Government established the Department of Practical Art under the Board of Trade to administer existing art schools and to establish museums as a means of public education in the field of art and design. The Treasury provided £5,000 for the purchase from the Exhibition of various objects of applied art which would serve as examples of good design and craftsmanship, and the Museum of Manufacturers was opened in Marlborough House on 6 September 1852 to house this initial collection. With new purchases and loans from private collections it soon expanded to include a wide range of exhibits arranged by material – textiles, metalwork, ceramics and woodwork. As the museum widened its range, so it changed its name, first to the 'Art Museum' and then to the 'Museum of Ornamental Art'. Similarly, its overseer, the Department of Practical Art, had changed its name in 1853 to 'Science and Art' and had also left the Board of Trade and come under the jurisdiction of the Committee of the Privy Council on Education. In 1857 the museum was moved to South Kensington where, opened by Queen Victoria, it became the nucleus of what was later called in 1899 The Victoria and Albert Museum. It became known affectionately as the 'Brompton Boilers' on account of its iron structure, and though this particular building was moved in 1872 to Bethnal Green, other buildings were added on the site from 1862 onwards to form a permanent base for the collections.

One man in particular had seen the museum through this long period of gestation. Henry Cole had been, together with Prince Albert, one of those chiefly responsible for both the Great Exhibition and the setting up of the museum. In 1852 he was appointed General Superintendent of the Department of Practical Art, and in 1853 became Joint Secretary with Lyon Playfair when the Department was enlarged to include science. From 1858 to 1866 he was sole Secretary of the Department and from 1866 until his retirement in 1873, he held the post of General Superintendent and Museum Director. When Lowe became Vice-President in 1859 Henry Cole was the man whom he had to deal with at the Department of Science and Art. Initially they got on very well together.

Lowe immediately impressed Cole as 'very intelligent indeed',[2] and within a month of taking office Lowe had taken his wife on a conducted tour of the Sheepshanks Collection of drawings and the other collections.[3] From the beginning Lowe supported the purchase of works of art, considering it, for example, in December 1859, a good investment to spend £100,000 on such objects. In the following year, Lowe made Cole restore £500 to the Department's estimates for the purchase of art examples, claiming that he would 'not reduce the Estimates because the Treasury reduced Taxation'.[4]

[2] Cole Diaries, 23 June 1859. [3] *Ibid.* 30 July 1859.
[4] *Ibid.* 19 April 1860.

As the International Exhibition of 1862 approached, Lowe wrote to Cole asking him to use up half of the unexpended Department balances, to the extent of £10,000, in buying up select articles for the museum.[5] Lowe saw himself at this time on the side of the angels of culture and although his chief, Lord Granville, would not support him in this, he wanted to ask for all that was needed for art purchases in the estimates, and not 'spare the Philistines'.[6]

Lowe also pressed for the appointment of a Select Committee of Inquiry into the South Kensington Museum and though the Treasury was reluctant,[7] Granville and Lowe secured one. It was appointed on 9 June 1860 with Lowe as its Chairman. It reported that the museum, together with similar institutions, should continue to receive state support since it provided opportunities for labouring men and their families for 'intellectual improvement and recreation'.[8] It also recommended that additional space for art collections should be provided by glazing over the quadrangular courts formed by the existing building. Subsequently Lowe pressed the Treasury to implement this. On 3 August 1860 Lowe wrote to Cole:

I have been thinking that we ought to write an official letter to the Treasury setting forth that a Committee was moved for at the suggestion of the Chancellor of the Exchequer, setting forth the favourable report of the Committee in general and its urgent recommendations about the buildings (both unanimously agreed to) and requesting them to place a sum on the estimates to enable us to fulfil the wish of the Committee.[9]

A week later Lowe asked Cole to prepare an estimate for him of £17,000 for the courts and £5,000 for the schools and residences; 'let me have it on Monday in order that I may try to get Gladstone's assent on Monday night in the House'.[10] The next day a triumphant Lowe reported that 'Gladstone gives me the £22,000.'

The building eventually began in 1862[11] and continued until 1868 when the quadrangle was finally completed. By this time Lowe had left the Committee of Council, but his support in the initial stages had been crucial.

[5] Cole Correspondence, Box 5, Lowe to Cole, 14 June 1861.
[6] Cole Diaries, 17 December 1861. [7] *Ibid.* 11 August 1859.
[8] *Report of Select Committee on South Kensington Museums*, 1860, pp. 533–4.
[9] Cole Correspondence, Box 5, Lowe to Cole, 3 August 1860.
[10] *Ibid.* Box 5, Lowe to Cole, 12 August 1860.
[11] *P.P.* 1862, XXXI, *9th Report of Department of Science and Art*, p. xii.

Lowe also supported Cole in his quest for the Soulages Collection. This was a collection of mainly Italian, but also some French, art in pottery (majolica), wood carving, bronzes and pictures which belonged to M. Soulage, a Toulouse lawyer. In October 1855 Cole had gone to Toulouse to inspect it and subsequently he negotiated its purchase at £11,000, and the collection arrived in England on 30 October 1856. It was put on exhibition at Marlborough House, but Palmerston, who was conducted round the exhibits by Cole, was not impressed. As Cole reported: 'once or twice looking at the *majolica* he said to me, "What is the use of such rubbish to our manufacturers?"'[12] According to the trust deed, if the State did not purchase the collection it was to be sold by the trustees, and in this way the Manchester Art Treasures Exhibition acquired it. When the exhibition terminated the Derby Government was in office and the Marquis of Salisbury, then Lord President, was more anxious than Palmerston had been to secure the collection. It was agreed that the Manchester Art Treasures executive should lend the collection to the Department of Science and Art on condition of receiving a rental, and also of giving the Department power to purchase objects from the collection – as much as it could afford from its annual budgets – until the whole was purchased. The purchases began at once to the extent of about £2,000 a year. However, in 1859[13] questions were raised in the House about the purchases and the Treasury criticised the Department for acting without official sanction and for incurring debt. Lowe, who was now Vice-President, sprang to the Department's defence. He drafted a letter showing that the transaction was in order[14] and he also had the satisfaction of hearing Gladstone, the Chancellor of the Exchequer, defend the purchase of the Soulages Collection in the House of Commons.[15] Privately, however, Lowe claimed that Gladstone's passion for majolica was more cautionary than aesthetic. He told Cole that Gladstone kept a piece of majolica on his table 'to warn him against public extravagance'.[16]

From 1859 to 1864 then, when Lowe had direct rule of the Department of Science and Art's affairs, he had pressed consistently

[12] Sir H. Cole, *Fifty Years of Public Work of Sir Henry Cole KCB*, London 1884, p. 292. [13] *Parliamentary Debates*, CLV, col. 370, 25 July 1859.

[14] Cole, p. 293; also Cole Correspondence, Box 5, Lowe to Cole, 6 December 1860. [15] *Parliamentary Debates*, CLV, col. 370, 25 July 1859.

[16] Cole Diaries, 31 October 1859.

for the expansion of its museum side. In 1868 however, when he became Chancellor of the Exchequer, his tune changed. His concern now was to cut public expenditure in every quarter and the Department was no exception.

Early in January 1869 Lowe asked Cole to keep his estimates down.[17] He also made it clear that his attitude towards museum purchases was now strictly utilitarian; he refused to buy armour 'because it had no use at the present day'.[18] At the time Cole was anxious to complete some new science school buildings and on 12 March 1869 Cole wrote to Lowe asking for an additional grant of £32,500 and adding that 'you [Lowe] may not care for public applause, but I think you would get it if you will be liberal to Science this year'.[19] Lowe apparently wanted neither to receive applause nor to be generous. He wrote back asking Cole to call upon him and explain why the building had begun without official approval.[20] From this moment relations between Lowe and Cole deteriorated rapidly, as did Lowe's relations with de Grey and Forster, President and Vice-President of the Committee of Council respectively.

The plan for new science buildings was allowed to go forward but Lowe was consistently obstructive. In April 1869 he cut the estimates without consulting the Department and though Forster fumed, Lowe had his way.[21] As the Department later reported: 'The usual vote of £32,500 having been reduced to £24,000 the progress of the work has been arrested proportionately.'[22] Lowe continued to hector the Department, demanding plans and asking for a model of the proposed buildings to be exhibited in the House of Commons. Cole duly complied, though he agreed privately with Forster that 'Lowe would make economy stink in the nostrils.'[23] Lowe struck his final blow on the issue when he put the arrangements for the science buildings under the supervision of the Office of Works. Cole recorded in his diary that this enraged both Forster and de Grey, who were 'ready for a fight',[24] but in fact Lowe had his way unchallenged.

Meanwhile other building went on unhindered, and early in 1873 the South East Courts, which had been begun in 1867, were

[17] Cole Diaries, 4 January 1869. [18] Cole Diaries, 11 January 1869.
[19] Cole Correspondence, Box 5, Cole to Lowe, 12 March 1869.
[20] *Ibid.* Lowe to Cole, 14 March 1869. [21] Cole Diaries, 13 April 1869.
[22] *P.P.* 1870, XXVI, *17th Report of Department of Science and Art*, appendix D, p. 317. [23] Cole Diaries, 26 June 1869. [24] *Ibid.* 4 March 1870.

opened to the public. The length of each court was 135 feet by 60 feet wide, and 'the paving of the corridors is executed in marble mosaic by female convict labour', the Department reported.[25]

The next round in the fight between Lowe and the Department was over the Bethnal Green Museum. In 1867 the 'Brompton Boilers' had been taken down and the plan was to re-erect them as a branch of the South Kensington Museum at Bethnal Green. From 1871 to 1872, Lowe tried to prevent this. At one stage he even offered the building to Sir A. Brady as a 'Technical University', claiming, it was reported, that he would not give a shilling to make it one of 'King Cole's hens and chickens'.[26] However, in the end, Lowe had to concede defeat. Even his attempt at the eleventh hour to refuse a grant of £5,000 for the state opening of the Bethnal Green Museum failed,[27] and the museum was opened on 24 June 1872.

By now relations between Cole and Lowe had degenerated from the friendship of 1859 into what Cole reported Lowe to have described as 'internecine war'.[28] The difficulties between the two were not merely over museum affairs. In June 1871 irregularities had been found in the books of a certain Mr Simkins, particularly with regard to receipts from the Office of Works. In December the Treasury attacked Cole for his failure to oversee the accounts and on 4 December Cole tendered his resignation to Lord Ripon,[29] though on the next day he retracted and requested that his resignation be held in abeyance.[30] Eventually the affair was smoothed over and Cole stayed, but he was becoming increasingly arrogant about his position and foolish in his antagonism of Lowe. On 8 April 1872 Ripon wrote to Cole warning him not to overspend on the estimates for Bethnal Green lest they were forced to close the museum shortly after it had been opened. As Ripon added: 'This would place us in a position with respect to the Chancellor of the Exchequer which neither Mr. Forster nor myself would like to occupy.'[31] Cole was, in fact, ready for retirement, but he was very worried that Lowe would use his position as Chancellor to deny him a good pension. Although Ripon reassured Cole that Lowe was friendly and would behave well in the matter of the

[25] *P.P.* 1874, XXI, *21st Report of Department of Science and Art*, p. ix.

[26] Cole Diaries, 31 January 1872.

[27] *Ibid.* 13 June 1872.

[28] *Ibid.* 15 April 1871.

[29] Earl de Grey became Marquess of Ripon in 1871.

[30] Cole Correspondence, Box 6, Ripon to Cole and Cole to Ripon, 5 December 1871.

[31] *Ibid.* Ripon to Cole, 8 April 1872.

pension,[32] Cole persisted in his animosity towards Lowe. He took delight in recording stories told against Lowe,[33] and even after his own retirement in May 1873 he took the opportunity to denounce Lowe in a speech at Spitalfield College of Art on 20 November 1873.

Lowe himself was transferred from the Chancellorship of the Exchequer to the Home Office in August 1873 and so ended a partnership which had begun with such willing co-operation in 1859 and which now ended in complete distrust. The museum side of the Science and Art Department had slowly grown over the period in terms of both collections and buildings, but Lowe's part in this development was at best equivocal. From a policy of whole-hearted support he had turned to one of obstruction, and though his motive was clear – he wanted to reduce public expenditure – officious methods served to obscure any good that he intended. As a result, and as Cole rightly observed, 'Lowe of '69 abused Lowe of '60.'

A similar pattern emerges if Lowe's policy towards the other two functions of the Science and Art Department are considered. The Department had the responsibility for administering grants in aid of science and art instruction and Lowe approached this as a purely administrative matter. Though he claimed, in certain of his speeches, an enthusiasm for science, he never developed a policy for its expansion through the Science and Art Department. Art instruction existed and Lowe was prepared to carry it on, but he formulated no policy for it. Like so many politicians, Lowe seems to have had no real concern for, or knowledge of, certain parts of the educational system which he administered. As a result, the Science and Art Department was subordinated to his other aims and particularly to his concern for economy. Paradoxically it was from the Science and Art Department that Lowe acquired what became a major administrative principle with him, namely, payment by results. Once acquired, Lowe never forgot it, and his subsequent policy towards the Science and Art Department centred on the systematic application of the principle of payment by results to its grant-aiding functions.

Payment by results had been introduced in 1856 by the Science and Art Department to encourage elementary schools to teach

[32] *Ibid.* Ripon to Cole, 20 November 1872.
[33] Cole Diaries, 17 January 1873, 22 August 1873.

drawing, and in 1859 under the Marquess of Salisbury and Henry Cole it had been expanded into a system for science examinations. Lowe recognised its value as a means of administering state grants for education, and in 1862 he widened its use and made it the basis of his Revised Code for grants in elementary schools. At the same time he brought its operation in the Science and Art Department under the same rules as those applied to elementary schools. Payments on teachers' certificates were ended and instead payments on pupils' results substituted, ranging from £5 for a first-class grade to one pound for a pass.[34] Although teachers disliked the loss of payments for certificates, Lowe's measure had the effect of increasing expenditure on science and art education.

In science schools the number of persons under instruction increased from 1,330 in 1861 to 3,111 in 1863. There was a similar increase in the total amount paid to teachers: from £1,298 17*s.* 6*d.* in 1861 to £3,210 13*s.* in 1863, and the proportional payment for each person instructed rose from 19*s.* 6½*d.* in 1861 to £1 0*s.* 10*d.* in 1863.[35] Lowe welcomed this increase in expenditure. He told the House of Commons on 9 May 1862, on moving the Science and Art estimate, that the extension of science education was the 'merit' of the scheme. However, it should not be forgotten that Lowe's main concern was not so much that the overall expenditure had increased, but that it was now spent more efficiently. There had been a reduction in unit costs and a consequent saving in value for money. As Lowe pointed out, when the Department had been founded some 8,000 pupils had been instructed at a cost of £3 5*s.* 6*d.* per head; now 91,000 were instructed at 8*s.* per head.[36]

By 1863 the success of payment by results in the Science and Art Department proved its own enemy. The Treasury under Gladstone was anxious about increasing costs[37] and a measure of retrenchment was introduced. By a Minute of 21 September 1863 certain restrictions were put upon the amounts teachers and pupils could earn in science. Teachers' earnings over £60 were reduced by a quarter and those over £100 by a half. Similarly, full grants

[34] *P.P.* 1863, XVII, *10th Report of Department of Science and Art*; also Cole Correspondence, Box 5, Cole to Lowe, 31 August 1862; Lowe to Cole 7 September 1862.

[35] *P.P.* 1865, XVI, *12th Report of Department of Science and Art*, p. vii.

[36] *Parliamentary Debates*, CLXVI, col. 1530.

[37] Treasury Papers, Out Letters, P.R.O. T/9/11, p. 229.

were payable for pupils on one subject only; other subject grants were cut by a half.[38] It was hoped by this to make a saving of about 20 per cent.[39] In fact there was only a temporary cut back on expenditure. In 1865 the Department reported that the attempts to curb expenditure 'had been found salutary', and indeed the total paid to teachers declined from £3,240 15*s.* in 1863 to £3,076 in 1864 and the proportional payment for each person instructed fell dramatically from £1 0*s.* 10*d.* to 15*s.* 3*d.*[40] By 1865 the proportional payment per student had fallen further to 13*s.* but this was its lowest point. In 1866 the total paid to science teachers was £5,002 7*s.* 6*d.* and the proportional payment per student had risen to 14*s.* 6*d.* This increase continued, and by 1868, £12,725 10*s.* was paid to teachers and the proportional rate per student instructed had risen to 16*s.* 10*d.* There were now 300 science schools instructing 15,010 students compared with 9 schools instructing 500 students in 1860.[41]

Lowe's period of rule as Vice-President had not greatly hindered the growth of science education in science schools. On the other hand, his policy had discouraged science in elementary schools. Even under the 1859 scheme, Lowe refused to allow elementary teachers to be distracted from their essential task of teaching the three Rs by taking on science,[42] and the Revised Code of 1862 re-emphasised this refusal. It was even with reluctance that Lowe and Lingen allowed elementary school teachers to run, in their spare time, evening classes in elementary schools under the Science and Art Department. However, on 21 August 1862 they agreed to allow this, though teachers with pupil-teachers were forbidden to devote their spare time to science teaching.[43] As a result science remained outside the elementary schools as a grant-earning subject until the introduction of 'specific' subjects in 1867 and of science as a 'class' subject in 1883, though evening classes for science steadily increased. Lowe took no credit for the overall growth of science instruction under payment by results. He told the Schools Inquiry Commission: 'the honour of it is due to Lord Salisbury and Mr. Adderley'. He praised its operation because it was 'efficient'. It cost the Government nothing in the way of providing

[38] *P.P.* 1865, XVI, 301, *12th Report of Department of Science and Art*, appendix A, p. 4, paras. 19–20. [39] P.R.O. Ed. 28/18, p. 127.

[40] *P.P.* 1865, XVI, *12th Report of Department of Science and Art*, p. vii.

[41] *P.P.* 1868–9, XXIII, *16th Report of Department of Science and Art*, p. vi.

[42] P.R.O. Ed. 28/11, p. 140. [43] P.R.O. Ed. 28/15, p. 123.

buildings or libraries, for science masters often taught in their lodgings, and yet thousands were gaining science instruction. It was, Lowe concluded, 'the most successful thing I have seen'[44] and he attributed this success entirely to payments by results and not to what was also a possible contributing factor, the state authorisation of teachers.[45] Lowe's role in the enterprise, however, should not be ignored. If others began the payment by results system, it was under Lowe's guidance that the Department worked out the details upon which its effectiveness and success depended.

Lowe supported art instruction under the Department in the same terms as he supported science. In 1860 he approved the attempt to encourage towns with a population of more than 15,000 to set up schools of art for artisans by sending them a letter to this effect.[46] He also considered that a strict use of payments by results was the most appropriate way to encourage the growth of art education. Prior to 1863, grants had been made on teachers' certificates and aid given through the distribution of medals and prizes for art. However, for reasons of 'economy'[47] a series of Minutes of 24 February, 3 March and 17 March 1863 abolished these payments and substituted a system of payment by results.[48] The Select Committee on Schools of Art which reported in 1864, and of which Lowe was a member, concluded that payment by results was not well adapted to Schools of Art and preferred capitation grants.[49] Lowe had opposed this in committee but failed to carry the rest of the members with him, by five votes to eight.[50] He had, however, successfully blocked the resurrection of payments for teachers' certificates by a vote of seven to six.[51] In any case, despite the Report of the Select Committee and much opposition from schools of art, payment by results under the Minutes agreed when Lowe was Vice-President, remained. The effect of the Minutes was to reduce for a period the amounts paid to teachers but there was no decline in either the numbers taught in art schools or in the number of payments made. In 1862 government payments to schools had been £9,395 15*s*. 8*d*.[52] but in

[44] S.I.C. IV, *Minutes of Evidence 1868*, Qs. 6650–1. [45] *Ibid.* Q. 6658.
[46] P.R.O. Ed. 28/12, p. 69. [47] P.R.O. Ed. 28/16, p. 17.
[48] For Minutes see *Report of Select Committee on Schools of Art*, 1864, pp. 277–281. [49] *Report of Select Committee on Schools of Art*, 1864, p. xvii.
[50] *Ibid.* p. xi. [51] *Ibid.* p. xxix. [52] *Ibid.* appendix, p. 348.

1864 they declined to £5,888 13*s.* 9*d.*[53] Individual masters certainly lost in salaries, as for example at Lambeth School of Art where in 1862–3 masters lost £81 8*s.* and in 1863–4 £64 13*s.* under the new system.[54] Individual schools of art also suffered a loss of income to a greater or lesser degree. For example, at Manchester School of Art, there was a reduction in the government grant from £641 in 1861 to £54 in 1863.[55] On the other hand, the Department of Science and Art reported in 1865 that the effect of the Minutes had been to increase the numbers successful in its elementary examinations: from the 11,934 students who obtained first- and second-class grades in 1863 to 16,144 in 1864. Similarly, the number of payments made to schools of art had increased from 4,672 in 1862 to 13,889 in 1864, and the total number of students taught art under the Department had risen from 87,389 in 1862 to 110,330 in 1864.[56]

By a Minute of 24 October 1862 Lowe did agree to a scheme which allowed payment by results for drawing in elementary schools. Payments were to be divided between the master of the school of art who gave the instruction and the managers of the school which supplied the children. The rates were 2*s.* per child to the school where the pupil was taught and 1*s.* per child for the master of the school of art in which the child was examined. In addition, bronze medals could be awarded to the teachers who were most successful in helping their pupils secure passes in the examination.[57] From 1866 there was a steady growth in the amount expended on teaching elementary drawing as a part of primary education. In 1866, 80,081 children were taught drawing in 580 schools at a total cost, including prizes and examples, of £3,497 9*s.* 8*d.* and in 1872 there were 1,770 schools teaching 194,549 children at a cost of £11,546 18*s.* 1*d.*[58] There was also a growth of evening classes in elementary schools and mechanics' institutes, giving instruction in places where there were no schools of art. By 1868 there were 130 such evening classes instructing 4,466 students.[59]

In summary, Lowe's extension of payment by results for Science

[53] *P.P.* 1865, XVI, *12th Report Department of Science and Art*, p. 153.
[54] *Report of Select Committee on Schools of Art*, 1864, pp. 252–4.
[55] *Ibid.* p. 271.
[56] *P.P.* 1865, XVI, *12th Report Department of Science and Art*, pp. xii–xiii.
[57] *Report of Select Committee on Schools of Art*, 1864, p. 277.
[58] *Return by Science and Art Department of Amount expended in U.K. on teaching Elementary Drawing as a Part of Primary Education, 1866–1875.*
[59] *P.P.* 1868–9, XXIII, *16th Report of Department of Science and Art*, p. xii.

and Art instruction had, on the whole, encouraged its expansion. The teaching of science in elementary schools had been discouraged, but the teaching of drawing continued and an impulse had been given to the growth of evening classes in both science and art.

When Lowe re-emerged in office as Chancellor of the Exchequer in 1868 he was once again in a position to influence the Science and Art Department. Now, however, his priority was to cut back on public expenditure and he made no exception either for the Science and Art Department in particular, or indeed, for the Education Department as a whole. W. E. Forster, who was now Vice-President of the Committee of Council, told the House of Commons on 19 July 1869 that there was pressure upon him from the Chancellor to reduce his estimates for the Science and Art Department[60] and this pressure continued in subsequent years. In January 1871 the Treasury was insisting that it had ultimate control over educational expenditure[61] and subsequently it followed this up with particular enquiries into discrepancies between the expenditure and estimates of the Science and Art Department.[62] The effect of such Treasury pressure was the introduction by the Science and Art Department of a new scheme of payments. In 1868 by a Minute of 24 August three levels of payments – elementary, advanced and honours – were established in science, and the payment for a first class at the elementary stage reduced to £3 from the £5 established in 1863. In 1869 by a Minute of 30 November this figure was reduced further to £2 and the second-class payment to £1. The same figure of £2 and £1 applied to the advanced grade, and £4 and £2 for the honours grade.[63]

The main purpose of this new scheme was the reduction of state aid and the encouragement of local support and fees for both science and art education. 'It is essential', the Department of Science and Art reported in 1871, 'that the science instruction of the artisan classes should not depend for its existence entirely on state aid,'[64] and on 8 March 1871 a letter was sent to all local committees of schools requesting them to impose fees. In 1872 the Department reported that fees in science schools were now a

[60] *Parliamentary Debates*, CXCVIII, col. 218.
[61] Treasury Papers, Out Letters, P.R.O. T9/13, pp. 520–1, 27 January 1871.
[62] *Ibid.* T9/13, pp. 539, 542–6.
[63] *P.P.* 1870, XXVI, *17th Report of Department of Science and Art*, appendix, p. 1.
[64] *P.P.* 1871, XXIV, *18th Report of Department of Science and Art*, p. ix.

'fair proportion' of the total cost, providing £3,873 as compared with the £14,289 which came from state grants,[65] but there was still concern that it was not enough. On 27 February 1873, a Minute was passed to oblige science students to pay fees, and it was stipulated that grants would be withdrawn if schools of science did not obtain the highest possible fees from their students.[66]

The general effect of these measures was to cut down government aid to science. For example, the total of payments made on results dropped from £20,115 in 1870 to £18,830 in 1871 and though, because expansion continued, the total in 1872 was £25,201, there was a steady decline in the average payment per student instructed: from 16*s.* 10*d.* in 1868[67] to 9*s.* 10*d.* in 1871.[68] However, in 1873 the Department of Science and Art reported that though there had been a 3.2 per cent fall in the number of science students in the schools, it appeared that the effect of the reductions in the scale of payments made in 1869 had 'now worn off' and there was an increase in the number of students examined: from 18,750 in 1871 to 19,568 in 1872; and also an increase in the number of examination passes from 22,105 in 1871 to 27,806 in 1872. Moreover, the cuts had stimulated a growth in fees so that they now amounted to a quarter of the grants paid by the State as payments on results.[69] By 1874 the number of science schools had continued to increase: to a total of 1,336, with 53,050 students under instruction. The total amount of payments by results was £36,769 and the proportional cost per student instructed was once more on the increase, to the sum of 13*s.* 10*d.*[70]

The effects on art education were less severe. There were no major changes in the regulations under which state aid was granted to schools of art and elementary schools and, according to the Chief Inspector for Art, H. A. Bowler, it was precisely because of this lack of change that the steady growth in the number of students under art instruction continued.[71] In 1868, 123,562 students were taught in the various schools which came under the Department's

[65] *P.P.* 1872, XXIV, *19th Report of Department of Science and Art*, p. ix.
[66] *P.P.* 1873, XXVIII, *20th Report of Department of Science and Art*, appendix A, p. 9.
[67] *P.P.* 1868–9, XXIII, *16th Report of Department of Science and Art*, p. vi.
[68] *P.P.* 1872, XXIV, *19th Report of Department of Science and Art*, p. viii.
[69] *Ibid.* p. ix.
[70] *P.P.* 1875, XXVII, *22nd Report of Department of Science and Art*, p. viii.
[71] *P.P.* 1871, XXIV, *18th Report of Department of Science and Art*, p. 214.

regulations for art, and this number increased annually to a total of 290,176 in 1873.[72] At the same time the fees paid in schools of art increased also – from £18,515 in 1868 to £23,432 in 1871 – a healthy total in comparison with the amount of the state grant to such schools, which in the latter year, for example, came to £13,100.[73] The total of payments in aid to schools of art and other classes in night schools, training colleges and science schools rose steadily: from £18,187 9*s.* 1*d* in 1869 to £34,182 6*s.* 3*d.* in 1874.

In summary then, Lowe's influence as Chancellor of the Exchequer upon the Science and Art Department caused some reduction in the growth of science education, but it was neither extensive nor long lasting. Art instruction suffered little under his rule. In general, his attitude to the Department had remained constant from his period as Vice-President in 1859 to his transference from the Exchequer in 1873. He supported its work provided that it could show itself to be securing value for money and that it did not become too great a drain on public expenditure. For Lowe remained steadfast in his view that state aid should always supplement self-help and never replace it. His policy was to administer what was there. It was in no sense creative.

72 *P.P.* 1874, XXI, *21st Report of Department of Science and Art*, p. xiii.
73 *P.P.* 1872, XXIV, *19th Report of Department of Science and Art.*

# CONCLUSION

Bell, Lancaster, Kay-Shuttleworth, Arnold, Forster – these have long been names to conjure with in the history of English education. Yet not one of them affected educational policies more than Lowe did. Lowe's comparative neglect requires explanation, especially since, in addition to his educational policies, he also produced significant ideas upon a variety of issues ranging from elementary to university education.

One reason for his neglect is not far to seek. His association with the Revised Code aroused the wrath of so many contemporary teachers and educationists that subsequent historians, relying upon this contemporary evidence, have treated Lowe either cursorily, or unsympathetically, or both. Similarly, the habit of writing the history of education in terms of progress has also militated against Lowe. For in this context, his ideas are so obviously not the ideas of twentieth-century educationists, his ways are so patently not our ways, that inevitably he has been written off as a villain and a reactionary.

However if, as Garrett Mattingly remarked, it matters to the living that they should do justice to the dead, then it is time some revaluation was made of Lowe. Certainly it is doubtful whether we should continue to dismiss so summarily a man who tried to relate education to the demands of his society, who provided a framework for elementary education in the Revised Code, who played such an important part in the genesis of the 1870 Act, and a man who advocated curriculum reform and held views of the university more radical than those held by the most revolutionary academic reformers of the present. It is possible to see Lowe as an illiberal liberal, a reforming conservative, an intellectual radical, a talented but mere administrator and an unrepentant elitist, but often these descriptions tell us more about those who make them than they do about Lowe. Some attempt must obviously be made to delineate the man in broad general strokes but, in addition to this, some assessment of his individual achievements must also be attempted if we are to come near to doing him justice.

First, Lowe must be seen in the context of his times. He was a mid-Victorian liberal trying to think himself out of the inherited ideas of the past and the prejudices of his present into the future. It was, as always, a slow and difficult process, but Lowe was at least conscious that he lived in a period when the rate of change was accelerating and he did try to come to terms with it. He brought certain advantages to this task. In the first place he was able to balance a keenly logical mind with a pragmatism which made any solutions he offered to current problems, on the whole, practical and possible, rather than theoretical and visionary. His policy with regard to the Education Act of 1870 is a case in point. Another advantage was his talent for administration which enabled him, on several occasions, to cut through the complexity of past administrative growth and produce a simplification. His revisions of government regulations for making grants to schools are an example of this. Thirdly, he had a shrewd appreciation of the importance of economics and he pioneered the application of efficiency tests and cost-benefit models to national educational policies.

On the other hand, these advantages had corresponding defects. Lowe's pragmatism meant that often he was unimaginative in his analysis of problems, and unadventurous in his production of solutions. Nowhere was this more apparent than in the time it took him to admit the need for some national system of education. Also, his talent for administration often resulted in a narrow legalistic approach to matters of detail and an unwillingness to see beyond the letter of the law to the spirit behind it. This was particularly apparent in his policy of the Revised Code, though it should be admitted here that it was Lingen more than Lowe who was responsible for the strict way in which the Code was operated.[1] Similarly, Lowe's obsession with the economics of education produced an attitude towards elementary education which was distinctly limited and which, though it rightly emphasised essentials such as the three Rs, failed to consider an education which would meet the full potentiality of which children were capable. To these defects of approach must also be added more personal characteristics which prevented Lowe from ever becoming a wholehearted supporter of educational expansion. Of these, the most notable was Lowe's lack of any feeling for the poor. Empathy was not one of his strong points. Moreover, his faith in

[1] See, for example, P.R.O. Ed. 9/4, Minute Book of Secretary, fol. 104, 12 January 1863, and fols. 168–9, 5 July 1865.

the value of self-help reinforced this lack of sympathy for those who could not help themselves. Consequently Lowe wanted to limit state action in education, and he also had no desire to educate children above their existing station in life. If a child could gain a higher station, Lowe would praise him but he would not directly assist him. There was a fundamental conflict here between his adherence to the idea of meritocracy and his faith in self-help; for even the most outstanding innate merit cannot rise very far in a society which demands acquired characteristics which only costly schools can supply and only people with money can afford. It was a conflict, however, which Lowe chose to ignore. Finally, Lowe had a personal prejudice against teachers. He considered teaching to be an unintellectual trade, and this view set the tone of his attitude towards teachers in particular and to education in general. With such an overall attitude it was impossible for Lowe to become an educational leader of any great stature.

Nevertheless, despite these limitations, Lowe achieved considerable success in his educational policies. In the first place, his simplification of the administrative system made possible that expansion of elementary education which occurred in England in the last forty years of the nineteenth century. Secondly, he devised a programme of basic mass education which, in its concentration upon the secular learning of the three Rs, met precisely the demands of a growing industrial society for a literate body of workers. Moreover, the particular means he chose to implement this – the Revised Code – not only secured better standards of basic education than had been achieved previously, but also made sure that the less able received attention in school. Thirdly, Lowe played a significant part in securing the 1870 Education Act. His advocacy of a national system, his provision of a practical administrative blueprint, his intervention in the Cabinet at a critical moment in the Bill's passage and his subsequent support for it as Chancellor of the Exchequer, all contributed to the eventual success of the Act. Fourthly, Lowe was successful in helping to extend the use of educational examinations as a means of social selection. Though examinations have their drawbacks, as an alternative to nepotism and patronage they are instrumental in producing a more egalitarian society in which merit may have its reward. In elementary, secondary and university education, Lowe was a consistent advocate of the value of examinations as a means of testing efficiency, rewarding merit and selecting for office. Ultimately, of course, as is becoming apparent, examinations and their uses for selection divide society as much as nepotism and patronage did, but Lowe aided a development which society has, on the whole, found more acceptable than the previous alternatives. Fifthly, Lowe was successful in producing, if not implementing, some interesting ideas about secondary education. His concern to introduce a curriculum in which modern subjects figured, and in which there was a balance between arts and general subjects was, at the time, radical and forward looking. His desire for a useful curriculum relevant to the future needs of students was also one which has since been re-echoed amongst educationists. His view too, that secondary schools would not become efficient until some system of examinations and government inspection was implemented, has been validated in subsequent practice. Finally, Lowe advocated a view of the universities which has slowly gained increasing acceptance. In his opinion, they should exist primarily to serve society as a whole, and not as isolated scholarly communities ministering to the desires of a minority of favoured academics. He wanted the universities to be open to the nation's most able students and to employ better teaching techniques so that students would be better educated. He wanted a wider university curriculum in which arts and science, both pure and applied, would flourish. In an effort to secure good standards he would have preferred a national council to examine university students and award degrees – and in this way he anticipated the Council for National Academic Awards – on the grounds that external examiners are always preferable to internally set and marked examinations. This view, at that time, fell on stony ground, but in his main aim, that of making the universities educators of public servants, he was eminently successful. He saw to it that the Civil Service examinations for the highest grade reflected university syllabuses and examinations, and in this way his policy had a buoyant effect on the universities, giving them a new purpose in what was an increasingly secular socity, so that from being seminaries for Anglican clergy, they became the nurseries of civil servants.

Against all this must be balanced the debit side of Lowe's policies. First, the policy of payment by results produced both short-term and long-term disadvantages. In the short term it temporarily depleted the teaching and pupil-teaching force. On a longer view it brought into the schools a dominance of the three Rs and an encouragement to mechanical learning which it has taken a long time to dispel. Though there is no evidence to support the myth that before Lowe's Revised Code there was a golden age in education, when a wide curriculum flourished and children learned by discovery under the guidance of non-authoritarian teachers, nevertheless, the Revised Code produced a particular emphasis in elementary education which was not to the good. Matthew Arnold put the matter succinctly when he wrote that 'the State has an interest in the Primary School as a *civilising agent*, even prior to its interest in it as an *instructing agent*. When this is once clearly seen nothing can resist it and it is fatal to the new Code.'[2] Lowe's Code lacked the ultimate vision of elementary education as a civilising agent. To him it was a cheap and efficient tool for basic mass education. Payment by results had three long-term effects. By using it as a means of measuring teachers' salaries, Lowe depressed teacher status and showed a complete misunderstanding of the teacher's task. He saw it in terms of an industrial factory system, as a piece-work trade, with payment at piece-work rates. He thus institutionalised views of the child and of the teacher's role which were quite inappropriate. What is essentially a humane process became in Lowe's view a mechanical one, and teaching, which should have developed as a profession and been rewarded as such, became increasingly seen as a trade paid at rates which never did justice to the function which it performed for society. The final long-term effect was on Inspectors. Giving them a key role in making this system of payment by results work, Lowe delayed the development of the inspectorate as advisers to the teaching profession. Instead they remained, until well into this century, even when they had lost their power over the allocation of grants and salaries, as primarily inquisitorial in their function.

Turning to secondary education, it is not so much a case of criticising Lowe's policy here, as regretting that he did not have one. His adherence in this field to the idea of *laissez-faire* totally inhibited him from seeing the case for a national system of secondary education. Lowe threw up some interesting ideas on the subject. For example, as has been indicated, he held that only a

[2] M. Arnold, letter of 26 February 1861, in George W. E. Russell (ed.), *Letters of Matthew Arnold*, 1895, I, pp. 161–2.

national examination system and state inspection would improve the standards of secondary education. Yet the crucial point of how to provide secondary education for those who were poor escaped him. He had plans for the appropriation of certain school endowments into a scholarship system to allow able poor boys to go to secondary schools but never developed them, and, as was the case with many of his contemporaries, the question of the education of girls gave him no concern. It may be urged in his defence that he was never in a position to establish a system of secondary education, and certainly the whole climate of opinion was against it in the seventies. Nevertheless, the most telling point against Lowe remains, that even when he had the opportunity to help the reform of endowed schools by supporting the Endowed Schools Commission, he let it go. Lowe was too much a prisoner of his times and his *laissez-faire* ideas, either to see or to grasp the opportunity to create a secondary school system.

Lowe's attitude towards the Science and Art Department and technical education showed a similar lack of creativity. He treated it as a purely administrative problem in which economising and securing value for money were his priorities. The development of scientific, art or technical education was not his main concern. In fact, Lowe's economies were marginal in their effect, and during his periods of control both science and art education continued, on the whole, the expansion that had gone on since the fifties. But here, as elsewhere, Lowe lacked either the vision or the enthusiasm to support their development wholeheartedly. The same trait was apparent in his dealings with the South Kensington Museum. He supported it energetically in 1859 but, as soon as he became Chancellor, his concern to make public economies soon overtook any educational enthusiasm he had for the museum.

In the end, it is precisely this lack of enthusiasm and humanity which emerges as a dominant characteristic in Lowe's public life and particularly in his attitude towards education. He was, in a way, too intellectual for politics, for his logical mind made him see things too much in terms of black and white and regard those who differed from him too much as enemies. As a result his political life was one of almost constant conflict and controversy. Lowe recognised this when he accepted, translated into Latin and published, an epitaph which he received on retiring from office. It went as follows:

*Robert Lowe's Epitaph*

Here be the bones of Robert Lowe
A treacherous friend, a bitter foe;
Whither his restless soul has fled
May not be thought, much less be said.
If to the realms of peace and love,
Farewell to happiness above.
If to a place of lower level
We can't congratulate the Devil.[3]

On the causes of Lowe's unremitting flair for controversy two reflections may be made. Firstly, it may have been partly the result of his physical appearance and disability which put him in the position of constantly wanting to assert himself and prove his equality, if not his superiority, to others. Secondly, it may be seen as the inevitable result of his personality. In a letter of 13 August 1873,[4] Gladstone made a penetrating analysis of Lowe which is particularly relevant to this point. Gladstone held that politicians were men whom it was, as a rule, 'most difficult to comprehend', but nevertheless he confessed to having isolated ideas about some of them, including Lowe. He wrote to Lowe as follows:

Such an idea comes to me about you. I think the clearness, power, and promptitude of your intellect are in one respect a difficulty and a danger to you. You see everything in a burning, almost a scorching light. The case reminds me of an incident some years back. Sir D. Brewster asked me to sit for my photograph in a black frost and a half mist in Edinburgh. I objected about the light. He said, 'This is the best light; it is all diffused, not concentrated.' Is not your light too much concentrated? Does not its intensity darken the surroundings? By the surroundings, I mean the relations of the thing not only to other things but to persons, as our profession obliges us constantly to deal with persons. In every question flesh and blood are strong and real even if extraneous elements, and we cannot safely omit them from our thoughts.

Gladstone went on to make two other observations.

I note, then, two things about you. Outstripping others in the race, you reach the goal or conclusion before them; and being there, you assume that they are there also. This is unpopular . . . Again, and lastly, I think you do not get up all things, but allow yourself a choice, as if politics

[3] Patchett Martin, II, p. 410.
[4] Gladstone Papers, B.M. Add. Mss. 44302, fol. 145, Gladstone to Lowe, 13 August 1873.

were a flower-garden and we might choose among the beds; as Lord Palmerston did, who read foreign office and war papers, and let the others rust and rot. This, I think, is partially true, I do not say of your reading, but of your mental processes.

Lowe's views on education certainly showed the characteristics which Gladstone had so accurately portrayed. For Lowe was aggressive in his opinions, seeing matters 'in a burning, almost a scorching light', emphasising a few issues to the exclusion of all others and, on the whole, reaching conclusions in such a way that compromise was impossible to admit. And yet it is impossible to end without indicating that Lowe was by no means humourless or wholly lacking in a capacity for friendship in his personal life. He could on occasion relax, even when others could not, as for example in May 1863, when he refused to let Henry Cole at the Science and Art Department arrange to open tenders on Derby Day of all days.[5] He was also capable of personal love and friendship. There is no reason to suggest that his two marriages were less than successful, and certainly he made long-lasting friendships with others, such as Benjamin Jowett, which withstood even differences of opinion. Nevertheless, he appeared to lack a real concern for persons and this, more than anything else, explains the unsympathetic way in which both contemporary and later commentators have treated Lowe.

[5] Cole Correspondence, Box 5, 18 May 1863, Lowe to Cole.

# SELECT BIBLIOGRAPHY

This bibliography is not exhaustive but it includes all the manuscript collections to which reference has been made and all the printed material which has been found useful.

The place of publication of books is London except where otherwise stated.



## A. MANUSCRIPT COLLECTIONS

*1. Public Record Office*

Education Department Papers
Ed. 9 Minute Book of Secretary, etc.
Ed. 28 Science and Art Department Minute Books

Treasury Papers
In Letters and Files
Treasury Board Papers 1557–1920 (T1)
Register of Papers 1777–1920 (T2)
Skeleton Registers 1783–1920 (T3)
Treasury Out Letters 1793–1922 (T9)
Subject Registers 1852–1909 (T108)

Granville Papers
Letters to Lowe. P.R.O. 30/29/24–68 especially letters to Lowe 1869–1873. P.R.O. 30/29/66

Russell Papers. P.R.O. 30/22/13–21
Cardwell Papers. Letters to Lowe. P.R.O. 30/48/5/22, 23 and 24

*2. British Museum*

a. Gladstone Papers. Add. Mss. 44086–44835
Series A. Correspondence
Special Correspondence. Add. Mss. 44086–44351
Correspondence with R. Lowe. Add. Mss. 44301–44302
Correspondence with W. E. Forster. Add. Mss. 44086–44087

Correspondence with G. F. Samuel Robinson, Earl of Ripon and de Grey. Add. Mss. 44286–44287
Correspondence with Earl Granville. Add. Mss. 44165–44180
Letter Books. Copies of Letters of Gladstone 1835–94. Add. Mss. 44527–51

Series B. Official Papers, including memoranda prepared for the use of the Cabinet 1834–95, 73 vols. mostly printed. Add. Mss. 44563–635

Series C. Cabinet Minutes. Add. Mss. 44636–48. 44636 (1853–1866), 44637 (1868–1869), 44638 (1870), 44639 (1871), 44640 (1872), 44641 (1873–4)

b. Ripon Papers. Add. Mss. 43510–43644
Special Correspondence. Add. Mss. 43512–43564
Correspondence with R. Lowe. Add. Mss. 43532. fols. 1–41b
Correspondence with Earl of Kimberley. Add. Mss. 43522

3. *Private Collection*

Lowe Mss. Collection of Lowe Papers in possession of Mrs R. T. Sneyd, The Malt House, Hinton Charterhouse, near Bath

Historical Manuscripts Commission, National Register of Archives. List No. 8681

4. *Victoria and Albert Museum*

a. Cole Correspondence K.R.C. Correspondence of Henry Cole. Boxes 1–19, 1836–76, especially correspondence with Public Officials, Boxes 4–7 and particulary Box 5 which contains 30 letters from Lowe

b. Cole Diaries. 33 vols. 1844–1882

5. The Times *archives*

Desk diaries indicating, by initials, *Times* leader writers. They begin in 1857

B. PRINTED COLLECTIONS

*The Political Correspondence of Mr Gladstone and Lord Granville, 1868–1876*. ed. A. Ramm. Camden Society. lxxxi–lxxxii. 1952

*The Political Correspondence of Mr Gladstone and Lord Granville, 1876–1886*. ed. A. Ramm. Oxford 1962

*Gladstone and Palmerston. The Correspondence of Lord Palmerston with Mr Gladstone, 1851–1865*. ed. P. Guedalla. 1928

C. OFFICIAL PAPERS

1. *Acts of Parliament*

3 & 4 Vict. c. 77, Grammar Schools Act 1840

16 & 17 Vict. c. 137, Charitable Trusts Act 1853
23 & 24 Vict. c. 136, Charitable Trusts Act 1860
25 & 26 Vict. c. 112, Charitable Trusts Act 1862
31 & 32 Vict. c. 32, Endowed Schools Act 1868
31 & 32 Vict. c. 118, Public Schools Act 1868
32 & 33 Vict. c. 56, Endowed Schools Act 1869
33 & 34 Vict. c. 75, Elementary Education Act 1870
36 & 37 Vict. c. 87, Endowed Schools Act 1873
37 & 38 Vict. c. 87, Endowed Schools Act 1874

2. *Hansard's Parliamentary Debates.* Third Series

3. Committee of Council on Education. *Minutes 1839–58*
Committee of Council on Education. *Reports 1859 et seq.*
Department of Science and Art. *Reports 1854 et seq.*

4. *Parliamentary Papers*

1835 VII *Report of Select Committee on Public Charities*
1852 XXII *Report of the Royal Commission on the University of Oxford*
1852–3 XLIV *Report of the Royal Commission on the University of Cambridge*
1854 XX *Papers relating to the Reorganisation of the Civil Service*
1854 XXVII *Report on the Organisation of the Permanent Civil Service*
1860 IX *Report from the Select Committee on Miscellaneous Expenditure*
1860 IX *Report from the Select Committee on Civil Service Appointments*
1861 XXI *Report of the Royal Commission on the State of Popular Education in England and Wales* (Newcastle Report)
1863 XVI Durham University Act 1861, *Commissioners' Report 1863*
1863 XLVI Durham University Act 1861, Commission. *Minutes of Evidence*
1864 IX *Report from the Select Committee on Education* (Inspectors' Returns)
1864 XX *Report of Her Majesty's Commissioners appointed to inquire into the Revenues and Management of certain Colleges and Schools, and the Studies pursued and instructions given therein* (The Clarendon Report)
1865 VI *First Report from the Select Committee on the Constitution of the Committee of Council on Education* (The Pakington Committee)
1866 VII *Second Report from the Pakington Committee*
1867–8 XXVIII *A Report of the Royal Commission on Schools not comprised within Her Majesty's two recent Commissions on Popular Education and Public Schools* (The Taunton Report)
1867–8 XXII *Civil Service Commissioners. Thirteenth Report*
1871 XI *Report from the Select Committee on Civil Service Writers*
1871 XVII *Civil Service Commissioners Sixteenth Report*
1872 XXIV *Report of Endowed Schools Commissioners*

1873 VII *Reports from the Select Committee on Civil Services Expenditure*

1873 VIII *Report of the Select Committee appointed to inquire into the operation of the Endowed Schools Act 1869*

1875 XXIII *Report of the Civil Service Inquiry Commission* (The Playfair Report)

1884 IX *Select Committee on Charitable Trusts Act*

1884 XIII *Report from the Select Committee on Education, Science and Art (Administration)*

1888 XXXV *Final Report of the Royal Commission appointed to Inquire into the Elementary Education Acts (England and Wales)* (The Cross Report)

1898 XXIV *Special Reports on Educational Subjects*

XXVI *Report of the Departmental Committee on the Pupil-Teacher System*

1956/57 XXV *Recruitment to the Administrative Class of the Home Civil Service and Senior Branch of the Foreign Service* (Cmd. 232)

5. *Miscellaneous Papers*

1860 LIII *Copy of Minutes and Regulations of the Committee of the Privy Council on Education reduced into the Form of a Code*

1862 XLI *Copies of all Memorials and Letters . . . on the Subject of the Revised Code*

1864 XLIV *Endowed Schools receiving Grants from Government in the years 1862–1863*

*Correspondence Relating to the Dismissal of Mr J. R. Morell*

1870 XLI *Return of Number, Salaries, and General Duties of Inspectors, etc*

1871 XXXVII *Return of the Number, Names and Salaries of the Inspectors . . . in Departments of the Civil Service*

1875 XLII *Return of the Number, Names and Salaries of the Inspectors . . . in Departments of the Civil Service*

D. NEWSPAPERS AND PERIODICALS

*The Times*. It is possible to identify which leaders Lowe wrote by consulting diaries in the possession of *The Times* archives department. They begin in 1857

*Educational Times*

*Educational Guardian*

*Journal of Education*

*Fortnightly Review*

E. SECONDARY SOURCES

ABBOTT, E. and CAMPBELL, L. *The Life and Letters of Benjamin Jowett, M.A.* 2 vols. 1897. vol. 3, 1899.

ADAMSON, J. W. *English Education 1789–1902*. Cambridge 1930.

ALTICK, R. D. *The English Common Reader*. University of Chicago Press 1957.

ARGLES, M. *South Kensington to Robbins*. 1964.

ARNOLD, M. *Schools and Universities on the Continent*. 1859.
*A French Eton*. 1864.

AUSTIN, A. G. *Australian Education 1788–1900*. Melbourne 1961.
*Select Documents in Australian Education 1788–1900*. Melbourne 1963.

BALL, N. *Her Majesty's Inspectorate 1839–49*. Edinburgh 1963.

BARON, G. 'The Origins and Early History of the Headmaster's Conference 1869–1914'. *Educational Review*. June 1955.

BENTHAM, J. *A Fragment on Government*. 1823.

BIRKS, Reverend T. R. *The Revised Code: What would it do? And what should be done with it?* 1862.

BISHOP, A. S. 'Ralph Lingen, Secretary to the Education Department 1849–1870'. *British Journal of Educational Studies*. XVI. No. 2. June 1968. pp. 138–163.
*The Rise of a Central Authority for English Education*. Cambridge 1971.

BOWLEY, M. *Nassau Senior and Classical Economics*. 1937.

BRIGGS, A. *Victorian People*. 1965.

BRYCE, J. *Studies in Contemporary Biography*. 1903.

BURCHLERE, Lady Winifred Anne Henrietta Gardner. *A Great Lady's Friendships: Letters to Mary, Marchioness of Salisbury, Countess of Derby, 1862–1890*. 1933.

BURN, W. L. *The Age of Equipoise*. 1964.

BUTTERWORTH, H. 'South Kensington and Whitehall: A Conflict of Educational Purpose'. *Journal of Educational Administration and History*. IV. No. 1. December 1971. pp. 10–11.

CAMPBELL, L. *The End of a Liberal Education*. Edinburgh 1868.

CAMPBELL, T. D. *Adam Smith's Science of Morals*. 1971.

CAVENAGH, F. A. *James and John Stuart Mill on Education*. Cambridge 1931.

CLARK, G. Kitson. *The Making of Victorian England*. 1962.

CHARLTON, H. B. *Portrait of a University 1851–1951*. Manchester 1951.

COHEN, E. *The Growth of the British Civil Service 1780–1939*. 1941.

COLE, H. *Fifty Years of Public Work*. 2 vols. 1884.

COLERIDGE, Rev. Derwent. *The Teachers of the People. A Tract for the Time*. 1862.

CONNELL, W. F. *The Educational Thought and Influence of Matthew Arnold*. 1950.

CRUIKSHANK, M. *Church and State in English Education*. 1963.

CURTIS, S. J. *History of Education in Great Britain*. 3rd edn. 1953.

DE MONTMORENCY, J. E. G. 'Lowe'. *Encyclopedia of Education*. ed. Foster Watson. 1921. II. pp. 104–16.

*State Intervention in English Education*. Cambridge 1902.

DOCKING, J. W. *Victorian Schools and Scholars*. Pamphlet No. 3. Coventry Branch of Historical Association 1967.

DUKE, C. 'Robert Lowe. A Reappraisal'. *British Journal of Educational Studies*. XIV. November 1965. pp. 19–35.

FABER, G. *Jowett*. 1966.

FARRAR, F. W. (ed.) *Essays on a Liberal Education*. 1868.

FITZMAURICE, Lord E. *The Life of Granville George Leveson Gower, 2nd Earl Granville 1815–1891*. 3rd edn. 2 vols. 1905.

FORTESCUE, Earl H. *Public Schools for the Middle Classes*. 1864.

GOSDEN, P. H. J. H. *The Development of Educational Administration in England and Wales*. Oxford 1966.

GRIFFITHS, D. C. *Documents on the Establishment of Education in New South Wales 1789–1880*. Australian Council for Educational Research 1957.

HALEVY, E. *The Growth of Philosophical Radicalism*. 1928.

HAMILTON, Lord G. *Parliamentary Reminiscences and Reflections 1868–1885*. 1916.

HAWTRY, Reverend S. *A Narrative Essay on a Liberal Education*. 1868

HOBHOUSE, A. *The Dead Hand*. 1880.

HOGAN, J. F. *Robert Lowe Viscount Sherbrooke*. 1893.

HOLMES, E. *What is and What might be*. 1911.

HOUGHTON, W. E. *The Victorian Frame of Mind 1830–70*. 1957.

HUME, Miss *Brief Comments on the Revised Speech of the Rt. Hon. Robert Lowe on The Revised Code. Feb. 13 1862*. 1862.

HURT, J. *Education in Evolution. Church, State, Society and Popular Education 1800–1870*. 1971.

JONES, L. G. F. *The Training of Teachers in England and Wales*. Oxford 1924.

KAY-SHUTTLEWORTH, Sir J. *Four Periods of Public Education*. 1862.

*Memorandum on Popular Education*. 1868. Reprint 1969.

KEKEWICH, Sir George W. *The Education Department and After*. 1920.

KELSALL, R. K. 'Intellectual merit and higher Civil Service recruitment: the rise and fall of an idea'. *History, Sociology and Education*. History of Education Society 1971.

KNIGHT, R. *Illiberal Liberal: Robert Lowe in New South Wales 1842–50*. Melbourne 1966.

LEESE, J. *Personalities and Power in English Education*. Leeds 1950.

LOWE, R. *Speeches and Letters on Reform*. 1867.

*Primary and Classical Education*. Edinburgh 1867.

*Middle Class Education: Endowment or Free Trade*. 1868.

LOWNDES, G. A. N. *The Silent Social Revolution.* Oxford 1937. 2nd edn 1969.

MALTHUS, T. R. *An Essay on the Principles of Population.* 2 vols. 1806.

MARTIN, A. Patchett. *Life and Letters of the Rt. Hon. Robert Lowe, Viscount Sherbrooke.* 2 vols. 1893.

MENET, Reverend J. *The Revised Code. A Letter to a Friend.* 1862.

MILL, J. S. *Essay On Liberty.* 1859.

*Principles of Political Economy.* People's Edition. 1865.

*Autobiography.* 1873.

MONTGOMERY, R. J. *Examinations.* 1965.

MONEYPENNY, W. F. and BUCKLE, G. E. *Life of Benjamin Disraeli, Earl of Beaconsfield.* 6 vols. 1910–24.

MOODY, T. W. and BECKETT, J. C. *Queen's Belfast 1845–1949: The History of a University.* 1959.

MORLEY, J. *Life of William Ewart Gladstone.* 2 vols. 1908.

MORRIS, N. 'State Paternalism and laissez-faire in the 1860's'. *Studies in the Government and Control of Education since 1860.* History of Education Society 1970. pp. 13–25.

NEWMAN, J. H. *On the Scope and Nature of University Education.* 1859. Everyman Edition 1955.

OWEN, D. *English Philanthropy 1660–1960.* Oxford 1965.

PATTISON, M. *Suggestions on Academical Organisation.* Edinburgh 1868.

*Memoirs.* Reprint Centaur Press, Fontwell 1969.

PARKIN, G. R. *Life and Letters of Edward Thring.* 1898.

PERKIN, H. *The Origins of Modern English Society 1780–1880.* 1969.

PINKER, R. *Social Theory and Social Policy.* 1971.

REID, T. Wemyss. *Life of the Right Honourable William Edward Forster.* 2 vols. London 1888.

RICARDO, D. *Principles of Political Economy.* 1817.

RICH, R. W. *The Training of Teachers in England and Wales during the Nineteenth Century.* Cambridge 1933.

ROBERTS, D. *Victorian Origins of the British Welfare State.* New Haven, Yale University Press 1960.

ROACH, J. *Public Examinations in England 1850–1900.* Cambridge 1971.

SELLECK, R. J. W. *The New Education 1870–1914.* 1968.

SELLMAN, R. R. *Devon Village Schools in the Nineteenth Century.* Newton Abbot 1967.

SENIOR, Nassau. *Political Economy.* 1850.

SILVER, H. *The Concept of Popular Education.* 1965.

SIMON, B. *Studies in the History of Education 1780–1870.* 1960.

SMITH, Adam. *An Inquiry into the Nature and Causes of the Wealth of Nations.* 1875.

SMITH, F. *The Life and Work of Sir James Kay-Shuttleworth.* 1923.

SPENCER, H. *Education. Intellectual Moral Physical.* 1919.

STURT, M. *The Education of the People.* 1967.

TOMPSON, R. S. 'The Leeds Grammar School Case of 1805'. *Journal of Educational Administration and History.* III. No. 1. December 1970.

TROPP, A. *The School Teachers: the growth of the teaching profession in England and Wales from 1800 to the present day.* 1957.

TU, Pierre N. V. 'The Classical Economists and Education'. *Kyklos. International Review for Social Sciences.* XXII. 1969. pp. 691–718.

VINCENT, J. *The Formation of the Liberal Party 1857–1868.* 1966.

WALCOTT, F. G. *The Origins of Culture and Anarchy. Matthew Arnold and Popular Education in England.* 1970.

WEST, E. G. 'Private versus Public Education. A Classical Economic Dispute'. *The Classical Economists and Economic Policy.* ed. A. W. Coats. pp. 123–143. Methuen 1971.

'The Role of Education in Nineteenth Century Doctrines of Political Economy'. *British Journal of Educational Studies.* XII. No. 2. May 1964. pp. 161–172.

'Resource Allocation and Growth in Early Nineteenth Century British Education'. *Economic History Review.* Second Series. XXIII. No. 1. April 1970.

WHITING, C. E. *The University of Durham 1832–1932.* 1932.

WINTER, J. 'The Cave of Adullam and Parliamentary Reform'. *English Historical Review.* LXXXI. January 1966. p. 39.

WRIGHT, M. W. *Treasury Control of the Civil Service 1854–74.* Oxford 1969.

## F. UNPUBLISHED SECONDARY SOURCES

BUTTERWORTH, H. 'The Science and Art Department 1853–1900'. University of Sheffield Ph.D. thesis 1968.

CLAYTON, J. D. 'Mr. Gladstone's Leadership of the Parliamentary Liberal Party 1868–74'. University of Oxford D.Phil. thesis 1959.

DOCKING, J. W. 'The Development of Church of England Schools in Coventry 1811–1944'. University of Leeds M.Ed. thesis 1966.

DUKE, C. 'The Department of Science and Art: Policies and Administration to 1864'. University of London Ph.D. thesis 1966.

JOHNSON, W. B. 'The Development of English Education 1856–1882 with special reference to the work of Robert Lowe'. University of Durham M.Ed. thesis 1956.

LEESE, J. 'The History and Character of Educational Inspection in England'. University of London Ph.D. thesis 1934.

ROLAND, D. 'The Struggle for the Education Act and Its Implementation 1870–73'. University of Oxford B.Litt. thesis 1957.

SULLIVAN, J. P. 'The Educational Work and Thought of Robert Lowe'. University of London M.A. (Ed.) thesis 1952.

# INDEX